BHAGAVAD GITA

THE DIVINE SONG

A New Translation and Commentary by
Rory B Mackay

Bhagavad Gita: The Divine Song / Rory B. Mackay — 1st ed.
ISBN 9780993267574

Hari Om Tat Sat.

CONTENTS

BHAGAVAD GITA

THE DIVINE SONG

Foreword

The Bhagavad Gita—The Song of God—is one of the world's most important spiritual documents in so far as it is the essence of the Upanishads, humanity's most ancient extant texts on the science of life. The Gita was written about 300 years before the birth of Christ and provides a timeless solution to the existential crises that we all face at some point in our lives.

The Upanishads are revealed texts, not the philosophical contentions of individuals or groups of individuals or the visions of mystics, which are often the basis of various religions. They come to us, not from us, much as the knowledge of electricity was revealed to Ben Franklin or the knowledge of gravity was revealed to Sir Issac Newton. Along with worldly sciences, the science of consciousness was revealed by the force that creates, sustains and destroys life to lead us out of the darkness of our material selves into the self-luminous light of our spiritual Self. It has been handed down in tact to this day.

This science is called Vedanta and sets us free of whatever doubts we may have about the nature of the material world, the nature of the human mind, and the God factor. It was passed on to me fifty years ago by my teacher and I passed it on to Rory Mackay, the author of this translation and commentary.

I have been teaching the Bhagavad Gita and other important Vedic texts to Western audiences in English worldwide for nearly fifty years. Unfortunately, my many duties have so far prevented me from giving written commentaries on the Bhagavad Gita. Fortunately, Rory's brilliant commentary on this amazing text shines the loving light that it rightly deserves. I heartily recommend it.

— James Swartz
ShiningWorld.com

Introduction

"Cast aside your despair and self-doubt. This self-indulgence is unbecoming of the noble warrior you are. It will not help this crisis, nor will it lead to enlightenment. Get up, Arjuna, and fight!"

I was twenty-one years old when I first picked up a copy of the Bhagavad Gita. The moment I opened it, the above words, spoken by Krishna in the second chapter, leapt out at me and have remained with me ever since—an exhortation at once inspiring and, at the time, perplexing.

As part of the Mahabharata epic, the Bhagavad Gita remains a prized jewel of India's cultural heritage; its story, characters and themes deeply embedded in the national psyche. Being a Westerner, I had only a passing familiarity with the Gita, but I knew that I held something special in my hands.

Delving into the ancient text, I found it both a fascinating and challenging read. Unfamiliar as I was with the Mahabharata, the first chapter was admittedly a struggle, filled with long, unpronounceable names and terms. But once I got to the second chapter, and Krishna began discussing the wonders of the Eternal Self, I was spellbound.

I can't remember how much more I read, but I soon floundered, in part because of what I saw as its overt religiosity (something that had put me off conventional Western religion). Moreover, as a committed pacifist, I couldn't reconcile the notion that God would command someone to fight and kill. Krishna's repeated injunction to Arjuna, a warrior overcome by doubt, is basically: "Go kill them, you wuss!"

Maybe I was a wuss too, because I decided the Gita wasn't for me.

It was around ten years later that, having scoured the spiritual scene in my search for answers, by sheer grace, and at a time of desperation and readiness to give it all up, I discovered Advaita Vedanta.

I devoured just about everything ever written by my teacher, James Swartz, and listened to audios of his talks every single day. One of the seminars was on the Bhagavad Gita. I dug out my dust-covered copy and read it again with a mind free of preconception.

That was when the Gita truly came alive for me. I came to see it as the masterpiece it unquestionably is; not only as a guide to Self-Realisation, but as a work of psychology and a comprehensive and surprisingly practical manual for daily life.

The Gita is a template for living; for overcoming suffering, finding our path and purpose, dealing with the obstacles of ignorance and attachment, and transcending the dualities of pleasure and pain, desire and fear, joy and sorrow. Krishna's timeless words invite us to turn within and discover our own innermost nature—which is, as it happens, is the key to liberation.

This seven hundred verse 'Song of God' (as the title translates) takes the form of a dialogue between the warrior-prince Arjuna and his divine mentor, Krishna. Whereas Krishna is an *avatar*, a direct embodiment of the Divine, Arjuna symbolises the proverbial everyman.

The Gita begins with Arjuna in despair at a moment of terrible crisis. It's important to note that, although his circumstances are unique, Arjuna's sorrow represents the basic suffering of all human beings. It's this suffering which eventually brings all of us to our knees, forcing us to confront life's 'big questions':

—*What is the purpose of life?*
—*Why am I here?*
—*How do I overcome this sorrow?*
—*What is my true nature and the nature of the world, God and reality?*

The Gita answers all of these questions and more. It deftly balances the profound and the practical, the cosmic and the

mundane, in a remarkable synthesis that provides sincere seekers with nothing less than a roadmap to freedom.

Because its message transcends time, culture and context,
the Bhagavad Gita is as relevant today as it was when composed
by the scribe Vyasa over two millennia ago, and will remain so
as long as human beings inhabit the Earth.

The Crisis Point

There comes a point in any mature person's life when they finally realise that, no matter what they try to do, be, have, or become, nothing in life is capable of removing their fundamental
sense of lack and insecurity. It's usually not until this point that,
out of sheer desperation, they begin inquiring about life, the self
and the nature of suffering.

Arjuna, embroiled in what will be the greatest war the world
has known, has reached such a crisis point. The situation is grim
and the future bleak. Greed, ambition and jealousy have divided
the royal family of Hastinapura, as two groups of cousins engage
in a deadly struggle for the throne. Arjuna and his brothers, the
Pandavas, have been robbed of their rightful claim to the kingdom by their cousins, the Kauravas, led by the ambitious and
ruthless Duryodhana.

By cheating at a game of dice, Duryodhana's uncle managed
to strip the Pandavas of everything, including their wife, kingdom and freedom. The brothers were exiled into the forest for
thirteen years, after which they were permitted to return and
reclaim the throne.

Upon their return, however, the obstinate Duryodhana re-
fused to concede, declaring that if they wanted the kingdom
they would have to fight for it. Though Arjuna and his brothers
had been willing to compromise and accept even a single house,
Duryodhana left them with no option but to declare war.

Although Arjuna was battling for a righteous cause—to free
his kingdom, restore order and correct a grave injustice—life
was making impossible demands of him. As we see in the opening chapter, Duryodhana had gathered Arjuna's own beloved

uncles, cousins, teachers and friends to fight against him. Upon seeing the face of his enemy, Arjuna's resolve crumbles.

Crippled by confusion and despair, the prince doesn't know what to do. Thus far he's done everything expected of him and everything that he could to try to make things right. Circumstances have only gone from bad to worse and now he must spill the blood of his own dearest kin.

That's when Arjuna turns to his beloved friend and charioteer, Lord Krishna. Arjuna regarded Krishna as a wise mentor and held him with the utmost regard. Indeed, when Krishna offered Arjuna the choice between having either him or his army fight alongside him on the battlefield, Arjuna opted to have Krishna by his side, even though that meant being vastly outnumbered by Duryodhana's forces.

Devastated at now having to fight his own family and friends, Arjuna seeks Krishna's help. Little did he know how profoundly life-changing Krishna's response would be.

The Battlefield is the Mind

The terrible war about to erupt between the Pandavas and the Kauravas forms the backbone of the Mahabharata. Historians believe it may have been based upon actual historical events in India's ancient past.

In the context of the Gita, however, this conflict should be considered in not just a literal but in a metaphorical sense. It becomes clear that the real battlefield isn't Kurukshetra, where the two armies meet—it's the battlefield of the human mind. The Gita's conflict symbolises the eternal war raging in the human heart and psyche.

Arjuna's situation is clearly an extraordinary one. Fortunately, few people will ever find themselves in such an extreme predicament: having to lead an army into battle against their own kith and kin.

But in order for the Gita's message to be relevant and applicable in a universal sense, it's important to understand that Arjuna's suffering represents the basic suffering of humankind. Though outer circumstances vary greatly, both the cause and the ultimate remedy for this basic human malady are the same for all people across all civilisations and time.

If the first chapter of the Gita lays out the problem: the universal suffering of worldly existence; the remaining seventeen chapters provide the solution.

The Curse of Self-Limitation

In order to understand the psychology of the Gita, it's necessary to consider the nature of human suffering.

In many ways, the human mind is a cauldron of conflict, desire, fear, and attachment. This inner conflict is such an integral part of our experience that we often either aren't even consciously aware of it, or we assume that life is meant to be full of stress and grief.

This inner turmoil, however, is unique to human beings. Whereas animals follow their nature without question, and without the burden of a self-concept, the faculty of intellect sets us apart from other creatures.

We human beings have the ability to self-reflect and to choose our own fate. Both a blessing and potentially a curse, the power of self-reflection is the cause of our bondage and also the instrument of our liberation.

According to Swami Dayananda Saraswati:

> It is the glory of man that he is conscious of himself. However, the self he is aware of is not a complete, adequate self. It is, unfortunately, a wanting, inadequate self.

The problem with self-awareness is that the 'self' we become aware of may not be acceptable to us—and it invariably isn't. By taking ourselves to be the body, mind and ego—which are by their very nature finite and limited—we experience an acute sense of lack and incompleteness at the core of our being.

The mind, reeling against this sense of self-limitation, then compels us to pursue an endless succession of desires. Rooted in lack, desire is a means to overcome our feelings of limitation and inadequacy. Thus, "I want" becomes the mantra of the human mind.

A person can only want what they think they don't already have. If you want to be happy, it's because you don't already feel happy. If you want to be whole, it's because you don't feel whole. Therefore, the more acutely you feel yourself to be lacking, the stronger your resultant desires, wants and fears.

The mind is extroverted by nature and our social conditioning only reinforces this. That's why we tend to fixate upon the objects of our environment and see them as the key to our happiness. We determine from an early age that if we could just get the world to match up to how we want it to be, then we'd be happy and complete.

The First Three Human Pursuits

It's on this premise that we spend our lives pursuing the various ends we believe will bring us a lasting sense of wholeness. Vedic tradition outlines four basic categories of human pursuit, which it calls *purushartha*, or 'human goals'. The first three of these are *artha*, *kama* and *dharma*.

1. Security and Wealth (*Artha*)

We all have essential requirements in life, such as food, clothing and shelter. We rarely stop at the basics, however. It doesn't matter if you already have a good job, a nice house, and a reliable car; there are always going to be better jobs, bigger houses and flashier cars out there.

The sense of not having enough is what fuels our ceaseless pursuit of *artha*, or wealth and security. Our hyper-consumer culture takes full advantage of this most basic drive and, in a thousand subtle and not so subtle ways, shamelessly fans the flames of human avarice.

Those stuck at this first human pursuit seek happiness in money, possessions, real estate, relationships, power and recognition. The problem is enough is never enough. Fulfilment is perpetually elusive, because no matter what you have, there's always going to more and better out there somewhere. It's a sad fact that even many billionaires worry about money, and no matter what they have, they never feel quite satisfied or secure enough.

2. Desire (*Kama*)

The second human pursuit is *kama*, or desire. When security is no longer your primary concern, and assuming you aren't a workaholic stuck in artha, your focus will likely shift to pleasure. You get bored, and you want to feel good, so you turn to food, sex, entertainment, socialising, alcohol, gaming, travel, and an endless array of other pleasures.

Living in our affluent modern society, without having to necessarily worry about day to day survival, kama becomes the primary drive for many people. It's for this reason that the entertainment industry is one of the biggest industries on the planet.

Unfortunately, desire is like fire. The more you feed it, the stronger it becomes. There's never a point when fire decides that it's had enough. It will keep burning and burning, and when one source of fuel is exhausted, it hungrily moves onto another.

3. Virtue (*Dharma*)

Any honest, intelligent person will eventually conclude that artha alone doesn't bring happiness, and kama may bring pleasure but little fulfilment. That's when a person may turn to the third human goal, which we call *dharma*.

As we'll see, dharma is an essential concept in the Gita. The term has different meanings depending upon the context. In terms of life goals, it relates to the desire to be virtuous; to do what is right.

The more mature you become as a person, the more you commit to dharma; seeking fulfilment through friendship, sharing, helping others and contributing back to the world and the society around you. Instead of trying to extract all that you can from the world, you begin thinking in terms of giving something back to it.

Obviously, not every human being reaches this point. Many get stuck at the level of artha or kama; revelling in the pursuit of money and sense pleasure. Generally, those who value dharma are people with a mature, cultured, and refined disposition.

Almost all human endeavour can be rooted in one or more of these three categories. Whatever you're doing, whether it's vying for a promotion at work, investing or donating money, pursuing a relationship, or picking up litter on the street, you're generally doing it to attain wealth and security, pleasure and enjoyment, or renown and fulfilment.

The Limitations Inherent in Seeking

Some people get pretty good at the game of life. Perhaps they achieve a measure of worldly success, wealth and recognition, marry the man or woman of their dreams and go on luxury cruises five times a year. Their quality of life is unquestionably good. But that doesn't necessarily have any bearing on their quality of mind.

As the rich and famous often lament, outer success is no guarantee of inner happiness. Indeed, it often seems that the more people have, the more they suffer because the more they have to lose.

One of life's great perversions is that everything in the phenomenal world is in a continual state of flux. Because things are constantly changing, it's impossible to hold onto anything. What you have today, you might lose tomorrow. What works one day may not the next.

You can spend the best part of a lifetime striving to attain the greatest object of your desire, only to find that, after the initial high wears off, you become accustomed to it and it no longer provides you with the same emotional high. Or perhaps the object itself changes. Your greatest delight one day can become the bane of your existence the next (if you don't believe me, go take a look at the nearest divorce court!).

The limitations inherent in seeking happiness through artha, kama and dharma are clear. Even when you do manage to manipulate life in such a way that you get exactly what you want, it often comes with a hefty price tag, so you must always be extremely sure that it's what you really want.

The truth is nothing remains fulfilling for very long. Things are constantly changing, and the human mind has a thirst for novelty. This, combined with the fact that others are also busily pursuing their own agendas and goals, conspires to deliver endless frustration.

The basic conclusion that any sane and rational individual will reach is that life is a zero sum game. You have the ability to transact with the world and pursue your goals, but there's absolutely no way that you can get what you want the whole time. Life being what it is, for every gain, there is a loss, and for every upside, a downside.

Samsara

Once you get sucked into the cycle of desiring and acquiring, it can be almost impossible to get back out of it. In the East, the term for this is *samsara*.

The word samsara comes from the root *samsri*, meaning, "to go round, revolve; to pass through a succession of states, as if moving in a circuit." Samsara relates to the cycle of birth, death and rebirth; "passage through successive states of mundane existence."

Samsara is a state of endless becoming. Never satisfied with what you have or what you are, you are compelled to keep performing action in the hope of attaining certain results; in the hope of becoming more than you are.

The problem is, as we've seen, life is a zero sum game, and no matter what you do, you'll never be completely satisfied with the results. Therefore, you have to keep doing and doing, all the while digging a deeper and deeper hole for yourself.

The wheel of samsara is kept in motion by desire. Desire prompts action, and this action creates a psychological tendency to repeat itself. Let's say that one day I discover chocolate cake for the first time. I pick up a spoon and taste it. I discover that I like it, and this simple action, taking a bite of cake, creates a desire to eat more cake. Each time I succumb to the desire,

I strengthen both the desire and the tendency to act on that desire. This tendency to repeat a thought or action is called a *vasana*.

The problem is, after a while, I'm no longer eating cake because I necessarily want to eat cake. I might actually be trying to lose weight. I'm eating it because my likes (cake) and dislikes (lack of cake) are now driving my psyche. So, who's really running the show here?

To make matters worse, every action generates not only a tendency to repeat itself, but a corresponding reaction. Before I know it, my cake vasana is out of control and I'm struggling with my weight and in danger of developing significant health problems.

Once we step onto the samsaric treadmill it can be almost impossible to get back off it again. We rely entirely on external supports to bring us happiness, even though this happiness is by its very nature fleeting. But, deliriously thirsty, we keep trying to squeeze whatever drops of pleasure we can get out of life. That's how the cycle of desire and action perpetuates.

The Fundamental Problem

It's important to realise that it's never really the object of our pursuit that we truly want.

Owing to our faulty self-concept, whether consciously or unconsciously, we consider ourselves to be deficient and inadequate.

What we really want is to feel different. That's the real reason we chase after things in the world. It's to add something to ourselves; to improve ourselves; to make ourselves acceptable in the eyes of others, and therefore acceptable in our own eyes.

This basic sense of self-dissatisfaction is the fundamental conflict at the core of the human psyche.

We experience it as a gulf between who we are and who we want to be; between our subjective wants and our objective reality. Everything that we do is an attempt to bridge this gap. Our actions are therefore motivated by the desire to be whole, complete, and free of the suffering that seems endemic to our very nature.

Chasing after the shiny, seductive objects of the world—whether it's fame, fortune, fast cars, soul mates, or even spiritual experiences—is at best a distraction. It's like trying to fix a car's engine by adjusting the wing mirrors.

Our failure to deal with the root of this problem dooms us to almost perpetual suffering, for nothing in this world of finite forms is capable of bringing us lasting happiness and wholeness.

Fortunately, there remains one final human pursuit. Most people aren't even aware that it exists. The fourth human goal is called *moksha*. In English, it means 'liberation' or 'freedom'—and this happens to be the Bhagavad Gita's primary topic.

The Highest Goal

Freedom is life's highest goal. In fact, freedom is life's only goal.

Whenever you're seeking artha, kama, or dharma, it's actually freedom that you want. By pursuing security, you seek freedom from your sense of insecurity. By chasing wealth, you seek freedom from poverty. By pursuing any desire, you seek freedom from that desire; freedom from the want that compels you to act—from the sense of lack, need, or insufficiency.

The problem is, seeking freedom in external conditions only ever leads to further bondage. As long as you depend upon any external factor for your freedom, you remain bound by your dependence upon it. The moment it changes, as it most certainly will, you've lost your freedom.

Moksha is the highest goal because it ends the need for all seeking. Instead of digging for scraps of happiness in the ever-changing and unpredictable outer world, you turn within and start seeking happiness in yourself.

This may not come easily, because you've likely spent a lifetime thinking of yourself as a lacking, deficient being, totally dependent upon others and the world for your happiness.

The problem isn't that you actually lack anything, however.

Rather, the problem is summed up in the words of the poet Walt Whitman:

You have not known what you are.
You have slumbered upon yourself all of your life;
Your eyelids have been the same as closed most of the
time.

That's where Vedanta comes in. According to Vedanta, the
distilled knowledge of the ancient Vedas, the issue is not one
of 'becoming free'. Vedanta points out that you cannot become
free, because you are already free.

The problem is one of ignorance; of lack of knowledge.

You are bound only because you take yourself to be what
you are not: ie., a separate, limited body-mind-ego. Only by inquiring into this assumption, which lies at the root of existential
suffering, will you come to realise the freedom inherent to your
very nature.

That may sound like a tall claim, but Vedanta has the means
to prove it, thereby removing the suffering of samsara.

Also called *jnana yoga*, or the yoga of Self-knowledge,
Vedanta is neither a philosophy nor a religion. It is a means
of knowledge. In this case, the subject is you. Therefore, the
knowledge it provides is Self-knowledge. The removal of ignorance regarding your true nature is the key to psychological and
spiritual liberation.

To understand the Bhagavad Gita, it's impossible to divorce
it from the context of Vedanta, because only then one can truly
grasp the full meaning of Krishna's words.

The Gita has the distinction of being one of the three primary scriptures of Vedanta; the 'triple cannon' which also includes the Upanishads and the Brahma Sutras. The Gita is both
a treatise on right action in the world (dharma) and liberation,
or enlightenment (moksha). Understood correctly, Krishna's
words provide a roadmap to psychological, emotional, and spiritual freedom.

The Liberating Power of Self-Knowledge

The actual teaching of the Gita doesn't begin until the eleventh verse of Chapter two. Prior to that it's a continuation of the Mahabharata narrative, laying out the reason for Arjuna's despair.

The Pandava prince doesn't know what to do. His mind is incapacitated with grief and he cannot see a way forward. It's at this point that Arjuna turns to his mentor and beseeches Krishna to accept him as his disciple. He asks Krishna to show him the way forward.

As we have seen, Krishna's initial response is, "Get up, Arjuna—and fight!"

Arjuna's confusion is understandable, which leads to Krishna revealing the ultimate Truth that leads to freedom from all bondage. This Truth is arguably the primary subject matter of the Gita: Self-knowledge.

Vedanta reveals that the root of our suffering is ignorance of our true nature. We've established that the cause of our desires and our suffering is the sense of being a limited, lacking, incomplete entity. As such a self is clearly unacceptable to us, we find ourselves constantly chasing the objects and experiences that we vainly believe will bring us freedom.

The only true freedom, however, comes from challenging this basic misapprehension about who we are.

Krishna immediately reveals to Arjuna the true nature of the Self* as complete fullness and limitlessness. This Self, which is the same in all beings, is eternal, deathless, ever secure, and untouchable by any worldly grief or suffering.

The Gita thus delves into the core teaching of the Upanishads. The person that we take ourselves to be is but a notion; a superimposition born of ignorance with no independent existence of its own.

---

* Please note: The word 'Self' is capitalised to distinguish it from what one might ordinarily consider the 'self', ie., the mind/body/ego. Any difference between the two, however, is purely notional, as we shall see.

Vedantic inquiry, through a process of negation, reveals that we cannot be the body, the mind or the ego.

As Krishna explains in chapter thirteen, there are only two categories in existence: the field of objects and the knower of the field. Anything known to us is an object, whether it's a physical object or a subtle object in our mind or imagination. The knower of these objects has to be other than the object.

The body is known to us as an object, as is the mind, intellect, ego, and the sense organs. The Self, therefore, cannot be any of those constituent parts. Rather, the Self is the knower of these objects and cannot itself be objectified.

This Self is pure awareness; the changeless screen upon which the phenomenal world appears like a desert mirage. All-pervading and eternal, this awareness is partless and indivisible.

Krishna tells Arjuna, "The Self is never born, thus it can never die." While bodies die, cast aside like worn-out old clothes, the Self simply adopts new bodies, for: "Ever-present and changeless, it is without beginning and end."

By taking ourselves to be a limited body and mind, subject to the ravages of time, sickness and death, we experience enormous fear, pain and suffering. But Krishna makes it clear that we "grieve over that which does not warrant grief."

If the Self is limitless and untouched by anything in this world, and we are the Self, then our sense of lack, inadequacy and want is illegitimate, for it is based on ignorance of our true nature.

The dawning of Self-knowledge—the realisation that we are by nature free, self-effulgent and the source of our own happiness—is the light that dispels the dark suffering of ignorance.

According to Krishna, those who attain liberation have mastered their own minds, have tranquil hearts and are "free of the anxiety of always having to acquire and hoard." Unburdened by binding desires, the liberated are, unlike the suffering samsari, content in themselves alone. With an ever full heart, they are unshaken by adversity and no longer depend upon anything external for their happiness.

According to Krishna, such people move about
as freely as air, devoid of all sense of limitation, fear
ing. Such is the bliss of Self-knowledge; the freedom t
from knowing one's true Self to be free of bondage
source of all joy.

Preparing the Mind

Alas, if all that moksha required was being told about the wonders of the Self, Arjuna would have been enlightened by the end
of the second chapter and there would have been no need for
the subsequent sixteen chapters.

Although Krishna beautifully describes the nature of the
Self, and Arjuna trusts his words, it's clear that words alone are
insufficient to end his suffering.

For Self-knowledge to take root and shift the locus of one's
identity from the limited ego to the limitless Self, one first must
have a qualified mind. Just as a field must be fertile and appropriately prepared prior to planting, so must the mind be open
and receptive to the knowledge. Certain groundwork has to be
in place, and this is the focus of the first section of the Gita.

The pull of the senses naturally draws the mind's focus onto
sense objects; to the world of form and experience. The immersive allure of the phenomenal captivates the mind and senses
so utterly that only precious few in any generation ever turn
inward to seek the Self.

The Gita repeatedly warns of the dangers of getting lost
in the world of the senses. In chapter two, Krishna states that
dwelling upon objects causes attachment, which, in turn, leads
to desire, from which suffering is born. A suffering mind becomes deluded, clouding one's judgement and preventing proper discrimination. "When the mind is no longer fit for the attainment of liberation," Krishna laments, "one's life is as good
as destroyed."

According to the Gita, the primary tool for cultivating a tranquil and pure mind, a mind capable of assimilating the knowledge of the Self, is *karma yoga*. It's no accident that Krishna
introduces karma yoga before the sections on meditation, devo-

tion and Self-knowledge. While the second chapter provides a snapshot of the contents of the entire Gita, the teaching unfolds in a deliberate and logical sequence.

The Gita can be divided into three sections, each consisting of six chapters. The first section deals with the topics of dharma, karma yoga, and the issue of action and renunciation. These chapters focus on preparing the mind for moksha, prescribing the proper lifestyle and the right mindset. The middle section of the Gita explores meditation, the nature of the Self and the creation, and *upasana yoga*, or devotional practice. The concluding section focuses on Self-knowledge and how to integrate this knowledge in one's life in order to attain liberation.

The Gita's deft interweaving of the spiritual and the practical, the divine and the worldly, marks it as truly unique. In fact, the eight century visionary Adi Shankara stated that if a person were to study only one piece of Vedantic scripture, it should be the Bhagavad Gita.

During Shankara's time, moksha was only seen as a viable goal for the *sannyasi*; one who formally renounces society, relinquishing all material pursuits for the attainment of enlightenment. Although there are still sannyasis in India today, modern society neither values nor recognises this as a legitimate life path.

For this reason alone, the Gita is important. It teaches that freedom can be attained without having to renounce society altogether; that a person can seek enlightenment without giving up a life of worldly action. In fact, Krishna specifically states that true renunciation doesn't mean giving up action altogether. It means giving up our attachment to the results of that action.

Understanding the Gita

As I learned when I first discovered the Gita, it's necessary to have a teacher to decode the teaching and to resolve any doubts and confusion. Without a qualified teacher, you'll only ever interpret the teaching according to your pre-existing beliefs and worldview. Confirmation bias is indeed one of the trickiest tendencies of the mind, for it keeps the truth obscured by a veil of ignorance masquerading as knowledge.

It should be no surprise that the Gita can be interpreted in different ways according to one's biases and sensibilities.

The Vedantin sees the Gita as an extension of the 'revealed knowledge' of the Upanishads, at the core of which we find the great saying, *Tat tvam asi*: That I am. These three simple words encapsulate the supreme truth of Vedanta, affirming the identity of the *jiva*, the personal self, as non-different to Brahman, the universal Self. Krishna explicitly states that He is the Self in all beings. The Gita, therefore, unfolds a vision of non-duality, using the conventions of language and duality.

As a Self-realised avatar, throughout the Gita Krishna refers to the Self in first person terms: as "I", "Me" and "Mine". Unless you grasp the nuance of his teaching, you might be tempted to take Krishna's words literally, just as many Christians take the parables of Jesus literally.

Instead of seeing Krishna as a personification of the universal Self at the core of all beings, some focus exclusively on the 'personhood' of Krishna. Vaishnavists, for example, take a dualistic and literal interpretation of the Gita. They refute that the Gita is a teaching on moksha, and interpret it as a strictly devotional text. They seek to worship Krishna as the 'Supreme Godhead', aiming to please Krishna and earn the chance to sport with him in the afterlife.

That is not the interpretation this commentary assumes. Arguably the most influential commentary ever written on the Gita was by the aforementioned Adi Shankara, who set the basis for Vedanta's teaching back in the eight century. Having found no better analysis, this commentary is in line with Shankara's teaching and the traditional Vedanta *sampradaya* (teaching tradition).

This work is heavily indebted to the excellent commentaries and teachings of Swami Dayananda Saraswati, Swami Chinmayanada, Swami Paramarthananda of Chennai, and my own teacher, James Swartz.

My intent was to distil the essence of the Gita in an accessible way for Western audiences, and for those who may not be overly familiar with it. I wanted to create the kind of commentary I wish I'd had when I first found this remarkable jewel; one that brings clear meaning and an understandable interpretation to the words.

In translating, I have endeavoured to remain faithful to the Sanskrit verses. I did, however, modify the beginning of the first chapter. The opening verses of the Gita can be difficult for those unfamiliar with the Mahabharata and Indian culture and historical context. The author, Vyasa, uses a narrative device in which a seer, Sanjaya, relates the entire story to Duryodhana's blind father, King Dritharastra. This can potentially be confusing and includes rather more detail about the warriors gathered on the battlefield than is necessary for understanding the Gita. I decided to set the scene in a simpler manner, describing the battlefield and the two armies gathered in short, descriptive prose. From then on, the translation remains largely faithful, with changes made only for clarity, meaning, and ease of reading.

It is my hope that this volume will be an opening for those who may wish to explore the Gita and the teaching of Vedanta in greater depth. To that end, I especially recommend Swami Dayananda's book 'The Teaching of the Bhagavad Gita' and, for the more committed, his multi-volume 'Bhagavad Gita Home Study Course, which is an outstanding work. Excellent general Vedanta books include 'The Essence of Vedanta' by James Swartz and 'Vedanta: The Big Picture', based on talks by Swami Paramarthananda.

In the spirit of karma yoga, I offer this book to the divine Self in all beings, and dedicate it to my teacher James Swartz and the noble *sampradaya* that has so greatly blessed my life.

BHAGAVAD GITA

CHAPTER ONE

Arjuna's Sorrow

¹ On the morning of the battle, the sun edged above the horizon, streaking the sky with red and gold. Two vast and terrible armies, numbering almost four million warriors and soldiers, sprawled across the fields of Kurukshetra, the abode of *dharma*.

²⁻¹¹ The largest of the two, the Kaurava army, stood facing West, commanded by the mighty Bhishma. The smaller army of the Pandavas faced East, led by Dhrishtadyumna.

Division after division of mighty warriors stood tall in golden chariots; their bows, maces, swords and lances glistening in the morning light. Men, horses and elephants filled the battlefield, clad in gold and bronze armour, banners waving in the wind.

¹²⁻¹⁹ With a roar, Bhishma raised his conch horn to his lips and sounded the war call. At that, the other Kauravas blew their conches, trumpets and cow horns and pounded at drums; a cacophony both tremendous and terrifying.

Arjuna, the Pandava prince, remained fearless and determined. Standing in a kingly gold chariot with his beloved mentor Krishna as charioteer, the prince raised his conch, *Devadatta*, to his lips. As he sounded the war cry, he was joined by Krishna, his brothers Bhima, Yudhisthira, Sahadeva and Nakula, and the other noble warriors gathered alongside them. The sound reverberated like thunder, piercing the hearts of all gathered upon the battlefield.

²⁰⁻²³ Arjuna then made a request of Krishna: "Take me forward, Krishna! Drive my chariot between the two armies. Let me see the faces of those I must fight."

²⁴⁻²⁵ Krishna complied. With a tug of the reigns, the white horses galloped ahead, sending a cloud of dust rising from the

ground. The chariot came to a stop at the centre of the battle-field. Krishna said, "Behold the Kauravas."

26-27 The moment Arjuna laid eyes on the men he was about to fight, his heart sank in horror. The opposing soldiers, armed to the hilt and ready to unleash the horrors of a war unlike any other, included many of his own family, friends and cherished teachers. His cousin, the twisted Duryodhana, had gathered Arjuna's own relatives to fight against him.

28-29 Seized by compassion, Arjuna said sorrowfully, "Krishna, these men are my family. How can I fight them in battle?" A moment ago the Prince had stood ready to vanquish his opponents. He was a seasoned warrior; his entire life devoted to dharma and heroic sacrifice. He was not a man given to fear or distress. But the moment his eyes beheld the great and noble men standing ready to fight him, all certainty vanished.

30 Overcome by despair, the bow slipped from his hand. The moment his great bow, *Gandiva*, hit the ground, time seemed to freeze.

31-37 Arjuna said, "Krishna, I see no good in this fight! I have little desire for riches, kingdoms or worldly pleasures. For what use is a kingdom if I must slaughter my own uncles, teachers and family? I cannot bring myself to kill these men, Krishna, even if they are sworn to kill me! What kind of satisfaction would such a victory bring? How could we ever be happy having destroyed our own people?

38-44 "They are fighting on the wrong side surely, but I would be no better if I were to slay them in battle. I cannot kill my own family. Family means everything. If fathers, brothers, uncles and cousins take arms against each other, families are destroyed, dharma perishes and society degenerates into chaos.

45-46 "How can a man kill his own flesh and blood out of greed and desire for victory? I cannot do it, Krishna! I would sooner lay down my arms and allow the enemy to kill me."

47 Having spoken these words, Arjuna sank down in his chariot, his heart overcome with anguish as he cast aside his bow and arrows. He had made his decision. He would not fight.

COMMENTARY

The opening chapter of the Bhagavad Gita sets the scene as two great armies prepare to battle for the fate of a stolen kingdom. While the teaching of the Gita doesn't begin until chapter two, this chapter presents Arjuna's predicament and subsequent despair upon realising that he must fight and kill his own family and friends. Thus, we begin with a war that must be fought and a warrior who will not fight.

This conflict isn't merely a dispute over land and power. Indeed, the opening lines refer to the battlefield as *dharmashetra*, meaning "place of *dharma*". This reference is not by chance, for it outlines one of the pivotal themes of the Gita. The battle of Kurukshetra is a battle of *dharma* versus *adharma*; that age old conflict of right versus wrong.

Arjuna happens to be a *kshatriya*, one of the warrior class whose sworn duty is to protect dharma, or righteousness. Those who violate dharma, such as Arjuna's enemy, Duryodhana, must be stopped. Dharma must always triumph over *adharma*, or else society will be destroyed.

The way to stop adharma is to first challenge it using non-violent means; to negotiate and try to find a peaceful resolution. Should this fail, the society's law enforcers must then take action. War is something that should be always avoided. Sometimes, however, when all other options have been exhausted, peace must be fought for.

As a defender of dharma, Arjuna has a duty to perform, but there's now a conflict between what he wants to do and what he must do. Upon seeing that the cruel Duryodhana has gathered his own family members, teachers and friends to fight against him, his resolve crumbles. He falters, not out of fear, but out of compassion. His mind now incapacitated, the noble prince can no longer perform his duty.

As noted in the introduction, the battle of the Gita has a largely metaphorical component. On one level it represents dharma and adharma, but it's also symbolic of the psychological and spiritual battle experienced by every human being. Indeed, Arjuna's grief represents *samsara*, the fundamental malady of humankind.

While mercifully few of us will ever find ourselves in as extreme a situation as Arjuna, the suffering of samsara is just as real irrespective of personal circumstances. Although its manifestation differs, samsara always has its root in faulty thinking; in ignorance-induced misidentification, the cause of inordinate sorrow and suffering.

Dharma

In order to understand the Gita, it is essential to have an understanding of dharma. Dharma is a nuanced topic. The word itself, which has no direct English equivalent, is derived from the root *dhr.*, "to hold, maintain, and support" and *dharman*, meaning "bearer or supporter".

Dharma, then, is the natural law underlying the creation; the invisible thread binding together the tapestry of life, ensuring that each constituent part works together, enabling the universe to function with cohesion and integrity.

In the context of the Gita, dharma is taken to mean 'right action', as opposed to adharma, which is 'wrong action'. Dharma refers to behaviour, action, and conduct in alignment with the natural order of life.

While values vary from culture to culture, along with personal predilections, dharma remains universal and constant. You might say it is built into the very structure of life as the unwritten code of creation.

The Yajur Upanishad states:

> Nothing is higher than dharma.
> Verily, that which is dharma is Truth.

Driving the entire creation, dharma is intrinsic to the functioning of society and the fate of the world. Therefore, upholding dharma is a matter of prime importance. That's why it is said that a person should be willing to sacrifice everything to uphold dharma.

Three Types of Dharma

Dharma can be understood in terms of three basic categories: universal, situational and personal dharma.

1. Universal Dharma

Universal dharma, or *samanya dharma,* relates to universal values, the most fundamental of which is non-injury. This isn't something that we need to be taught. We all have an innate understanding of non-injury based upon our shared values and mutual expectation. After all, when you leave your house, you expect to be able to walk down the street without having someone jump out and steal your wallet.

No living being wants to be hurt, therefore, non-injury is the foremost aspect of universal dharma. We all want to be treated with kindness, sympathy, and compassion. Wilfully injuring another grossly violates dharma and always brings unfortunate karmic repercussions.

Truth is another key aspect of dharma. Everyone knows it's wrong to lie, because no one likes being lied to. Purity and self-restraint are other key dharmic values. It makes sense to live as cleanly as possible in terms of body, diet, thought, word, and deed, for our own well-being, health and peace of mind. Similarly, self-restraint prevents us from falling victim to our mind's petty whims and impulses, which often lead to nothing but trouble.

It's worth noting that even those who routinely violate dharma, such as thieves and liars, still have an instinctive knowledge of right and wrong. We know this because they, in turn, don't want to be stolen from or lied to. That's why a thief will always hide his loot. So it's not that such people don't understand dharma; it's just that, for various reasons, they choose not to follow it.

There is, however, always a price to be paid for violating dharma. We must face not only outer consequences, but also inner repercussions, in the form of mental conflict, guilt, fear and sorrow.

2. Situational Dharma

A society creates laws to ensure that dharma is maintained. Unlike dharma, however, laws are not universal. Some may even be adharmic depending on who is running the society. Furthermore, laws are changeable. They may apply at certain times, but not others. Murder, for example, is considered the worst of all crimes. However, at times of war, soldiers on the battlefield are expected to kill when ordered. So, while a civilian will end up in jail for killing someone, a soldier could end up in jail for refusing to kill.

Dharma, then, has a situational component, which we call *vishesha dharma*. Every situation has its corresponding dharma; specific rules that should be observed and not broken. When you go to the grocery shop, you have wait in line to pay for your purchases. If you go to see a movie, you are expected to sit in your seat and remain quiet during the showtime. When you drive, you are expected to stay on the appropriate side of the road. Everyone must abide by these rules, or else chaos erupts.

On an individual level, we all have specific types of dharma in relation to our roles as a parent, child, teacher, student, employer, employee, citizen, spiritual seeker, and so on. Such dharma will at times change depending on our circumstances, roles, and stage of life.

3. Personal Dharma

It's important to understand that everything in existence also has its own *svadharma*, or personal dharma. This is inbuilt and rooted in the essential nature of that particular object or being. For example, it is the dharma of the sun to shine, of water to flow, birds to fly, flowers to bloom and bees to make honey.

Human beings also have their own dharma, which manifests as universally occurring personality archetypes. This dharma isn't self-selected. It is inherent to our innermost nature.

Depending on their svadharma, some people have a natural proclivity to be artists, healers, or mathematicians, while others might be compelled to work in science, law enforcement, business, or politics.

All beings must follow their nature and act according to their dharma. In this way, we each make an appropriate contribution to life, supporting the entirety of the creation.

Violate Dharma At Your Peril

Following dharma feels good. Regardless of the outcome of your actions, you experience a sense of harmony and satisfaction when you do the right thing and remain true to your nature. If you want to live a happy and largely incident-free life, all you need to do is commit to following dharma impeccably.

Violating dharma, on the other hand, always brings guilt and inner conflict. Even a sociopath knows when they've crossed the line and will feel bad, even if it's just because they know there will be repercussions to face.

Whenever you violate dharma, you can guarantee that consequences are inevitable. Sometimes the repercussions are swift. If you hit me, my immediate reaction might be to hit you back twice as hard. Other times, the consequences may take longer to fructify. Perhaps I go to the police, file a report, and the next morning a police officer comes knocking at your door. Either way, even the slightest transgression of dharma causes ripples.

Unlike human beings, animals and plants naturally follow their dharma. They have no choice in the matter. A bird will always behave like a bird. It won't one day decide that it should dive into the water and become a fish. An apple tree will always yield apples and not pears. Sugar will always be sweet and fire will always be hot. Dharma is innate. Without it, life would exist in a perpetual state of chaos. No meaningful action could take place due to constantly shifting variables. Instead, we live in a lawful universe; a dharma field.

Human beings, however, are often at odds with their own nature. Endowed with the capacity for self reflection and self determination, we are the only species capable of contravening dharma. If the battlefield of the Gita is witness to a conflict between dharma and adharma, so too is the human mind.

The core of this conflict is a clash between what we desire and value and what we know is right.

A mature person can recognise the importance of doing the right thing regardless of their personal desires and preferences. Such a person knows that the ends never justify the means, and is aware of the cost of violating dharma. Accordingly, they can discriminate between what should and shouldn't be done.

An immature person lacks this crucial discrimination. Their desires are so strong that they see nothing wrong with taking shortcuts, breaking the law, or hurting others in order to get what they want.

An adharmic life is a costly one, causing endless conflict and retribution. More than anything, it keeps one drowning in the whirlpool of suffering that is samsara.

The Wheel of Samsara

The basis of samsara is always a sense of lack. Those who feel whole and complete in themselves have few desires. After all, what's there to desire when you know that you are the source of your own happiness?

The basic human problem is that while we all know that we *are*, we don't know *who* we are. We all know that we exist, but have a fundamental lack of knowledge about our true nature and identity.

This is a universal problem, irrespective of age, gender, nationality, or social status. It isn't something confined to the modern age, either. It was just as much a problem in Arjuna's time, thousands of years ago, and will continue to be as long as our species graces the planet.

The problem of samsara is simple. Because you take appearance to be real and believe yourself to be a limited body-mind entity, you experience a great sense of incompleteness and lack. This feeling of lack is called *dukkha*, which means "unsatisfactoriness".

Regardless of your personal circumstances, whether good or bad, the body, mind and ego are always by their very nature limited, and forever haunted by the spectre of their own inevitable demise.

As a result of this basic sense of lack, limitation and inadequacy, you desperately try to control your life as best you can. The mind becomes a bubbling cauldron of want and desire. Driving your entire psyche is an endless array of likes and dislikes, desires and aversions. A person can only want what they feel they lack, so the greater your sense of self-limitation, the stronger your desires.

The problem is, no matter how much you strive and how much you get, it's never enough. It's never sufficient to resolve that fundamental sense of incompleteness at the core of your being.

Until you deal with the root of the problem—dukkha, and the belief or assumption that you're a lacking, limited ego—it's impossible to escape the whirlpool of suffering that is samsara. You just keep drowning in it, over and over again.

The Vicious Cycle of Samsara

This sense of self limitation gives rise to three particular qualities which, together, comprise the cycle of samsara.

1. Binding Desire/Attachment (*Raga*)

Raga is born of a sense of incompleteness. Because your deepest desire is to be whole and complete, you actively seek the objects and circumstances which you believe you will complete you.

'Desire' isn't strong enough a translation for raga. Raga refers to those intractable, binding desires that form the basis of emotional attachments and addictions. It's more than just a desire; it's a psychological dependency.

These attachments are always self-centred in nature. When you're driven by raga, your primary concern is fulfilling your own emotional needs. You're determined to get all that you can out of whatever people, relationships, or situations you con-

sider necessary for your happiness. Often you don't much care
whose toes you have to step on along the way, and whether or
not you are following dharma.

2. Sorrow (*Shoka*)

Raga inevitably leads to *shoka*, or sorrow.

You can never be free as long as you remain emotionally
dependent on any external factor for your happiness. Someone
who needs crutches to walk might feel secure, but it's a false
security. The moment someone takes those crutches away, a fall
is inevitable.

The loss of a psychological crutch, whether it's a relationship, a job, or a cherished possession, causes terrible suffering.
Whether it manifests as anger, bitterness, depression or grief,
the stronger your attachment, the greater your sorrow.

3. Delusion (*Moha*)

Sorrow and anger, in time, result in delusion. When your mind
is overcome by attachment, you can't see clearly. You can no
longer discriminate between right and wrong; between what
you should and shouldn't do. Before you know it, you're living
an adharmic life. The more adharma you commit, the more you
suffer and the more suffering you inflict on others.

This, of course, only reinforces the basic sense of inadequacy that initiated the samsaric cycle.

This cycle is one of perpetual frustration and suffering. You
find yourself continually performing the actions you think will
bring happiness and wholeness. Unfortunately, nothing in this
world is capable of delivering lasting happiness. Even the attainment of a desire will eventually turn to suffering because, given
that everything in this world is in a state of constant change,
objects are incapable of providing lasting happiness.

Yet, owing to ignorance and the momentum of past actions,
the vasanas (subtle tendencies, or psychological compulsions)
compel you to keep chasing rainbows in the hope of eventually
finding your pot of gold.

Sadly, this just keeps you stuck in an ever greater spiral of attachment, sorrow and delusion. Once the wheel of samsara starts turning, it can be almost impossible to get off it.

Re-educating the Mind

We always tend to assume that outer circumstances are the cause of our suffering, when the real fault lies closer to home.

A problem can only be solved when you deal with it at the level of the problem. Trying to escape samsara by rearranging the outer circumstances of your life will have no effect whatsoever. The issue all along was one of faulty thinking; specifically, this false notion of who you think you are and what you think you need in order to be happy and whole. Because the problem arises in the intellect, that's the only place it can be solved. The way out of samsara is, therefore, to re-educate your mind.

As it happens, that is precisely Krishna's role in the Gita. Recall that the battlefield of Kurukshetra symbolises the human psyche. Arjuna represents the mind ensnared in samsara, and Krishna represents the higher mind; the ever-liberated Self.

Recalling an analogy in the Katha Upanishad, the very chariot in which Arjuna and Krishna ride is the perfect metaphor for the human being. The chariot itself represents the physical body, the horses are the sense organs, the reins are the mind, the rider of the chariot is the ego, while the driver is the intellect.

At first it might seem strange to have Arjuna as lord of the chariot while Krishna sits beneath him as charioteer. But it's no mistake that Krishna drives the chariot. After all, one's chariot, one's life, should always be directed by a higher principle—and what is higher than God?

Without a discriminating intellect, without the power to think clearly and make proper decisions, the senses run amok as the ego blindly tries to gratify its lower impulses, irrespective of dharma. Without a competent driver at the reins, the horses will gallop uncontrollably, or perhaps not move at all.

Purposeful action is only possible when the senses and mind are kept in check by the intellect. The problem is, as we have seen, a samsaric mind is an incapacitated mind.

It's here the Gita begins, with Arjuna lost in the throes of samsara. His mind paralysed by doubt and confusion, he can no longer act, even though he knows the duty before him.

Almost every human being will experience such a crisis point at some time or another; and it can either make or break that person. Whereas one person's despair might turn them to drink, drugs, or even suicide, another might start inquiring. He or she begins to question things. Is this really all there is to life? What is it that I can't see? How have I contributed to my own problems—and what can I do about them?

Arjuna has given up the battle before it's even begun. But he's not alone. The divine Krishna stands by his side, and, as we shall see, Krishna has much to say.

CHAPTER TWO

The Power of Knowledge

¹ Arjuna sat motionless, his vision blurring with tears as he stared across the battlefield.

²⁻³ Krishna looked down at him, and he spoke in a voice filled with impassioned resolve: "Arjuna, the hour of battle has come. Cast aside your despair and self-doubt. This self-indulgence is unbecoming of the noble warrior you are. It will not help this crisis, nor will it lead to enlightenment. Get up, Arjuna, and fight!"

⁴⁻⁵ "Krishna, how can I fight these men?" Arjuna said. "These are great souls, worthy of my devotion. I'd rather beg on the streets than take up arms against my teachers and friends. If I were to kill them, any victory would be stained with their blood.

⁶ "Even if I should attain the most prosperous kingdom on earth, what pleasure could I take from it? How could I live with myself knowing who I had slain? Besides, how can we even say for certain who should win this war? Who is to that say we should be victorious and not they?"

⁷⁻⁹ The prince shook his head. "I don't know what to do. My mind is in darkness. I can't see a way forward. I'm your student, O Krishna. I seek refuge in you. Please teach me. Share with me your wisdom. For I shall not fight." With that, Arjuna fell silent.

¹⁰⁻¹¹ Krishna's face softened, and he said, "You speak with compassion, Arjuna, but your sorrow is misplaced. The wise grieve neither for the living nor the dead.

¹² "There was never a time that I did not exist, nor you, nor any of these kings gathered here. Nor will there come a time when we cease to exist in the future.

¹³ "Just as the indweller of the body experiences childhood, youth and old age, so too at death, does he simply gain another body. Knowing this, the wise do not grieve.

14-15 "While the senses give rise to heat and cold, pleasure and pain, these experiences are fleeting; they come and go and must be endured. Those who remain even-minded in both pleasure and pain have true discrimination and are fit to attain liberation.

16-17 "Listen carefully, Arjuna, for this is the knowledge that leads to freedom. The unreal does not exist, and the real never ceases to exist. The wise understand this, for they know That which pervades this entire universe to be indestructible. One cannot bring about the destruction of That which never changes.

18-19 "While bodies are subject to change and death, the eternal Self, reflected as man's indwelling consciousness, is impervious to destruction. Anyone who thinks that the Self can kill or be killed is ignorant of his own essential nature.

20-22"This Self is never born, so it can never die. Ever-present and changeless, it is without beginning and end. When the body dies, the Self remains. Just as worn-out old clothes are cast aside, this indwelling consciousness discards worn-out bodies, replacing them with new ones.

23 "The Self cannot be pierced by weapons, nor burned by fire. Water cannot wet it and wind cannot dry it.

24-25 "Untouchable by anything in this world, the Self is all-pervading, immovable and eternal. Unmanifest, it cannot be reached by the senses, and is free from all modification.

26-27 "Even if you believe the Self to be subject to birth and death, your sorrow is misplaced. Death is inevitable for the living, and rebirth inevitable for the dead. Therefore, you ought not to grieve over the inevitable.

28 "All beings arise from the unmanifest. At birth they assume manifest form, before again returning to the unmanifest at death. What indeed is there to grieve about, Arjuna?

29 "Some look upon the Eternal Self as a wonder. Others hear of it and speak of it as a wonder. Yet few truly understand it.

30 "Again, I tell you this, Arjuna: this Self, animating the bodies and minds of all living beings, is imperishable. It cannot be lost. If the Self, the inmost essence of all beings, can never be lost, what reason is there to grieve?"

31-32 Sensing that Arjuna was yet unconvinced, Krishna then appealed to Arjuna's vanity. "You must also consider this from the standpoint of your duty, Arjuna. For a warrior, there is no greater virtue than a battle for a righteous cause. It is your duty to challenge wrongdoing, and you will be rewarded accordingly. This is your mission and your calling; it is your dharma.

33-36 "By refusing to follow your duty you incur consequences. You will forfeit your honour and fall into disgrace. Others will see you as a coward; a traitor who fled in the face of battle. They will speak ill of you for generations to come. To a noble man, who cherishes his honour, what could be more painful than such disgrace?

37-38 "If you die on this battlefield, you will gain heaven. If you win, and you shall enjoy the fruits of your victory here on earth. So, I say to you, Arjuna—arise, and resolve to do your duty! Knowing that pleasure and pain, gain and loss, victory and defeat are one and the same, you must prepare yourself to fight. Do this, and you can only triumph."

39 There was a moment of silence as Krishna's words sunk in. The world around them remained frozen in time as Krishna continued: "I have explained to you the true nature of the Self. Now listen as I share the ancient wisdom of karma yoga. This yoga will free you from the bondage of action and the turmoil which engulfs your soul.

40 "With its practice, no effort ever goes to waste, nor can any undesirable results be produced. Even the smallest application will free you from great fear.

41-44 "Those who seek Me alone have true discrimination, and they attain their goal with singleness of purpose. Those who lack discrimination find their mind wandering in all directions, lost in a sea of distractions. Selfish and vain, their hearts are full of desire. Though they claim to be virtuous, they act only for their own pleasure and power. Blind of heart and mind, they are unable to attain liberation.

45 "The wise, however, are capable of mastering their own mind. Of tranquil heart, they are free of the anxiety born of the need to acquire and hoard. That is true power!

46 "For the Self-Realised soul who understands the nature of reality, the scriptures are as much use as a puddle when the land is flooded.

47 "Hear now the essence of karma yoga. You have the choice to act, but no choice over the results of that action. The results of action are never under your control. Desire for the fruits of your labour should never be your sole motivating factor. Neither should you be given to inaction.

48 "Remain steadfast in the spirit of karma yoga, Arjuna. Perform every action without attachment to the outcome, and accept what comes with grace, whether it be success or failure. You will thus attain inner peace in the midst of action. This evenness of mind is the essence of yoga.

49 "One gains success by performing one's duty with the karma yoga attitude. Action prompted by desire and anxiety over the results will always cause misery.

50-51 "Therefore, seek refuge in this knowledge. Surrender to the Self, and let every action be a form of joyful worship, relinquishing all concern over the outcome. Doing this, you free yourself from the bondage of action and your mind will easily attain liberation.

52-53 "A life of karma yoga creates a tranquil heart and dispels the delusions of the mind. One becomes dispassionate toward the things of this world, all of which come and go of their own accord. No longer fixated on the objects of the senses, the mind becomes serene and steady, and it comes to rest in contemplation of one's own Self. Being established in Self-knowledge is the gateway to liberation."

54 Arjuna listened with deep fascination and had many questions. "Krishna, tell me more about a person with such wisdom; one who is unperturbed by the things of this world and whose mind abides in the Self?"

55-56 Krishna smiled. "Such a person renounces all desires as they appear in the mind, for they are content in themselves alone. Unshaken by adversity and no longer yearning for happiness, they are free from longing, fear and anger.

⁵⁷ "This person, whose mind is illumined by the blissful radiance of Self-knowledge, is truly discriminating. Even-minded in all situations, they are unattached to outcomes. They neither rejoice upon gaining the pleasant, nor do they grieve when experiencing the unpleasant.

⁵⁸⁻⁶¹ "Much as the tortoise withdraws its limbs into its shell, the wise person withdraws their sense organs from the external world and rejoices in contemplation of the Self. Ceasing the relentless pursuit of sense pleasure, the mind is naturally drawn inward. Worldly craving ends when a person comes to know the wholeness of their own essential nature. Only those who tame the mind and who still the stormy seas of desire can sit in contemplation of the Self; their minds ever absorbed in Me.

⁶²⁻⁶³ "Dwelling upon sense objects creates attachment. From attachment, desire is born. Desire, when thwarted, gives rise to anger. Anger deludes the mind, clouding judgement and making one forgetful of one's true nature and highest purpose. Discrimination is then lost, and the mind becomes incapacitated. When the mind is no longer fit for the attainment of liberation, one's life is as good as destroyed.

⁶⁴⁻⁶⁵ "Those, however, who master the mind and senses live free of attachment and aversion; their minds ever clear and tranquil. Self-knowledge is easily established in such an intellect, and this Self-knowledge ends all sorrow.

⁶⁶⁻⁶⁷ "Without a peaceful, stable mind, contemplation upon the Self is impossible. When one lacks the ability to contemplate, there is no peace. Without peace, how can there be happiness? A mind that indiscriminately follows the impulses of the wandering senses is like a ship swept off course. A soul set adrift can never attain liberation.

⁶⁸ "Therefore, Arjuna, be the master of your mind and senses! Use discrimination, and focus your mind on your true goal. Only full knowledge of the Self will set you free.

⁶⁹ "The wise see light amid the dark night of the worldly; and that which the world calls 'day' is but a night of ignorance to the enlightened.

70 "Just as all rivers flow into the already-full ocean leaving the ocean unchanged, so do worldly objects arise in the minds of the wise leaving them unchanged. This is not so with those whose desires compel them to continually chase the objects of the senses. Such a mind can never know peace.

71 "He or she who relinquishes all binding desires and moves through the world devoid of longing, setting aside all sense of "I", "me" and "mine", gains peace.

72 "The Self is then realised as one's true nature. Knowing this Self to be limitless, deathless and free, delusion is vanquished, freeing the soul from bondage to the things of this world. This, Arjuna, is enlightenment."

COMMENTARY

If someone were to only read a single chapter of the Bhagavad Gita, I would recommend this second chapter. The entire essence of the Gita is condensed into these seventy two verses, covering everything from the nature of the Self, birth, death and reality, to duty, karma yoga, the mind and emotions, and, most crucially, how Self-knowledge leads to enlightenment. If the first chapter set the scene and presented the basic problem of samsara, the second reveals the solution. The sixteen chapters that follow are largely an elaboration of what is laid out here.

The Fundamental Problem

Arjuna ended the first chapter overcome by sorrow and despair. Unable to see a way out of his predicament and unwilling to slay his own kin, the warrior-prince found himself unwilling to fight for his kingdom. For him, the battle was over before it had even begun. Casting aside his bow and sinking to the ground, he then turns to Krishna for guidance.

Krishna's initial response is perhaps unexpected. He chastises Arjuna, urging him to overcome his emotionality and to get on with his duty: "Get up, Arjuna—and fight!"

Perhaps wondering if Krishna didn't quite understand him, Arjuna reiterates his doubts. How can he kill these great men who are his teachers, uncles, and cousins? What satisfaction would such a victory bring? Arjuna's mind is so crippled by doubt he's even begun questioning which side should win the war.

Although he has declared that he will not fight, Arjuna makes an important request. He beseeches Krishna to accept him as his student. "I seek refuge in you," he says. "Please teach me. Share with me your wisdom."

Krishna has already given Arjuna his counsel, which Arjuna didn't accept. But Arjuna is looking for something more from

Krishna. He's not looking for battle advice. Arjuna is looking for a way out of samsara. He's looking for freedom.

It's this search for freedom that drives all beings. Our outer problems, which might be termed topical problems, are incidental. They come and go. Life being such as it is, the moment you solve one problem another presents itself. Arjuna's outer problem has unearthed a deeper problem: that of attachment and sorrow.

While topical problems vary from person to person, the underlying problem of samsara is fundamentally the same in all human beings. This universal problem comes with a universal solution. Unlike life's topical problems, samsara has a 'one size fits all' solution.

The cause is self-ignorance; the act of misapprehending the nature of the self. As we have seen, this ignorance manifests as a basic sense of lack and limitation. The entity that you take to be yourself isn't a whole, complete self. Rather, it's an incomplete, wanting, deficient self. As no one can be happy with such a self, this gives rise to a cycle of desire, attachment, grief and delusion.

It's important to understand that ignorance cannot be removed by action. Although the Gita and other Vedantic texts may prescribe yoga, meditation, mantras, and devotional practices, these are palliative in their effect. They don't eliminate the underlying problem, although they do help prepare the mind for the ultimate treatment: *jnana yoga*, the yoga of Self-knowledge.

The Problem is You and The Solution is You

There are four stages to dealing with any problem. First, you have to be aware of the problem. Once you've identified the root of the problem, you'll most likely try to deal with it by yourself.

A lot of the time that simply won't work. The mind naturally tends to assume that its problems are caused by external factors. So you immediately set about trying to rearrange the external conditions of your life. You might try getting a new job, a new house, or a new partner. You change your hair, get a new wardrobe, or maybe you book a holiday or enroll in college.

Unfortunately, no matter how well you try to makeover the outer conditions of your life, the fundamental problem remains. You can have all the wealth, health and success in the world yet still feel empty and miserable inside.

If that's the case, you eventually must concede that the problem isn't 'your life'. The problem is you. No one likes to admit that they are the source of their own problems. But, on the upside, if you are the problem, you are also the solution.

Once the real issue has been discovered and you realise that you are unable to solve it by yourself, the next step is to acknowledge your helplessness and find someone who can help. This requires a degree of self-honesty and humility.

It's this stage Arjuna has reached at the start of the second chapter. He's faced with a seemingly insurmountable problem. Unable to see a way forward, he turns to his friend and mentor Krishna, who happens to be the teacher of all teachers. The final stage is to then apply the solution. In this case, the remedy is, as Krishna reveals, Self-knowledge.

Now that the teacher and student have been brought together the Gita is about to begin. The relationship between teacher and student is an important one in Vedantic tradition. Self-knowledge can only be gained with the help of a teacher. Independent attempts invariably fail owing to the immense concealing power of ignorance. As long as your intellect is afflicted by self-ignorance, the teachings will be viewed and (mis) interpreted through the murky lens of ignorance. That's why a qualified teacher is required to cut through this ignorance with the blade of discrimination.

At this point, Krishna is no longer Arjuna's charioteer. He is now his *guru* (a Sanskrit word that literally means 'dispeller of darkness'). The teaching commences in the eleventh verse, which is also where Shankara begins his commentary.

Is Sorrow Your Nature?

Arjuna's sorrow is the sorrow of all human beings trapped in samsara. Topical problems vary from person to person, but this fundamental suffering is the same in all.

But where does this suffering come from? If you experience a lot of sorrow in life, does that mean you are a sorrowful person? Does this sorrow come from your own self, or does it come from something else?

If suffering is inherent to your self, there's no possible solution. The nature of a thing can't be changed, so if sorrow is your nature, you'd better get used to it, because that sorrow will forever be with you!

Sorrow, however, cannot be your nature. If it was natural to you, it wouldn't be a problem. In fact, you'd happily accept it. It's only when something is unnatural to us that we try to rid ourselves of it. Just as the physical body tries to expel toxins and foreign bodies, so, too, do we want to eliminate anything unnatural to us.

In short, if this sorrow was inherent to your nature, you wouldn't want to eliminate it. You, therefore, cannot be the source of your sorrow.

The Two Categories of Existence

Vedanta distinguishes two categories in existence: *atma* (the Self) and *anatma* (that which is not the Self)*. In other words, there is awareness, the knower, and the various objects, the known, that appear in awareness.

Differentiating these two orders of reality is the essence of Vedanta's teaching methodology and the key to liberation. Arjuna's core confusion, and the confusion of all human beings, is an inability to discriminate between the two.

---

* In actual fact, *anatma* is later negated and all that is shown to exist is *atma*, otherwise Vedanta would be a dualistic philosophy. This provisional acceptance of a subject/object duality is a necessary part of the teaching.

If the Self, awareness, is not the source of your sorrow, then it must surely be the world of objects appearing in awareness?

However, Krishna immediately tells Arjuna that his "sorrow is misplaced." The Sanskrit literally translates as "you grieve over that which deserves no grief". Krishna is saying that Arjuna's grief is illegitimate. His problem is not actually the situation at hand.

A problem can only be solved if it is a legitimate problem. If I mistakenly believe that I have a certain medical condition, I can't be cured of it, because I don't have it in the first place! All that I have is a mistaken belief. I'm superimposing a condition on my body that it doesn't actually have.

A cure will only work if it belongs to the same order of reality as the problem. If I have a physical problem, an imaginary cure won't work. Likewise, if I have an imaginary problem, a physical cure won't work either. I can only cure my imagined illness by removing the superimposition that caused it.

Krishna reveals Arjuna's problem to be of a similar nature. Sorrow is superimposed upon the Self due to ignorance; to non-recognition of the true nature of the Self.

If this sorrow is only due to confusion and the non-apprehension of our nature, then it's not actually caused by objects; by the world of experience. Like my imaginary medical condition, my sorrow and grief is caused by ignorance and nothing more. The only way to cure ignorance is to apply knowledge.

Self-Ignorance

Human beings are born ignorant. At birth, you can't tell your fingers from your toes. You know nothing of the world, your environment, or yourself.

As the mind, senses and intellect develop, you soak up information like a sponge. Bit by bit, the operating system of your personality is installed. You begin to adopt certain roles: son or daughter, brother or sister, pupil, student, friend, or whatever else. A sense of ego begins to develop along with this; the sense of being a separate, defined 'self'.

While this sense of self feels solid and real, it's a completely arbitrary, *ad hoc* assemblage of ever changing variables. These variables include assorted memories, impressions, thoughts, beliefs, likes and dislikes, as well as extensive cultural and social conditioning.

Your sense of self is based upon certain assumptions. These assumptions are rarely, if ever, challenged. While you learn all about the world and your environment as you grow up, the one thing you never learn about is *you*—the you that sees, hears, thinks, feels, and does—the you behind the succession of roles and masks that you adopt.

You are, by definition, self-ignorant. By a process of superimposition, you assume yourself to be something you are not, and this, the Gita explains, is the source of your suffering. It can only be solved by learning the truth about who you are.

Who Are You?

As a means of self-inquiry, Vedanta employs a rigorous, step by step process of logic to eliminate all non-essential variables; to strip away our many layers of self-misidentification. In this way, we find what is true by negating what is false.

1. Are You the Body?

Because our primary identification is with the physical body, the notion "I am the body" should be our first line of inquiry.

It seems like a safe assumption for most people. It intuitively feels true. The body is the first thing we become aware of as apparently 'ours'. I can move my arm and not yours, therefore the arm must be mine, and by implication 'me'. It also seems to us that our body is always present; that it's there all the time.

However, the Mandukya Upanishad reveals that the physical body is only experienced in one of the three states we experience every day. It is present in the waking state. But when you're asleep, you can inhabit any body your mind cares to dream of. You can be young or old, a man or woman, a tiny mouse or a bird soaring across the sky. In dreamless sleep, you experience no body or objects of any kind.

Although you only experience the physical body in one of these three states, the mind automatically identifies with it. You never say, "my body is fat," "my body is tall," "my body is old," or "my body is hungry." Instead, you say, "I am fat," "I am tall," "I am old," "I am hungry". The body is invested with a sense of "I-ness". You *become* the body.

However, this is a superimposition of subject onto object. Because the body is known to you—in other words, perceivable as an object—it cannot be the subject; it cannot be "you". It's important to remember that the knower is always distinct from the known.

The body is experienced as an object of perception. While there is clearly an association with this particular body, it remains an object of perception. Furthermore, like all objects in the world, the body is subject to constant change and has no independent existence, as we shall see later.

2. Are You the Mind?

The next level of inquiry is to examine your identification with the mind, intellect and ego.

Together these comprise what Vedanta calls the subtle body (discussed in detail in chapter four's commentary). The locus of your identity hinges not upon only your physical body, but also your thoughts, beliefs, interpretations and emotions. Some people have a stronger identification with their subtle body than their gross body.

However, the same logic of negation applies to the subtle body. Just as the physical body is an object that you, the subject, are aware of, so too are the mind, intellect, and ego.

Your thoughts, beliefs and sense of identity are intangible, arbitrarily constructed and constantly changing. Yet they seem so very real and you invest them with a tremendous sense of ownership and 'my-ness'.

In our minds we create a whole subjective world, which we then superimpose on the objective world and mistake for reality. Most people are unable to separate the objective world from their subjective interpretation of it. That's why identification

with mind and thought can be even harder to break than identification with body.

3. Are You the Ego?

Identification with the sense of being a 'doer', an agent of action—which we call the *ahamkara*, or ego—is the hardest of all
to break. Yet the Gita does just that, as we'll see in chapter four's
commentary. Suffice to say, in order for you to be the doer, you
would need to be aware of and have control over every single
factor that determines your thoughts and actions. Clearly, that
is impossible.

The inescapable conclusion is that mind, intellect, and ego
are all known to you as subtle objects of perception. Because
you know your mind, you cannot be your mind. Because you
know your thoughts and feelings, you cannot be your thoughts
and feelings. Finally, because you know the part of yourself that
takes itself to be the 'doer' of actions, you cannot be that doer.

When all objects are negated as that which is known, what
remains is you: the knower, which is pure awareness. This is the
awareness in which your body, mind, thoughts and ego appear;
the light by which all things are known.

The Self

The Upanishads, the source texts of Vedanta, tend to talk of the
Self in poetic, grandiose terms. This can make the Self seem like
something cosmic and transcendent; something far removed
from the everyday little person we're all familiar with.

In actual fact, the Self is your ordinary, everyday awareness.
It's the same awareness that's been looking out of your eyes
your entire life and in which every single sight, sound, object,
thought, emotion, desire and fear is experienced. The Self is the
ever-present awareness in which the world of objects, including
the gross and subtle bodies, exist as objects of perception.

In everyday conversation the word 'awareness' is often used
in reference to being aware of something. You might say, "I'm
aware of the tree," or "I'm aware of what happened at work yesterday." This implies that awareness is inconstant; that it comes

and goes and that it can potentially be absent. Such awareness might even seem to be a scarce commodity, given that campaigners are always eager to 'raise awareness'!

Awareness, however, is independent of content. In fact, it's the eternal context in which all content appears. Regardless of what you are or aren't *aware of*, awareness is constant. It's always there. There's no way to either gain or lose this awareness.*

The Nature of the Self

The heart of this chapter's teaching is a meditation on the nature of the Self. Vedanta contends that the Self, awareness, is not dependent upon the body, but rather the body is dependent upon the Self. After all, without the Self how would the body be known?

This Self is both immanent and transcendent. It is both personal in that it is intimately known to you as the very essence of who you are, yet impersonal in that it is universal. There is, in fact, no difference between the individual self and the universal Self. Only the point of reference differs.

This Self can't be described in terms of attributes, because it has none. As the Brahma Sutras state:

> Just as light, which has no form, appears to be endowed with different forms because of the object which it illumines, the Self, which has no attributes, appears as if endowed with attributes.

Awareness is the nature of the Self, but it can never be objectified or conceptualised. That's why we can't describe it positively, but only in terms of what it is not; ie., birthless, deathless, timeless and limitless.

---

* In this context, the words 'awareness' and 'consciousness' are synonymous and used interchangably. I generally favour 'awareness' because, for many, 'consciousness' tends to be equated with the content of one's psyche, such as thoughts, memories, beliefs, and so on.

About the only positive statement that can be made about the Self is that it is self-evident and self-revealing. Just as the sun doesn't require any other source of light in order to be revealed, awareness is revealed by its own light.

In describing the nature of the Self to Arjuna, Krishna reveals:

1. The Self is Limitless

"The Self is That which is limitless, imperishable and unchanging. It is That which gives all beings existence and resides within them as their innermost essence."

Limitless is a strict definition. For something to qualify as limitless, it must be limitless at all times. It can't be limitless some of the time and then limited at other times.

An object can never be limitless. In order to exist as an object, limitation is necessary (which is to say, an object must necessarily have boundaries). Therefore, the Self can't be an object. It can't be an object because it itself is the eternal subject; that by which all objects are known.

Being limitless, it's impossible to find the beginning or the end of it. There is no place it is not, no thing it is not, and no time it is not.

You can actually verify this in your own experience. Take a moment to close your eyes and turn your attention within. Become aware of the fact you are aware. Can you find a beginning or an end to your awareness? Does it have a boundary or does it contain everything? Is it a young awareness or an old awareness? Is it a male awareness or a female awareness?

All you can say about awareness is that it is awareness, and that it has no discernible boundary, form or ability to be objectified in any way.

"This Self is never born, thus it can never die," Krishna reveals. Because the Self is limitless, it is also deathless. Death can only affect a limited entity subject to change and modification.

If the Self is limitless then it must be the very basis and totality of existence. Furthermore, it's impossible for us to be anything other than the Self—because, again, that would necessitate limitation (ie., if you weren't the Self, that would mean there was something the Self is not, which would make it limited).

2. The Self is Beyond Time

"Ever-present and changeless, it is without beginning and end."

Time only applies to the world of objects. In order to be affected by time, the Self would have to be both an object and subject to limitation. Krishna negates this. He tells Arjuna, "There was never a time that I did not exist, nor you, nor any of these kings. Nor will there ever come a time when we cease to exist in the future."

Clearly, he is not talking about their bodies, because bodies have a finite existence. Therefore, the Self must be other than the body.

The Self, which is of the nature of awareness/consciousness, is not a part, product, or property of the body. Although independent of the body, it nevertheless pervades and enlivens the body. It is not limited by the body's boundaries or dimensions. Furthermore, it is not 'born' when the body appears, nor does it 'die' when the body is lost.

We all have this idea that we were born at a certain time in a certain place and that prior to that we did not exist. While it's true that the body was born at a specific time and place, and you have the birth certificate to prove it, the notion that you did not exist prior to this body is unprovable. It's unprovable because in order to say there was a time you were non-existent, you would have to be there (which is to say, you'd have to exist!) to know it. Non-existence, therefore, will always remain a concept and nothing more.

3. The Self is Non-dual

"Untouchable by anything in this world, the Self is all-pervading, immovable and eternal."

There is only one Self. More than one Self would necessitate limitation. Awareness is a partless whole. It has no division. While the world of form appears to the senses as a duality of 'this' and 'that', all objects are all united as appearances in a singular awareness.

Although without form, awareness pervades all forms. Like space, it contains all things. Just as space is one, in spite of all the many objects appearing in it, so is the Self one.

Swami Dayananda says:

> The Self is not many; there is only one Self. Because the forms, *upadhis*, are many, there are many people, whereas the Self is one whole consciousness, not bound by time.

While the world's billions of bodies and minds all differ, each apparently unique, the Self animating your body and mind is no different from the Self animating my body and mind.

A good metaphor is that of electricity. Electricity powers countless appliances, yet it is one; it has no division or differentiation. The electricity powering my light is no different from the electricity powering my computer.

The above quote introduced the word *upadhi*, which is an important concept to understand. Upadhi means 'limiting adjunct'; an object which apparently lends its attributes to something else, making that thing appear to be other than it is. For example, if clear water is kept in a red bottle, the water will appear to be red. The bottle is an upadhi, lending its quality of 'redness' to the colourless water.

The concept of upadhi explains why the Self, which Krishna says is limitless and unbound, appears to be limited and bound. Owing to the upadhi of the body-mind sense complex, the Self seemingly takes on the properties of the body and mind, which are finite, limited and subject to birth, death, suffering and decay. But these attributes belong to the body and mind, not the Self.

While it's true that the body and mind are constantly changing and subject to pain and sorrow, the Self is unaffected by pain and sorrow. That's because the Self is of a different order of reality to the body-mind-sense complex, just as a mirror is of a different order of reality to the objects reflected in it. You can change the objects in the room all you like but, while this will change the reflection in the mirror, the mirror itself will not change.

4. The Self is Actionless

"Know Me (the Self) to be beyond doing, ever changeless and free. Actions do not affect Me. I have no personal desire to act, nor do I long for any particular results. The one who knows the Self as actionless is no longer bound by karma."

Being limitless, non-dual, and beyond time, the Self is also actionless. Awareness has no doership. To do anything requires motion, and motion necessitates form, limitation and time. That's why the Self cannot perform any action any more than space can act. Space is already everywhere and in everything, so where can it go and what can it do?

Much as the sun shines upon the world, allowing all life to exist and action to take place, while itself actionless, the Self is that which enables all action to take place but is not the doer of action.

Because the Self is actionless and you are the Self, that means, in spite of appearances, doership doesn't belong to you either. There's another factor responsible for action, which we will explore in the fourth chapter when we examine the topic of action and inaction.

5. The Self Cannot Be Experienced As An Object

"Unmanifest, it cannot be reached by the senses, and it is free from all modifications."

The Self can't be experienced as an object any more than the eye can see itself or a camera can take a picture of itself. However, the existence of both the eye and the camera is known by virtue of the images, the objects, they reveal. The camera can't take a picture of itself, but the fact the pictures exist is proof that the camera exists.

The existence of an object presupposes a subject. Although the Self, being subtler than the body, mind and intellect, can't be experienced as an object, it clearly exists, for it is that which lends existence to all objects.

6. The Self is Self-Evident and Self-Revealing

"The Self is that which is all-knowing, all-pervading, timeless, the cause and ordainer or all things, beyond form, radiant as the sun, beyond knowing and unknowing."

Another metaphor for understanding the Self is to think of a cinema screen. The Self is the light revealing the movie on the screen. As you're watching the movie, you get completely absorbed by the images dancing upon the screen. If it's a good movie, you'll identify with the characters and get carried away by the plot, which, for the duration of the film, becomes utterly real to you. Your pulse quickens as the drama unfolds. The sad parts make your eyes well with tears; the funny bits make you laugh, and moments of horror make you squirm or squeal.

All that you are experiencing the whole time, however, is light projected upon a screen. The moment the light stops, the picture disappears and the imaginary world of the movie fades along with it.

Although you were probably so immersed in the projection that you weren't consciously aware of it, the ever-present light was in fact the essence of everything you saw. Even so, this light was uninvolved and unaffected by the images on the screen.

Similarly, the Self is that which allows the entire creation to exist and unfold while remaining actionless and unaffected. By its very nature, awareness is self-evident and self-revealing. Like the sun, the light of awareness is self-revealing and doesn't require any other light to reveal it. It is that by which all things are known, and that on which they depend for their existence.

Existence and Borrowed Existence

Verse sixteen contains one of the most important sentences in the entire Gita: "The unreal does not exist and the real never ceases to exist."

The ability to distinguish between the real and the unreal is the key to liberation. But first we need a definition for both.

Every object has two components to it: an essence and a form. The essence of an object is its real nature; that which is intrinsic, permanent and independently existent. The essence relies on nothing else for its existence. This is Vedanta's definition of 'real'. The Sanskrit word for it is *satya*.

By contrast, the form of an object, its incidental nature, doesn't exist independently. It borrows its existence from satya and is time-bound and subject to change and loss. Any form is only temporary; a configuration that exists for only a limited time, like a wave on the surface of the ocean. Thus, unlike satya, all forms are perishable and impermanent. The term for this is *mithya*, meaning 'unreal'.

In short, satya is the independent cause and mithya is the dependent effect. Shankara uses the analogy of a pot and clay. While it might at first seem reasonable to conclude that "the pot exists", in actuality the pot has no inherent existence of its own. We superimpose 'is-ness' onto the pot, believing that the object possesses an inherent existence; ie., that it is satya; real.

The pot, however, borrows its existence from the clay. 'Pot' is just a name and form given to the clay. As such, it is time-bound. There was a time when the pot didn't exist and if it breaks, there will be a time when it ceases to exist. The clay will remain but the pot will be gone. The pot, therefore, is mithya and the clay is satya.

Mithya, which is simply a configuration of name and form, always relies upon satya for its existence.

The ability to differentiate between satya and mithya is crucial to liberating the mind. This is what Krishna means when he says, "The unreal does not exist and the real never ceases to exist."

In the context of this discussion, the Self alone is satya, real, and the entire phenomenal world, including the gross and subtle bodies, is mithya; only apparently real.

The Satya-Mithya Confusion

Confusing satya and mithya is the root of all our sorrows.

By a process of mutual superimposition, we superimpose the quality of satya (existence) onto an object, believing that the object itself possesses an inherent existence of its own rather than a temporary, borrowed existence.

At the same time, we superimpose the qualities of mithya onto satya. That's why we take the body and mind's attributes to belong to the Self. Like the clear water which, due to its proximity to the red glass bottle, appears to be red, the Self then appears to possess the properties of the body and mind. That's why we say, "I am happy," "I am sad," "I am fat," "I am thin."

This is an error of perception caused by ignorance. As Krishna said, the Self is free of all attributes, and without limit or objectification. If the Self is limitless and without attribute, how could it—how could *you*—possibly be happy, sad, fat, or thin?

As long as you identify with the body or mind, you are subject to its miseries. But the moment you shift your identity from mithya to satya, from the body and mind to awareness, you are freed of all limitation.

The Ultimate Truth in Three Words

The whole of Vedanta can be encapsulated in three words: *Tat tvam asi:* 'That thou art'.

'That' refers to Brahman, which is another name for the Self; the reality underlying all that exists. Brahman is satya; the intrinsic, all-pervading, unchanging existence from which all phenomenal objects derive their borrowed existence.

Everything that exists is Brahman. Brahman plus name and form is what we perceive as the phenomenal world, in the same way that clay plus name and form is what we perceive as the pot.

'Thou' refers to the *jiva*, the individual; the body-mind-sense complex which, subject to *avidya* (ignorance), takes itself to be a person with its own inherent existence.

The final part of the equation, 'art', links the two.

Therefore, it means, 'you are Brahman.'

Were this knowledge a self-evident fact, there would be no need for the Gita or Vedanta. Human beings, knowing their identity as the changeless, ever-present Self, would not be subject to samsara. Samsara is born of ignorance of this fact.

As the sage Nisargadatta Maharaj once said:

> To take appearance for reality is a grievous sin and the cause of all calamities. You are the all-pervading, eternal and infinite awareness/consciousness. All else is local and temporary. Don't forget what you are.

The inability to discriminate satya from mithya creates endless suffering for the jiva. The whole purpose of Vedanta is to resolve this confusion.

By declaring "That thou art", the "thou", the jiva, is essentially negated. It is revealed as mithya; as appearance alone. You are "That"; the Self, the underlying reality that is satya.

Shankara further summarised the essence of Vedantic teaching in a single sentence:

> Brahman alone is satya (real), the world is mithya (unreal), and the jiva is non-different from Brahman.

We have established that the world is mithya. Like the wave rising from the ocean, all perceivable objects are time-bound, limited and have no intrinsic existence of their own. They depend upon another factor for their existence.

Think of a gold ring. Although we call it a 'ring', the ring has no independent existence of its own. All that's there is gold plus a name and form. By melting it down, the ring—the name and form—is destroyed, but the gold remains. Was it ever really a 'ring' at all? It was really just gold in ring shape.

In the same way, the entire mithya world borrows temporary existence from satya, which is the Self. That's why the sentence ends by affirming that the jiva, although mithya, is non-separate from the Self.

The idea that you are a body and mind subject to time, decay and death is a notion created by ignorance and superimposed upon the Self. Swami Dayananda calls it "an error of self-identity, which only the teaching can resolve".

The Battle is With Ignorance

Krishna makes it clear that although the world of form appears to be a duality with countless different bodies and forms, the Self is one, deathless and eternal. While bodies are subject to pain and death, the Self cannot be injured or harmed in any way.

Krishna says that the Self can neither kill nor be killed and implores Arjuna to do his duty. Many have misinterpreted the Gita over the years, believing this to be a justification for killing. Perhaps they fear it could be used as a convenient line of defence for murderers in court!

The context of the Gita, a brutal war, is extreme. What Krishna is really saying when he exhorts Arjuna to "get up and fight" is to "get up and follow your dharma". In terms of the Gita's teaching, the battlefield is metaphorical. It not only represents dharma, but is a metaphor for the human mind. The war we must wage is the greatest of all wars—the war against self-ignorance.

Having identified the problem as ignorance, the only solution is knowledge. Knowledge destroys ignorance as the sun dispels the darkness of night. To gain knowledge, all you need to do is find and utilise the appropriate means of knowledge. This means of knowledge is jnana yoga, the yoga of Self-knowledge, also called Vedanta. With its root in the ancient Vedas, this knowledge is the heart of Krishna's teaching.

Vedanta has a number of teachings to systematically strip away ignorance. We'll explore these in the chapters to follow. Vedanta is much like uninstalling an old operating system and installing a new one. The old operating system, based on ignorance, caused you to misidentify with the body-mind sense complex and all its woes. This new operating system reorients your identity to awareness. All that you need is to do is to consistently expose your mind to the teaching, work through any doubts, then steadfastly apply this knowledge to the mind (chapter six's commentary explores these three stages of Vedanta in greater detail).

A Qualified Mind

If, to begin with, you find this vision of non-duality hard to grasp, you aren't alone. In a sense, Krishna jumps in at the deep end as he eloquently reveals the ultimate truth of existence. If the student possessed a suitably qualified mind, if they could immediately grasp and assimilate this teaching, that might be all they needed.

Such students are rare, however, and Arjuna is not one of them. If he had been, there would have been no need for further teaching and the Gita would have promptly ended at this point.

It should be noted that, for the vast majority of people, it takes time to fully understand, assimilate and integrate this teaching. Ignorance is rarely felled with one swing of the axe. That's why you must stick with the teaching until it gradually becomes clear and your doubts are systematically resolved. As with most things in life, persistence is key.

So what do you do when you've received the highest of all teachings and it still hasn't taken away your suffering?

In the space of a single paragraph, Krishna goes from expounding the ultimate nature of reality to appealing to Arjuna's sense of duty and vanity. Although he has revealed Arjuna's true essence, and the essence of all beings, to be the limitless Self, the limited apparent self, the jiva, still remains. And, like all things in the relative world, it has a dharma to follow.

Following dharma is prerequisite for preparing the mind for liberation. That's why the Gita swings between two main topics: dharma and moksha; right action in the world, and liberation from worldly attachment.

In order for Self-knowledge to work, you must consider the quality of your mind. Unless care has been taken to cultivate a steady, tranquil mind, the mind will always return to its default. For the samsari, this will be a mind gripped by relentless desires, attachments and aversions; a mind habituated to vainly seeking happiness and fulfilment in worldly things.

Such a mind will find it impossible to assimilate Self-knowledge. That's why this teaching will mean nothing to the average person. It takes a mature and sophisticated mind to value this knowledge, much less to actualise it.

Originally, Vedanta was intended for yogis; people with highly disciplined, refined and crystal clear minds. If the student has a suitably pure, open mind, simply listening to the words of a teacher may be enough to set them free. As we've seen, such people are rare—and never more so than in today's chaotic, value-compromised society with all of its stresses, conflicts and distractions.

While there are countless seekers of enlightenment, only a few will ever attain their goal. Their success or failure is not down to the capricious hand of fate, but to the extent to which they have cultivated a mind fertile enough for the seeds of Self-knowledge to germinate.

In order for Self-knowledge to bear fruit and liberate the mind from samsara, the student must have certain qualifications; certain qualities of mind. It's the presence or absence of these qualifications that determines whether you attain moksha or not.

In order to achieve anything in life, you require qualifications. This only makes sense when you think about it. If you want to study a certain field at university, you must first meet the entry requirements. To proceed without having the necessary grounding in the subject would be a waste of everybody's time.

If you want to run a marathon or climb a mountain, first of all you must make sure you have the necessary level of fitness and stamina. To attain this qualification, you must commit to a regular regimen of exercise, strength training, healthy eating, and so on.

Vedanta is no different. In order for the teaching to work, the mind must first be prepared. Vedanta itself is actually quite easy. You sit, listen to the teaching, work through any doubts with the help of a teacher, and then apply this knowledge to the mind. The knowledge then works its own magic, just as switching on a light in a darkened room automatically removes the darkness. The challenging part, however, is ensuring that the mind is, and remains, qualified.

The Four-Fold Qualifications For Enlightenment

In Tattva Bodha, Shankara outlines a set of four main qualifications. These are:

1. Discrimination

Discrimination means the ability to differentiate between the real and the unreal; to exercise good judgement and to make decisions based upon sound values and a clear understanding of dharma.

Lack of discrimination keeps you bound to samsara and oblivious to the true nature of the Self. By taking appearance to be real, you remain victim to the mind's rampant likes and dislikes, and subject to its conditioning and basest instincts. Like a puppet on a string, you remain bound by samsara's cycle of desire, attachment, and sorrow — which, as we've seen, incapacitates the mind, making discrimination impossible, thus perpetuating the problem of samsara.

Swami Paramarthananda says:

> Discrimination enables us to see the limitation of pursuing worldly goals as a means of fulfilment and the necessity of instead pursuing moksha. With discrimination, we can differentiate between passing worldly pleasures and lasting spiritual liberation, between illusion and truth, between ignorance and knowledge. Discrimination keeps us on the right path, enabling us to see with clarity and to be clear about our true goal.

2. Dispassion

Clear discrimination naturally leads to dispassion with reference to sense objects. When you understand that all objects are impermanent and incapable of delivering lasting happiness, an attitude of dispassion naturally develops. Rather than clinging to things, you relinquish binding attachments and allow things to come and go without overt stress and grief.

Swami Paramarthananda elaborates:

> Realising that our attachment to worldly objects is only a form of bondage, we no longer make that our top priority in life. Certain things are still needed for our survival, such as money, food, and shelter. But our primary pursuit is now liberation from dependence upon objects, and this is only achieved by the Self-knowledge that leads to moksha.

This echoes the words of Ramana Maharshi when he said, "Let what comes come, and let what goes go. See what remains."

3. The Six-Fold Inner Wealth
The third qualification relates to discipline, and is sixfold in nature:

I. Mastery of the Mind. First, you must learn to control the mind and senses. Until you master these faculties, you remain a slave to them. Rather than being blindly led by your conditioning and vasanas (the tendency to repeat past thoughts and actions), you must take a stand and assert control of your own mind.

This is the hallmark of a mature person. As Swami Paramarthananda notes, this doesn't entail suppression, but sublimation by "learning to consciously regulate, channel and direct our thoughts to avoid anxiety, stress and depression."

The mind is your primary instrument and must be conditioned and used in an appropriately healthy way; one that is always in line with dharma. You alone choose where your mind dwells. You have the power to refuse to entertain thoughts and desires that are harmful to your spiritual and psychological well-being and which obscure your true goals and highest purpose.

II. Mastery of the Senses. Once you've mastered the mind, you naturally gain control of the senses. This means that you are no longer victim to compulsive desires and addictions, not to mention the need to continually feed your senses. Instead, you act as a gatekeeper to your senses rather letting them run away with themselves, which invariably leads to an agitated or dull mind. Mastery of the senses means that you choose how you direct your senses, both in terms of what's coming into them and what's going out from them.

III. Withdrawal From Sense Objects. This qualification follows on from the previous two. The ability to withdraw from sense objects is an important part of inner discipline.

A mind that's continually hooked to worldly objects and sense pleasures is a mind subject to extroversion, and this can be a great impediment to the pursuit of Self-knowledge. You never have the necessary time, energy or motivation to pursue moksha as long as you are fixated on worldly goals, desires and pleasures.

This qualification ties in with discrimination and dispassion. When you take a more objective, dispassionate view of worldly pleasures, and are clear about your true goal, it's easier to disengage and prevent the mind from being consumed by cravings for sense objects. By consciously directing your mind and senses, they naturally withdraw from sense objects much as a tortoise withdraws into its shell.

IV. Forbearance. Forbearance is to the ability to weather life's inevitable storms and stresses. As Krishna says, the opposites of life—the dualities of heat and cold, light and dark, pleasure and pain, praise and criticism—are unavoidable and must be endured with even-mindedness. The qualified seeker accepts the 'pinpricks of life' without complaint and unnecessary drama.

V. Focus. The ability to focus the mind is essential. Without a steady mind, capable of sustained reflection upon the teaching, Self-knowledge will never be more than an abstract concept.

The committed seeker has single-pointedness of mind and a clear goal in sight. With fortitude, nothing can shake them from their path.

VI. Faith. The teaching of Vedanta is challenging. It might at first seem counterintuitive. It may go against every 'common sense' assumption you've ever had about yourself and life. That's why it's necessary to proceed with an open, inquiring mind and be willing to have faith in the words of the teaching and the teacher.

This is not a blind faith, however. It's no use to simply accept the word of an outside authority with no way of verifying its truth for yourself. This has led to enormous catastrophe throughout human history. Here, your faith is provisional, pending the results of your own investigation and inquiry.

4. Desire For Liberation

Last, but by no means least, is the desire for liberation. This is what Krishna later calls, "The desire that is not opposed to dharma."

Without the burning desire to be free, you will never devote the necessary time and energy to getting free. There will always be something more tantalising to pursue in the world of objects. Failing to recognise the value of Self-knowledge, you will continue suffering the agonies of samsara as you endlessly and futilely seek permanent happiness in the world of impermanence.

Only when you realise that freedom can never be attained through emotional dependence on the world of objects will your desire for liberation provide the necessary motivation to commit to moksha.

Each of these qualifications naturally leads to the next. First, discrimination is necessary, for discrimination allows us to see that, unlike finite worldly goals, only moksha can deliver lasting fulfilment. From this comes dispassion, lessening the bonds of attachment to material objects. Only then do we cultivate sufficient desire for liberation. This desire provides the necessary motivation and commitment to work with the teaching until the knowledge is assimilated and the mind is freed from suffering.

Karma Yoga

All of these factors must be in place in order for Self-knowledge to work. Clearly, at this stage, Arjuna has some qualifications but not others. He has faith in Krishna and a desire to be free. He is a cultured, refined man; intelligent, disciplined and committed to dharma. However, it's clear that his discrimination and dispassion are currently compromised.

So how do you go about attaining these qualifications? Vedanta doesn't leave you high and dry. In this chapter, Krishna reveals the primary means for cultivating these qualifications—*karma yoga*.

The essence of karma yoga is understanding that while you have the right to act, you have no control over the fruit of those actions. The moment you shoot the arrow, you have no say over whether it hits the intended target.

As a karma yogi, your responsibility is to do the best that you can and dedicate all your actions to the divine, taking whatever results come as *prasada*, a divine gift.

By practicing karma yoga and relinquishing attachment to the results of your actions, you cultivate a steady, stable, tranquil mind; a mind fit for self-inquiry. Your happiness no longer depends upon getting your own way. Which is just as well, because as we all know, it's impossible to get what you want all the time.

The results of action are ever unpredictable. To base your happiness on unpredictable factors is to invite a lifetime of fear, frustration and unhappiness. A materialistic, results-driven mind is one subject to enormous anxiety, stress and strain. That's why Swami Paramarthanada defines success as the ability to face life's successes and failures, its ups and its downs, with evenness of mind.

As a karma yogi, you are no longer driven solely by the desire to attain specific material ends. Your primary goal is moksha, which is freedom from emotional dependency on worldly objects. You act not according to your desires and aversions, but according to dharma.

A life of dharma and karma yoga is the ultimate stress reliever. Grief over the past and anxiety about the future melt away when you cease living solely for the whims of your ego and make your every action an offering to the divine Self. The vasanas are gradually rendered non-binding, thus reducing the psychological pressure of extroverted desires and aversions.

For the seeker of liberation, this purification of the mind is a vital first step. The mind has to be fit in order for Self-knowledge to take root, otherwise the teaching will never be more than mere words; words that, while inspiring, have no lasting effect.

As Krishna says:

> Without a peaceful, stable mind, contemplation upon the Self is impossible. When the mind lacks the ability to contemplate, there is no peace. Without peace, how can there be happiness?

The Gita offers other tools for taming the mind, such as meditation, devotional practice and the yoga of the three *gunas*. These are unfolded in subsequent chapters. The primary means, however, is karma yoga, which will be explored in greater depth in the next chapter.

Enlightenment is Not Chasing Experience

Chapter two ends with Arjuna asking Krishna to describe the characteristics of a Self-Realised person. Krishna has already shared the essence of the teaching and prescribed karma yoga as the means for purifying the mind. Arjuna, however, being a practical and pragmatic man, wants to know exactly how this will benefit him.

Obliging his request, Krishna paints a vivid picture of one who has attained moksha and whose mind is free from the bondage of samsara. Such a person is called a *jnani* ('knower of truth') or a *jivan-mukta* ('one who is liberated while living').

It should be emphasised that moksha is not about chasing experiential states. Because the human mind is experience hungry and forever seeking experiential highs, many sincere spiritual seekers get waylaid by the mistaken belief that enlightenment is about attaining certain states of consciousness or experience.

That is one of the downsides of the yoga approach. Yoga presents enlightenment as just another experience; a better experience—the experience to end all experiences!

While the materialist seeks happiness by manipulating the objects of the outer world, the yogi seeks happiness by manipulating the objects of his or her inner world. Both are seeking experiential states of pleasure.

It's essential to remember that all states and experiences, however exalted, are still mithya and, like a dream, are ultimately fleeting and unreal. Just like the objects of the gross world, the world of subtle experience is limited and subject to time. Even the greatest state of spiritual rapture, like all things phenomenal, can never last.

That's why chasing spiritual experiences is no more the means of attaining liberation than chasing worldly objects. Becoming attached to spiritual highs and 'enlightenment experiences' will, like any attachment, lead to binding desire, sorrow and delusion, thus perpetuating the cycle of samsara.

Liberation has to be without condition, otherwise it's not liberation at all. That's why we define moksha as freedom from dependence on objects or experience for your happiness. Moksha is the firm knowledge that, whatever you happen to be experiencing—and, given the nature of the mithya world, your experience will be changing from moment to moment—you are always whole, full, and complete.

Another danger lies in making enlightenment into an ideal. Creating an ideal of what an enlightened person is like and then trying to live up to that ideal won't lead to liberation. It may, however, get you lost in a more sophisticated and 'spiritualised' self-concept: a spiritual super-ego. Sadly, if there's anything worse than a regular ego, it's a spiritual ego!

It might seem paradoxical, but enlightenment isn't something that you have to acquire or add to yourself. You can't *do* anything to 'become' free. Vedanta reveals that you are already free. You are already the Self; deathless, eternal and all-pervading. Your problem is simply lack of knowledge about who you are.

That's why knowledge alone can liberate you. It does this by removing the ignorance that has prevented you from appreciating the wholeness and freedom inherent to your very nature.

The Self-Realised Person

Krishna describes a Self-Realised person not so we will try to emulate or impersonate them, but to inspire us to commit to purifying the mind and attaining Self-knowledge.

He states that the Self-Realised person "renounces all desires as they appear in the mind." This clarifies that enlightenment is not some super-human state in which all thoughts, desires and sense of duality utterly vanish. The jivan-muktah still possesses a body and mind, and for the duration of his or her lifespan, that body and mind will continue functioning as they are designed to.

Desire may arise according to past conditioning. However, the jnani, the knower of the Self, is no longer dependent on external factors for his or her happiness. Therefore, the desire is no longer binding. It doesn't automatically compel action.

Gone is the compulsion to chase or acquire worldly objects and pleasures in order to feel whole. The jnani derives their happiness and joy from the Self alone. Why would you continue seeking love and happiness in the ever-changing and unpredictable mithya world when you know there's a limitless source of love and happiness within you?

That's why Krishna says, "Worldly craving ends when a person comes to know the wholeness of their own essential nature."

Fear is also absent in the mind of the jnani. Fear is a byproduct of duality; the sense of being separate from everything else.

With the removal of the sense of duality, fear begins to dissolve in the light of Self-knowledge.

The jnani's mind remains dispassionate, tranquil and stable. Such a person is, to use a Christian term, 'in the world but not of the world'. At this point, karma yoga is no longer a practice, but a natural way of responding to the world. The jnani is naturally discriminating and unattached to outcomes. They take the good with the bad and no longer look to the outer world to complete them.

What is samsara but a desperate entanglement with (and emotional dependency on) worldly objects? If, owing to self-ignorance, you don't know that wholeness is your nature, this sense of incompleteness will compel you to seek fulfilment through external objects. Liberation is the removal of this misguided compulsion.

How to Commit Spiritual Suicide

Krishna then briefly examines samsara from the point of view of attachment. Dwelling upon sense objects, he tells us, causes attachment. Attachment inevitably leads to desire.

Advertisers know only too well that if a child sees a toy advertised enough times they'll begin to want that toy. With the right amount of exposure, what began as a subtle spark of desire will soon ignite into a burning flame. When all the other kids start showing up at school with this cool new toy, heaven help the parents, because you can be assured that this desire will erupt into a ravenous inferno.

Desire never travels alone. It comes with many problems, both when it's fulfilled and when it's obstructed. Krishna examines what happens if desire is thwarted.

When your desires are not met, you become angry. Whenever you're angry, it's almost always because you're not getting what you want in some way. To go back to our example, the avaricious child is likely to throw an enormous tantrum if his parents say that he can't have the toy.

Anger has consequences. A mind agitated by anger and sorrow loses perspective and the ability to discriminate.

Consequently, you forget your higher nature and your values and priorities become muddled. As a spiritual inquirer, your mind becomes too turbulent to contemplate the teaching. Losing discernment, you perhaps begin acting on impulse, expressing your emotional disturbances in often dysfunctional ways and violating dharma left, right and centre.

This amounts to nothing less than spiritual suicide. Losing yourself in a spiral of materialistic and emotional reactivity only reinforces your basic sense of lack and incompleteness.

Contemplation on the Self becomes impossible and liberation unattainable. Krishna uses the metaphor of a ship swept off course, lost at sea and helplessly buffeted by the crashing waves of samsara.

The solution to this is reiterated by Krishna throughout this chapter:

> Be the master of your mind and senses! Use discrimination, and focus your mind on your true goal. Only full knowledge of the Self will set you free.

CHAPTER THREE

Karma Yoga

¹⁻² Arjuna said, "But Krishna, if knowledge is preferable to action, then why are you telling me to fight this terrible war? Your seemingly contradictory words confuse me. Tell me which is the better path for gaining liberation."

³ Krishna responded, "There are two paths in this world: the path of knowledge for renunciates and the path of karma yoga for those who pursue action in the world.

⁴⁻⁵ "A person does not attain liberation by simply refusing to perform action. Indeed, such a thing is impossible. No one rests for even a second without performing some kind of action. All beings are driven to action by the nature of existence and the interplay of the three gunas.

⁶⁻⁷ "Those who refrain from action but whose minds dwell upon sense pleasure and worldly objects are insincere and deluded aspirants. But those who, having mastered their mind and senses, remain unattached to objects and act with the karma yoga spirit, attain freedom.

⁸⁻⁹ "Therefore, do what is to be done, Arjuna. Action is necessary just to maintain the body and stay alive. Fulfil your duties. Act selflessly, without attachment to results. Selfish action binds you to karma. Selfless action, without thought of personal gain, liberates. The wise perform action not for themselves, but as an offering to the Divine.

¹⁰⁻¹³ "All beings have been created and all their needs provided for by the Creative Intelligence of life. Honour life and repay this gift by sanctifying your actions. By fulfilling your duty to life, you will thrive, as promised by the scriptures. Anyone who enjoys the fruits of life without offering anything in return is a thief. Those who eat, having offered the food to the Lord, are released from bondage, whereas those who prepare food only for themselves consume only guilt.

¹⁴ "Living beings are born of food. Food is born of rain. Rain itself is born of sacrifice, and sacrifice is born of action.

¹⁵ "Every selfless act is born of Brahman, the imperishable and all-pervasive source of all being. Therefore, to retain this mindset of giving is to live in harmony with the Self.

¹⁶ "Those who fail to live in harmony with the cosmic order, and who live only to indulge in sensory pleasure, have wasted their lives, Arjuna.

¹⁷⁻¹⁸ "But those who realise the Self, and are satisfied with the Self alone, enjoy eternal contentment. Such people, having found the source of joy and fulfilment within, no longer seek happiness or gain in the external world. Secure in themselves and dependent on no objects whatsoever, they have nothing to gain or lose by any action.

¹⁹⁻²¹ "Therefore, Arjuna, do what is to be done without attachment, and you will attain the highest goal of life. By acting in this way, you will attain liberation and inspire others to follow your example.

²²⁻²⁴ "For Me, there is nothing to be done, Arjuna. There is nothing for Me to gain in this world or any other. I am not driven by any need of My own, yet I continue to act. If I were to refrain from action, others would follow My example. They would become confused and lazy and society would unravel.

²⁵ "The ignorant, attached to the results of their actions, work only for their own gain. The wise, unattached to the results, work for the welfare of the world, without thought for egoistic concerns.

²⁶ "The wise should not lecture the ignorant who remain attached to the results of action. Instead, they should encourage them by performing all actions with compassion and non-attachment to the results.

²⁷⁻²⁸ "All actions are born of the *gunas* of *prakriti* (material existence) which influence mind, body and senses. Deluded by identification with the "I-sense", a person erroneously thinks, "I am the doer". But the knower of truth understands that the body, mind and senses act automatically according to the interplay of gunas.

29 "Deluded by the play of prakriti, the ignorant become identified with and bound by the body-mind-sense complex and its actions. Those who understand this truth should not disturb the minds of the ignorant.

30 "Renounce all actions to Me, and with a mind that is discriminating, devoid of expectations, and without any sense of "mine-ness", anxiety or frustration—fight (act)!

31 "Those who follow this teaching faithfully and without fault, will be freed from bondage to action and its results. They will attain liberation.

32 "Those, however, who seek to find fault with the teaching and who do not follow My vision, who are deluded and devoid of discrimination, will not progress and will remain the cause of their own suffering.

33 "Even a wise person must act in keeping with his or her own nature. Because all beings automatically follow their own nature, what use is it trying to control them?

34 "The mind and senses are conditioned to respond to sense objects with attraction and aversion. These binding compulsions must be overcome, for they impede one's path to freedom.

35 "It is better to perform one's own dharma imperfectly than to succeed in the dharma of another. A life spent trying to follow the dharma of another leads only to frustration and danger."

36 Arjuna ventured a question. "Krishna, what is it that drives a person to commit lowly, self-debasing actions, even though they know it is wrong?"

37-39 Krishna answered, "Desire is responsible, which gives rise to anger. Born of the guna of *rajas*, this unceasing greed and attachment is an intractable foe. Just as fire is covered by clouds of smoke, a mirror coated by dust and a foetus concealed in the womb, knowledge is obscured by this binding desire. The insatiable fire of lust is the constant enemy of the wise, Arjuna.

40-41 "Selfish desire manifests in the senses, mind and intellect, blinding one to wisdom. Therefore, Arjuna, guard your senses and vanquish this inner enemy; the destroyer of knowledge and wisdom.

42-43 "It is said that the sense organs are subtler than the body; the mind subtler than the sense organs, and the intellect subtler than the mind. Subtlest of all is the Self. Knowing the Self as that which is supreme, steady your mind and slay the hidden enemy of selfish desire."

COMMENTARY

The third chapter opens on a note of confusion. Krishna had previously told Arjuna that knowledge alone will end the suffering of samsara. He then proceeds to discuss the path of karma, or action. If only knowledge leads to liberation, then why all this talk of action?

In Arjuna's mind, the path of knowledge and the path of action are exclusive and distinct. He sees it as an either-or-choice. Either you're actively involved in worldly affairs, or you renounce the world altogether and become an ascetic.

Now on the brink of a terrible battle, Arjuna's inclination is to take the latter choice. He's in a grim situation and is looking for a way out of it. That's why the path of renunciation has a sudden appeal to him.

The Stages of Life

To understand Arjuna's confusion, it's helpful to know something about Vedic *ashrama* system. The Vedas outline four specific stages of life, each with a certain focus and duties: the student stage, the householder stage, the retirement/ascetic stage and, finally, the renunciant stage.

The first stage covers a person's first twenty-five years or so of life. As a *brahmacharyi*, the student goes through formal education, preparing for his or her future profession. For some, this would also involve time living with a guru to gain spiritual knowledge.

The second stage is the householder (*grihastha*) stage. The individual reaches maturity and is expected to maintain a job, contribute to the society, and get married and start a family. The pursuit of wealth (artha), enjoyment (kama) and virtue (dharma) are largely the focus of this life stage.

The householder stage draws to a natural conclusion when the children have grown up and established lives and families of their own. At this point, the individual retires from professional and social life, and they enter the *vanaprastha* stage. They can remain married but their spouse is now seen a friend rather than a lover. Historically, the retiree was expected to leave their home and live in the forest in order to spend their time in solitude, prayer and contemplation. This stage, in which one's focus shifts from worldly gains to spiritual knowledge, leads to the final ashrama: the renunciant, or *sannyasa* stage.

The *sannyasi* fully devotes him or herself to the pursuit of Self-knowledge and moksha. Renunciation is no longer tentative, but absolute. A sannyasi has no home, no possessions, and no family duties, attachments, or social obligations. Shaving their hair and wearing nothing but orange robes, they live as wandering ascetics, devoting all their focus to Self-realisation.

These days, few people enter the latter two ashramas. Renunciation has limited appeal, and in most modern societies is not viewed as a legitimate life path. However, the scriptures are clear that all human accomplishments should culminate in moksha. Any life that doesn't lead to Self-Realisation is an incomplete one.

In Indian society, a person can potentially skip the middle two ashramas and jump straight to sannyasa, spending the rest of their life as a renunciate. This option only appeals to those with an intense thirst for spiritual knowledge and little interest in worldly life. Such sannyasis have no involvement in worldly affairs; no duties, no families, no responsibilities, and no impetus to pursue karma.

Given his dire predicament, it's perhaps no surprise that Arjuna has a sudden interest in relinquishing his duties and taking to a life of renunciation. What he doesn't realise is that knowledge and action aren't mutually opposed. Ideally, the path of action eventually leads to the path of knowledge and can be used to prepare the mind for that knowledge. Therefore, the ultimate goal of both is the same: moksha.

There Are No Shortcuts

Krishna warns that simply abstaining from action will not make one a sannyasi, nor will it lead to liberation. Unless the mind is suitably prepared, a life of renunciation will only result in misery. After all, outer detachment is impossible without a corresponding inner detachment.

You can certainly try to isolate yourself from the world. You could even sell your belongings and go live in a cave in the Himalayas. But if your mind is still attached to objects, your meditation won't be on the Self. It will be on whatever you think you're missing out on in the world. You'll keep wondering what your old friends are doing, and what life could have been if only you'd had a family and gained worldly success. Rest assured, your mind will mercilessly devour itself with an endless flood of doubts, envy and regret.

As Krishna explains in the second chapter, the more your mind dwells upon a particular object, the more you want it. Desire and attachment, whether fulfilled or obstructed, create further bondage in the form of anger, depression, greed, or envy. Such qualities lead to delusion, and leave the mind unfit for self-inquiry.

As the saint Ramakrishna used to say, the biggest obstruction to enlightenment is attachment to "women and gold", meaning relationships and money. It's no use, however, to simply suppress your desires and compulsions. Whatever is suppressed must eventually return to the surface, usually in greatly magnified form. The only solution is to sublimate these desires with inquiry and dispassion, and this only comes with maturity.

Krishna knows that Arjuna is unsuited to a life of renunciation. The Pandava Prince is looking for an easy way out, but dereliction of his duty is not the answer. The path of renunciation only works for someone with a dispassionate and contemplative temperament; one who has mastered his or her binding desires and attachments. This necessitates an objective and mature mind, and such a mind must be cultivated.

The Problem of Likes and Dislikes

According to Swami Dayananda, "The objective world does not create any problem for you. The problems are caused by a mind dominated by likes and dislikes."

As we've established, the samsaric mind is driven by a sense of lack and inadequacy. Owing to self-ignorance, you take yourself to be a limited body-mind entity. This causes a deep sense of existential limitation. Unable to experience wholeness in yourself, you seek instead it in the world of objects. You figure that if you could just get the external world to measure up to how you want it to be, you'd finally experience lasting happiness. This is the fundamental delusion of the human mind.

From this basic sense of lack, desire arises. You can only ever desire what you believe you lack, otherwise the desire would be pointless. As you grow up, the mind acquires a vast array of likes and dislikes. These come in two varieties: non-binding and binding.

A non-binding like or dislike is more of a preference than a compulsion. You might prefer chocolate ice cream to vanilla, or tea to coffee. You might favour one pair of shoes over another. But generally, non-binding likes and dislikes don't cause psychological suffering. You won't, for instance, end up incapacitated with grief if there's no chocolate ice cream in the freezer.

When the Gita addresses the problem of likes and dislikes, it isn't referring to the non-binding variety. Even Krishna had certain preferences and predilections, such as playing the flute.

Binding likes and dislikes are the real enemy. These deep-rooted compulsions drive a person's entire psychology. All of your actions and reactions, behaviour, goals, beliefs and prejudices are governed by these likes and dislikes. Life becomes little more than an exercise in trying to get the external world to match up to your sense of 'want' and 'don't want'.

Such a mind is incapable of objective vision. Accordingly, we each inhabit what Swami Dayananda calls a "private world of fantasy and fancy."

The World Wasn't Put Here To Make You Happy

When life is governed by desire and aversion, happiness is always precarious, because it depends on the successful fulfilment of those desires.

The belief that the world is here to make you happy is perhaps the greatest of all human delusions. 'Make you happy' essentially means that it should conform to your desires. What you want is to try to force the objective world to conform to your subjective ideal.

Self-dissatisfaction and the need to acquire and accomplish is the very core of the samsaric mind.

Vedanta reveals that happiness is not the attainment of desire. Happiness is the absence of desire; desire itself being a manifestation of lack and limitation.

On the problematic nature of desire, Swami Dayananda says:

> Desire produces other desires. Its nature is to continually perpetuate itself. Like a fire that leaves a black trail of charred earth never says, 'Enough! Don't give me any more fuel! I have burned up so many houses already,' desire, too, will never complain.

Whether obtained or obstructed, desire begets further desire. The nature of life is such that your desires cannot be fulfilled all the time. As the saying goes, you win some, you lose some.

Failing to get what you want leads to anger and depression, which result in delusion and a compromised mind and intellect. Unable to discriminate, and under the sway of your desires and aversions, you may find yourself compelled to perform actions not always in line with dharma.

The Gita makes it clear that action should always be determined by dharma rather than our personal likes and dislikes. As well as being subjective and particular to the individual, likes and dislikes are fickle. Much of the time we don't even know what we want, or what we want changes from moment to moment depending on our mood.

As well as predisposing us to adharma, a mind driven by likes and dislikes is prone to agitation and despair. For such a mind, moksha is unattainable, and a lifetime is wasted chasing shadows.

Therefore, we need a way of managing the mind, lest we forever be its slave.

The Solution is Karma Yoga

As we learned in the previous chapter, the steady application of karma yoga neutralises the mind's binding likes and dislikes, cultivating the tranquil, abiding mind necessary for the assimilation of Self-knowledge.

As Krishna says:

> A person does not attain liberation by simply refusing to perform action. Indeed, such a thing is impossible. No one rests for even a second without performing some kind of action.

In other words, life is karma, or action. Every being has an inherent nature, as determined by the three *gunas*, or properties of matter (a topic that will be unfolded in depth in later chapters). Abstaining from action is impossible. A person's own nature will compel them to act, whether they like it or not.

A recent psychological experiment found that participants would rather administer electric shocks to themselves than sit alone in a room doing nothing. The pressure of their vasanas and psychological compulsions made it impossible for them to sit quietly and refrain from action without experiencing considerable discomfort.

Since it's impossible for us to refrain from acting, our actions should at least be dharmic and done in the correct spirit. That's why, in the words of Swami Paramarthananda, Arjuna is recommended to:

> Take to the way of active service, contributing to the society; in the process refining the mind and removing the sharp edges of the personality. Just as a knife is sharpened on a rough surface, only in the rough and tumble of life does the mind get mellowed, matured and prepared.

Karma yoga is the means of doing that.

A Contributory Mindset

Two factors come into play with karma yoga. The first is action and the second is one's attitude with regard to the action.

Action should always be determined by dharma. Our primary aim is not simply doing what we want, but doing what is right.

Sadly, we live in a desire-based rather than a dharma-based culture. It's plain to see that our grasping, materialistic, egoistic behaviour is casting the entire social and environmental ecosystem into jeopardy. Pursuing personal greed above all else, the human race is living like it's the last generation on the planet, endangering the very world upon which we, and future generations, depend.

Instead of living with an extractive mindset, in which we constantly seek to 'get more out of life', karma yoga impels us to adopt a contributive, ecological mindset.

Life owes us nothing. It has already given us everything—everything that we have and everything that we could ever need. When one is given a gift, it's natural to reciprocate by offering something in return.

That's why it's appropriate to live with an attitude of appreciation and a desire to contribute more to the world than we take from it. In this way, our life becomes a devotional offering; an expression of gratitude and worship. The focus of our life shifts from getting to giving.

Action motivated by personal desire will always be rife with anxiety because our happiness depends upon attaining certain results. On the other hand, action performed out of dharma is free from bondage. Every act becomes an end in itself, and anxiety over the results and the need to 'get something back' disappears. Vedanta calls this *samatvam*, or evenness of mind.

A Pragmatic Approach

One of the great problems in life is that while we have a choice with regard to the actions we undertake, we have no say over the results of those actions.

It's true that to a certain extent you can predict what the results are likely to be. If you go to the gym regularly and lift heavy weights, it's safe to assume that you'll build muscle.

However, cause and effect isn't always as simple as A+B=C. An infinite number of factors, both seen and unseen, come into play when determining the result of an action.

You might have your eye on a cute man or woman from the office. But perhaps they have their attention on somebody else. They're also subject to their own personal likes and dislikes; another salient factor over which you have no control.

When you don't get what you want, you might tend to berate yourself and think of yourself as a failure. However, because the result was never in your hands, any notion of failure is illegitimate. The results were determined and delivered by an inviolable set of universal laws governed by *Ishvara*, as we'll explore in a moment.

On one level, karma yoga is simply a pragmatic approach to dealing with life. You still undertake action with the desire to attain a certain result. After all, if there was no desire for a result, you'd have no need to take the action. But you recognise that you have no control over that result. Your job is to release the arrow using all your skills of precision. Whether or not it hits the target is then determined by factors outside your control.

At this point, you might start stressing. But worrying over the results is a waste of energy and produces nothing but mental and emotional agitation. The results are now up to Ishvara, as governor of the field of existence.

As a karma yogi, you accept whatever result comes, irrespective of your personal preferences. You receive the fruit of all action as *prasada*, a divine blessing. The karma yogi's response is always one of graceful acceptance. If the arrow doesn't hit its target, you can assume it wasn't meant to hit its target. If it was, it would have. This doesn't necessarily mean that you won't try again. The karma yogi is not fatalistic. You still do your duty and follow your dharma, but you accept whatever results come without undue stress and resistance.

This may be a difficult proposition for those deeply entrenched in their likes and dislikes. But, by accepting whatever result comes as appropriate, even if it wasn't what you intended, you neutralise the mind's likes and dislikes and begin cultivating a peaceful, even mind. That's the primary aim of karma yoga.

Who Created the World?

In order for karma yoga to work, it's necessary to have an understanding of what we call *Ishvara*. After all, if you're expected to surrender the results of your actions and accept whatever comes as being appropriate, then you need to know that there's an underlying order to the cosmos. The belief that life is a random accident and that the universe is a disorganised chaos is a huge impediment to Self-knowledge.

In the last chapter we established through systematic analysis that you, as the Self, are not the body, nor the mind, the senses, or the ego. These are all objects belonging to the phenomenal world of matter and form.

The Self is the noumenon at the root of all phenomena: an eternal, unchanging substratum of existence; and its nature is pure, unconditioned awareness/consciousness.

The Self alone is satya, real, and the phenomenal world of objects is mithya, apparently real.

Anything objectifiable, including your body, your thoughts, the outside world and the entire universe, is but an appearance in the substratum of awareness. It depends upon the Self for its existence just as a pot depends upon the clay out of which it is formed.

However, an important question then arises. If I am the Self, and the entire universe appears in me, then who is responsible for its creation?

I certainly didn't create the stars, the planets, trees, rivers, animals, and people. I'm not responsible for the laws that govern the universe: the cycles of birth and death, creation and dissolution, gravity, oxygen, respiration.

As a jiva, a person, I clearly had no part in this—I can barely change the batteries on my remote control! As the Self, pure non-dual awareness, I can't have had a hand in it either. The Self, being limitless and beyond time and causation, is what we call *akarta*—it's not a doer. It's incapable of action because there's nothing other than it.

So, where did this creation come from? Who or what is responsible for this vast, intelligent, interconnected universe of form and experience?

The Concept of God

For anything to exist, there must be a creative principle with the knowledge, the power and the material to create it.

If I show you my watch and ask you, "Do you believe that somebody made this watch?" your response would have to be "yes". You didn't see the watch-maker create the watch. You don't know anything about him; his age, where he lives, or what he looks like—or, indeed, even if it was a man or a woman. But that doesn't negate the fact that the watch-maker clearly had to exist. You can't have an effect without a cause. The very fact that the watch exists presupposes a creator of the watch.

The same logic applies to the world. The world clearly exists and the mere existence of a thing necessitates a creative principle.

Now, clearly no rational being on Earth can lay claim to being its creator. This is where the idea of God comes in. Many religions purport that God is the Creator of the universe and that He lives in Heaven and can only be known through faith. This is the notion accepted by most religious people.

However, it is an insufficient explanation for an inquirer with a questioning intellect. For a start, it may raise more questions than it answers. Where does this 'God' come from?

Is there a Mrs God? Where is Heaven, how did He create the world, and what He does on His days off?

Accordingly, those who find this notion unsatisfactory tend to reject the concept of God altogether. That's why the topic of God can be a thorny subject for many people, Westerners in particular. The very word has been abused by religion for so many centuries that it has become a somewhat distasteful one for many.

In seeking to explain the nature of the cosmos and its creation, blind faith in theological doctrine is insufficient. One of the primary qualifications in Vedanta is to have a clear and discriminating mind. A certain degree of faith is necessary but this isn't blind faith. It is faith pending the results of your own analysis.

Religion and Science Both Have Their Limits

We live in a scientific age, in which the physical sciences have helped us understand the world around us in great depth. Like anything, however, it has its limits.

For decades, the most brilliant scientists on the planet have struggled to come up with a 'theory of everything'; a way of understanding every aspect of creation. Unfortunately for them, their reach will forever exceed their grasp.

Physical science is a means of knowledge for understanding the physical world based on observation and inference. It isn't, however, a means of knowledge for anything beyond what Vedanta terms *prakriti*, the material aspect of existence. Even today, science has no understanding of consciousness/awareness and can offer nothing other than competing theories based on assumption alone.

A means of knowledge is always specific to that knowledge. For example, your eyes are a means of knowledge for visual objects alone. You can't use your eyes to know sound, touch or taste. It would be wrong to assume, however, that just because your eyes can't smell an object and your nose is blocked up, that smell doesn't exist.

Similarly, science is a valid means of knowledge for the physical and manifest, but not for the non-physical and unmanifest. Problems arise when science descends into scientism and people purport that if something can't be quantified by our current scientific paradigm that it doesn't exist. Such an ironically unscientific assertion can be a great impediment to knowledge.

Whereas science by its nature can't penetrate beyond the phenomenal, most religions fail to offer anything other than empty and often distorted dogma, mistaking subjective symbols for objective fact.

Disenchanted by the failings of conventional religion and the inability of science to deal with anything other than the material aspect of existence, many people refute the existence of God altogether.

Fortunately, Vedanta provides a different, better and wholly more logical understanding of God. Vedanta is a means of knowledge for understanding the totality of creation; both the phenomenal and the noumenal; the manifest effect and the unmanifest cause.

According to Vedanta, all debate about whether God exists or not is erroneous. Why? Because God is all that exists.

The World Appears In You

The Self, formless awareness, is all that actually exists. It is satya, the very ground of existence. Eternal and unbound by time, the Self is non-dual; an undivided whole unaffected by anything in the phenomenal world.

Our intuitive, common-sense assumption is that, because we take ourselves to be a body and our body is born at a certain place and time, we appear in the world. But if you really examine your experience, you'll realise that the world actually appears in you. The only place you can ever experience the world is your awareness.

Awareness is your carrier of reality; your medium for experiencing the world. You will never experience anything outside of awareness. Everything that you see and perceive appears in this awareness—in you; the Self.

This Self is all-pervading, formless and non-dual. The technical term for it is *Nirguna Brahman*, meaning 'the Self without form or attribute'. It is the eternal subject; the unchanging substratum from which all objects arise and into which they resolve.

In order for anything to be known, there must be a changeless principle by which everything is experienced. Experience is constantly changing, but the knower of the experience, the Self, remains unchanged. If it did change and modify to each new experience, there would be no continuity between experiences.

This entire world of form is nothing but an appearance in the Self. It appears by virtue of a creative principle called *maya*. Maya causes an apparent subject-object split, creating a world of duality out of non-duality.

Maya is the power that causes actionless, formless, non-dual awareness to apparently appear as an entire universe of gross and subtle forms. *Avidya*, self-ignorance, then causes awareness to identify with these forms; and thus you take your body and mind to be your self.

Just Like a Dream

This world of multiplicity is projected in awareness much as the dream-world appears in the mind of a dreamer.

When you're dreaming at night, where does this dream-world come from? You yourself didn't create it. A power in your mind generates the dream state and your consciousness appears to take on different forms, shapes, and experiences. Neither real nor unreal, the dream-world occupies a different order of reality to your waking world.

Your dreams can take you on the most incredible journeys. You might encounter all kinds of wondrous and terrible things, and experience every conceivable emotion. It's not until you wake up that you realise the entire dream was just an appearance in your consciousness. Your mind served as both the cause and the effect of the dream; its content and very substance.

When you're dreaming, which part of the dream is your consciousness? Which part of it is you?

Actually, your consciousness pervades the entire dream. The dream appears within you—and is you—but you are not the dream. You stand apart from it. When you wake up, the dream vanishes, but you are still there.

In the same way, this phenomenal universe appears in the Self, awareness. The Self pervades every aspect of this creation. Just as the dream can't exist without the dreaming consciousness, the universe can't exist independently of the Self because it derives its entire existence from it.

While the Self without form or attribute is called *Nirguna Brahman*, the Self associated with form and attribute, with maya, is called *Saguna Brahman*. Another name for Saguna Brahman is *Ishvara*, or God.

The Nature of Ishvara

Any creation requires not just an intelligence to create it (the efficient cause) but also a material out of which it is made (the material cause). In the case of a pot, the material cause is the clay, and the efficient cause, the intelligence necessary to fashion the pot, is the potter.

Ishvara is the Self associated with the material universe at a macrocosmic level. You might think of Ishvara as the universal potter; the impersonal cosmic intelligence which, wielding the power of maya, shapes and sustains the entire universe.

However, a problem arises. Out of what does Ishvara create the universe? If the material is different from Ishvara, that would necessitate something outside of Ishvara. Where would such a material come from? If there was Ishvara plus a material, then which qualifies as the actual creator? We'd end up with an infinite regress and, like Russian dolls, we'd have an endless number of Ishvaras.

It's for this reason that Vedanta posits Ishvara as both the efficient and material cause of the objective universe. Ishvara is not only the intelligence that shapes the universe, but also the very material out of which it is made.

In this way, Ishvara doesn't stand apart from the creation. Ishvara is the very creation itself: the entirety of all things both seen and unseen.

Think of a spider. A spider not only creates its web but also provides the substance out of which the web is spun. Similarly, Ishvara is the creative principle that shapes and governs the laws of the universe and also the very material out of which it is formed.

Therefore, everything that exists in phenomenal reality is Ishvara. Everything is governed by Ishvara, and everything belongs to Ishvara. As Swami Dayananda beautifully put it, "Some religions say there is only one God. Vedanta says there is only God."

Unaffected by the Creation

Usually the act of creation changes the substance of which it is created. If you want to make cheese, for instance, milk has to be processed a certain way. Once you get the cheese, you can never return the milk to its original state.

By contrast, the creative power of maya, as wielded by Ishvara to create the objective universe, never affects the Self. Maya creates the appearance of multiplicity, but the Self is never changed in any way.

By virtue of *upadhis* (limiting adjuncts), the Self can appear to take on certain forms and limitations. We've already explored this on the microcosmic, individual level. When awareness is associated with the upadhi of a body-mind-sense complex, it seems to take on the qualities of that body and mind. Courtesy of the upadhi and avidya (ignorance), the Self appears to *become* a jiva (individual). Therefore, the Self 'becomes' Mike, Sandra, Fido the dog, a tadpole, or a tree.

At the macrocosmic, universal level, when awareness is associated with the upadhi of maya, with the entire creation, it appears as Ishvara, the Controller and wielder of maya.

An Impersonal Creative Force

Ishvara's creation, the phenomenal universe, is not unlike a dream in many respects, but it is a dream appearing in the Cosmic Mind of Ishvara. That's why it's experienced as the same by all the seemingly separate jivas, which are indeed also part of Ishvara.

Owing to our naturally extroverted senses, we jivas are fascinated and enthralled by Ishvara's creation, which we take to be reality by superimposing satya on what is ultimately mithya— which is to say, taking something to be real when it is only apparently real.

Ishvara and maya are essentially the same. Maya is the power to create, and Ishvara is that which shapes the creation out of its own form. The creation is, as James Swartz says, "An orderly and intelligently designed matrix; a universe of physical, psychological and moral laws. [...] The whole creation is made up of knowledge."

Ishvara is the factory of knowledge that makes creation possible. Forms are created according to certain templates. When you are born, for instance, the cells of your body don't have to struggle to figure out how to work. They are already programmed with the intelligence that allows them to function perfectly.

The entire universe operates according to this inbuilt intelligence allowing stars to live and die, planets to spin in orbit, cells to divide and metabolise, and electrons to revolve around their nucleus.

When any form is created, it functions according to the pre-encoded template provided by Ishvara. Ishvara therefore is a storehouse of knowledge, whether it is tree knowledge, animal knowledge, people knowledge, mind knowledge, or matter knowledge.

Ishvara creates out of itself and provides the intelligence for all life to flourish according to set patterns. As the creative principle of maya, Ishvara governs and manages everything, setting and upholding the laws of the creation.

These laws are universal and inviolable. They aren't open to negotiation. Ishvara is an impersonal creative force. Just as the sun shines on all beings alike, the laws of the creation apply equally to all beings without a hint of reservation. If two men fall off a cliff, one a saint and the other a sinner, neither will be exempt from the snare of gravity. Ishvara shows no favouritism.

If the functioning of the universe were changeable and Ishvara's will fickle, no meaningful action could take place. What use would fire be if some days it was hot and other days it was cold? The laws of Ishvara remain constant because the creation is an ordered system and not a chaos.

Personalising God

Understanding Ishvara is tricky, which explains why we have so many different concepts of God. Chapter nine's commentary explores our three-fold way of understanding God. A person's understanding is entirely dependent upon their level of maturity, knowledge and intellectual comprehension.

Because it's hard for the untamed mind to contemplate the formless, non-dual nature of the Self (Nirguna Brahman) or to understand Ishvara as the totality of the manifest creation (Saguna Brahman), religion creates symbols, personifying God in various forms for our convenience.

In Hinduism alone, there are said to be 33 million gods! These are all simply facets of a single God; different faces of Ishvara, which is non-separate from the Self. This topic will be explored in much greater depth in the middle chapters of the Gita.

In the Gita, Ishvara appears in the form of Krishna, who is an avatar, or divine incarnation. Like many of the Vedic scriptures, the Gita takes the form of a dialogue. To facilitate this, the divine must necessarily be represented in form, thus creating a provisional duality.

Of course, there are dangers with creating symbols for God. The irony is that while theologians say that God created us in His image, we have essentially create God in our image. Because we humans consider ourselves the highest form of life on the planet, we conceptualise God as a more powerful version of ourselves, complete with a personality and human traits such as will, anger, love, and vengefulness.

This anthropomorphised conception of God can lead to problems because, the human ego being what it is, we may then be inclined to proclaim that "our God" is better than "your God".

What we fail to realise is that our personal God is just a symbol for the impersonal, universal consciousness which, for lack of a better word, Vedanta calls Ishvara.

When literalists get stuck on the level of form, of personal deities, sectarianism arises. This has been a problem with religion from the very start. It's easier to worship a personal God than an impersonal, formless God, but the inquirer shouldn't forget that all forms, whether mundane or divine, are still mithya. Only the formless Self is satya, the ultimate reality.

While Ishvara is the universal creative force that allows this entire universe to appear, Ishvara is still mithya. As the moon borrows its light from the sun, Ishvara borrows its existence from the Self.

Evil is a Product of Ignorance

Vedanta makes it clear that Ishvara is both the intelligence that shapes the creation and the very substance of the creation. If you want to know God, all you need do is look around you. Everything is Ishvara and everything belongs to Ishvara.

God is, therefore, in every form and aspect of the creation. There is no division. You don't need to seek God. You simply need to understand that everything is God. Arguing over 'your' God and 'my' God is clearly ridiculous, as is the notion that God doesn't exist, because God is everything existent. To deny God is to deny your own existence.

However, the idea that Ishvara is everything can pose a problem for some people. People find it easy to accept Ishvara in pleasing forms; in sunsets, waterfalls, twinkling stars, kittens and chocolate cake. But if Ishvara is everything, that also must include the uglier things in life, such as disease, famine, greed, hatred and violence. If God is capable of being evil, then how can one accept such a God?

Firstly, this phenomenal universe is a duality. There can never be up without down, heat without cold, pleasure without pain, and birth without death. A certain amount of suffering is inevitable and inescapable, as is the fact that all forms are finite and perishable.

Furthermore, Ishvara governs the universe through a set of natural laws, including the law of dharma, which is woven into the fabric of the creation. Dharma is, in fact, Ishvara functioning in form.

The greatest tragedies in human history (and today, sadly), such was wars, genocide, violence and ecological destruction are not caused by Ishvara, but the human mind's ignorance of Ishvara.

Because human beings are the only species on Earth bestowed with free will, they are also the only species capable of using that free will to violate dharma. Violating dharma, usually for the sake of satisfying one's personal desires and aversions, always results in suffering.

The root of our suffering on a personal and global scale, and the true cause of man's inhumanity to man, is ignorance of our true nature and the nature of reality.

The Two Powers of Maya

Maya has two predominant powers: the power to conceal and the power to project.

The power of concealment renders us unable to apprehend the true nature of the Self. The mind and senses are our primary means of knowledge. The upadhi of maya makes us seem to be limited to flesh and bone and the thoughts and desires streaming through our mind. Until we learn to practice self-inquiry, we are inclined to identify with the body-mind-sense complex.

Maya's power of projection causes us to superimpose meaning and value onto objects, overwriting objective reality with an entirely subjective interpretation.

The power of maya to delude is so immense that avidya, self-ignorance, is near universal.

The Upanishads state that the moment we perceive duality, fear is born. From fear comes the need to protect and acquire, and so we are pulled into the seemingly inescapable vortex of suffering that is samsara. Fear, desire, and an endless flood of likes and dislikes become the engine of the jiva's psyche, and in order to attain our desires, we become willing to contravene dharma. Evil is born, therefore, not from Ishvara, but from ignorance of Ishvara.

Everything Is Ishvara

If everyone knew that duality was simply a trick of maya—or an "optical delusion of consciousness", as Einstein put it; that we are all the same Self, and that God is everything that exists around us, the human race would change in an instant.

With this knowledge, everything becomes sacred. This entire creation is a blessing and everything in your life is a gift from Ishvara.

You've been given a body on loan, along with enough oxygen to last a lifetime, and all the resources you need to survive and thrive. (Any scarcity of those resources is again down to the adharmic behaviour of mankind under the delusion of separation).

You realise that Ishvara doesn't owe you anything, for all of this has been been given to you.

When you receive a gift, the appropriate response is to express gratitude and give something in return. That's why everything in life ought to be seen as a blessing, and every action should be a form of worship.

This understanding is essential in order for karma yoga to work. It's not until you know that everything is divine that you can truly surrender the results of your actions to Ishvara.

You gracefully accept whatever comes as right and proper, even if it doesn't happen to align with your likes and dislikes. You know there's a higher order operant at all times; an order that may or may not deliver what you want, but which always delivers what is ultimately appropriate for the totality based on the outworking of karma.

The results of your actions aren't a product of random chance. This is a lawful universe. Because Ishvara controls these natural laws and dispenses the fruits of all actions, it's only appropriate to have an attitude of devotion and worshipful reverence to Ishvara.

Only when you understand that this is an intelligent and benign creation can you relax and accept life as it unfolds, while continuing to follow your dharma and play your part in the tapestry of creation.

CHAPTER FOUR

Actionless Action

1-3 Krishna said, "I have taught this imperishable yoga since time began. Handed down from generation to generation, the teaching has passed to countless sages and kings. But over time, this knowledge has been lost in the world. Today, I share this secret knowledge with you, for you are my devotee and friend, Arjuna."

4 Arjuna was perplexed. "How can you have taught this since time began?"

5 Krishna said, "You and I have passed through many births, Arjuna. I remember them all, whereas you have forgotten.

6-8 "I am the changeless and unborn Self, the Lord who dwells in the heart of all living beings. Yet through the power of my own maya, I appear to take on material form. In every age, whenever there is a decline in right living, I come into being to restore dharma, to protect the good and destroy adharma.

9-10 "The one who knows Me as his own divine Self overcomes bodily identification and attachment and is not reborn into this world. Such a soul is united with Me. Free from craving, fear and anger, totally resolved in Me, and purified by Self-knowledge, many have reached unity with My nature.

11-12 "People seek Me in many ways. In whatever way they worship Me, I bless them accordingly. Those desiring success in worldly things worship the world. Their actions in the world quickly attain results.

13 "The apparent difference between people in terms of social division, temperament and karma is created by Me. Even so, know Me to be beyond doing, ever changeless and free.

14-15 "Actions do not affect Me. I have no personal desire to act, nor do I long for any particular results. The one who knows the Self as actionless is no longer bound by karma. Knowing Me in this way, the seekers of ancient times still performed action.

Therefore, Arjuna, do the same and perform your duties as the sages of ancient times did theirs.

16-17 "Even the wisest of men can be confused by the distinction between action and actionlessness. I will now share the secret by which you will be released from the bondage of samsara. You must understand the nature of right action, improper action and actionlessness.

18-19 "The wise see actionlessness in action and action in actionlessness. With this understanding, one is a yogi, and has attained everything there is to attain. The one whose undertakings are devoid of selfish desire, whose actions are purified by the fire of knowledge, the sages call wise.

20 "Relinquishing attachment to the results of their actions, always contented, and no longer dependent on external supports, the wise may be fully engaged in action yet are free of the notion of doership.

21-22 "Devoid of expectation and all sense of possession, such people, having mastered the body, mind and senses, do only what is necessary to sustain the body. They are happy with whatever comes by chance. Unaffected by life's dualities, free from jealousy and even-minded with regard to success and failure, the wise are no longer bound by action and its results.

23 "They are free and without attachment, their minds remain rooted in Self-knowledge. The karma of the liberated, who perform action only to bless the world, is completely resolved.

24 "The means of offering is Brahman. That which is offered is Brahman. Brahman offers Brahman into the sacrificial fire, which is also Brahman. Brahman is indeed reached by those who see the One in all things.

25-31 "Worldly aspirants may offer material sacrifices. Karma yogis offer selfless action. Renunciates offer their lives into the fire of Self-knowledge. Some renounce the enjoyment of sensual pleasure through discipline. Some share their wealth, follow prayerful disciplines, meditate, practice yoga, or study the scriptures and practice Self-knowledge. Some perform *pranayama*, regulating each inhalation and exhalation, thus gaining control of the mind and the physiological forces. Others moderate their food and diet. All those who understand the nature of service through action are rewarded with a purified mind.

³² "Through this spirit of sacrifice, one realises the Eternal Self. For the one whose actions are motivated solely by egoic desire, nothing is gained in this world or beyond. All offerings are born of action, whereas the Self is actionless. Knowing this, you will be liberated.

³³ "The discipline of Self-knowledge is superior to religious rituals or material offerings. All actions are resolved by the light of Self-knowledge.

³⁴ "Always seek a teacher who has attained Self-realisation. With reverence and devotion, ask the proper questions and this wise soul will share the vision of Truth and teach you knowledge of the Self.

³⁵ "This knowledge will free the mind of delusion, and you will see all beings in yourself and in Me.

³⁶⁻³⁷ "Even the greatest of wrongdoers can cross all karma with ease by the raft of knowledge. Just as a blazing fire reduces wood to ashes, so does the fire of Self-knowledge reduce all karma to ashes.

³⁸ "In this world, there is no purifier equal to knowledge. Having prepared the mind through the practice of karma yoga, the power of knowledge naturally leads to Self-realisation.

³⁹ "One who has faith in the teaching and the teacher, who is committed to attaining knowledge, and who is master of his or her senses, attains the highest goal. In gaining this knowledge, one gains absolute peace.

⁴⁰ "But the one who lacks discrimination, who has no faith in the teaching and whose mind is indecisive and doubtful, wastes his life and attains no peace in this world, or any world beyond.

⁴¹⁻⁴² "Those established in the Self are no longer bound by action, attachment or doubt. Therefore, Arjuna, take the sword of knowledge and slay whatever ignorance or doubt appears in the mind. Arise, and take action with the spirit of yoga!"

COMMENTARY

The fourth chapter covers a number of important topics, ranging from the nature of samsara, rebirth, and Krishna's purpose as an *avatar*, to the paradox of action and actionlessness, and how to transcend karma.

Krishna As Avatar

Krishna's opening statement that He has taught this knowledge since the beginning of time naturally perplexes Arjuna. The Krishna that Arjuna knows—his friend, mentor and confidante—is a man of a certain age, born at a certain time and place, which makes his statement seemingly impossible.

It's necessary to understand that, henceforth, when Krishna uses the terms "I", "Me" and "My" he is rarely speaking as a jiva (as Krishna, the individual), but as an embodiment of Ishvara.

The term for this is *avatar*—a word that will be familiar to many people, even if its original meaning isn't. Its literal meaning is 'descent'; specifically, the descent of God into physical form. As Krishna explains:

> Through the power of my own maya, I appear to take on material form. In every age, whenever there is a decline in right living, I come into being to restore dharma, to protect the good and overcome adharma.

An avatar is Ishvara appearing as a particular name and form—in this case, the noble Krishna. While mortals beings are born of ignorance, the avatar is born of compassion, and remains free from the bondage of self-ignorance.

The purpose of an avatar is to protect dharma and destroy adharma.

All natural systems have some form of protection or defence. When the body becomes sick, for instance, a system of defence kicks in. Lymphocytes, programmed to detect and eliminate foreign microorganisms, are pumped through the bloodstream;

maintaining the natural dharma of the body (health) by destroying adharma (illness and infection).

At the macrocosmic level, the universe works on the same principle. The entire creation is an integrated system. Whenever there's a significant disturbance, and the laws of dharma are threatened, it stands to reason that universal Intelligence will respond in the appropriate way to restore balance. Just as a functioning immune system keeps the individual healthy, so does Ishvara keep the creation healthy by virtue of a 'cosmic immune system'.

When dharma is broken, which is to say, when a system no longer functions as it should, Ishvara has ways of restoring the balance. Humankind violates dharma out of ignorance. The solution, therefore, can only be knowledge, which is why Ishvara has provided us knowledge in the form of the teaching—in this case, the 'divine song', as sung by Krishna.

The Difference Between an Avatar and a Jiva

Some may wonder about the difference between an avatar and a jiva. After all, it's already been established that all beings are expressions of the one universal Self, so how can the question of difference be resolved?

First of all, there is no real difference between Ishvara and the jiva. According to Swami Dayananda, only the costumes differ. On a theatre stage, one actor might play a king, and the other a beggar. One role commands respect and adoration, while the other elicits pity. In reality, there is no difference, because both are only actors and both earn the same wage regardless of their role.

Furthermore, Swami Dayananda says:

> Because of our costumes, we appear to be different. In His role of Ishvara, the Lord's body is all-pervasive: He is all power; all knowledge. In your role as a jiva, you are limited in power, knowledge and other respects. These appearances do not represent real differences.

The question of difference is actually a question of knowledge—or lack of knowledge. Ishvara, the Self associated with the power of maya, has complete knowledge of the creation and of Itself. The jiva, which is the Self associated with a particular body-mind-sense complex, has only limited knowledge specific to that body and mind, and is born ignorant of its true nature as the Self.

Therefore, as an avatar, Krishna is Ishvara appearing in physical embodiment with full knowledge of his divine nature. As a jiva, Arjuna is also Ishvara as a physical form, but with a mind subject to avidya (self-ignorance).

What Is a Jiva?

Thanks to the power of maya, the formless, indivisible Self appears to take on form and limitation; and from non-duality a world of duality is seemingly created.

At the macrocosmic level, the upadhi of maya makes the Self appear as Ishvara, the entire universe of gross and subtle forms. At the microscopic level, the upadhi of an individual body/ mind allows the Self to appear as the jiva, a finite person with a birth and subsequent death, and subject to all kinds of limitation in between. The jiva is, therefore, awareness associated with a particular body-mind-sense complex.

In actuality, there is only the Self, but under the spell of self-ignorance, we superimpose the notion of jivahood onto the Self. By identifying with name and form alone, we're like the ocean believing itself to be a single wave, thus 'losing' its vastness and seemingly becoming locked into a limited, time-bound form.

As long as self-ignorance remains, the jiva's existence is characterised by a sense of limitation and fear. Because it's not inherent to our nature, this limitation is unacceptable to us, and so we spend our lives striving to overcome it. Taking ourselves to be a doer and enjoyer, we perform countless actions, believing our happiness, wholeness and peace of mind to be dependent on the attainment or avoidance of certain objects.

As Vidyaranya Swami writes in Panchadasi:

Jivas perform action for the results they believe will make them happy. They then pass from birth to birth like insects that have hatched and fallen into a river. They are swept from one whirlpool to another by samsara's restless currents, never attaining peace.

The glue binding the jiva to samsara is the need to continually perform karma, action, in order to find scraps of happiness in the external world and thus allay our existential sense of limitation and fear.

Until one is committed to following dharma above all else, the jiva's actions are largely driven by its accumulated desires and aversions, which in turn are determined by the impetus of past action.

These likes and dislikes exist in the form of vasanas; self-repeating and self-perpetuating grooves in consciousness. Whenever you perform a certain action, or even think a certain thought, it leaves a subtle imprint in the mind. Depending on the result of that action, it creates a tendency in the mind to either repeat or avoid it. The more this happens, the stronger this tendency, or vasana, becomes.

When you wake up in the morning, you probably don't even have to consciously think about what you're going to do. Perhaps you stagger to the bathroom, brush your teeth and go make coffee. The momentum of your past actions, reinforced every day, created the vasanas that determine what you will do each morning.

These vasanas can be positive or negative; helpful or harmful. Automatic and often largely unconscious, they drive and compel action, shaping a person's mind, reactions, behaviour, relationships and entire life.

A Wheel In Perpetual Motion

Samsara is often referred to as the *samsara chakra*, which means the 'wheel of samsara'. Like a wheel, it spins in perpetual motion, driven by the momentum of past actions which, in turn, generate yet more action.

It should be noted that this cycle outlasts the span of a single lifetime. As Swami Dayananda put it:

> Nothing in this world really ends. Matter does not get destroyed, nor does energy. One form may get converted into another, but it does not disappear altogether. There is no logical basis for thinking that the conscious being comes to an end.

According to the Gita, the jiva—the conscious being wielding this particular body-mind complex—does not die when the body dies. Just as physical matter is recycled into new forms, so too is subtle matter.

The jiva's subtle body might be likened to a traveller, moving from body to body, led by the trail of its karma. When one body dies, another is assumed. Death only means that the jiva's association with a particular gross body has come to an end.

So what is it that keeps a jiva in this cycle of death and birth, moving from body to body?

When an action is performed, the karma accrues results, both good and bad. This karma fructifies in the form of vasanas; the psychological pressures that compel the jiva to keep performing action.

Some of these results are experienced in the present lifetime, but most must be carried over to some future time. This karma remains on the jiva's 'account', so to speak. Accordingly, the jiva will be reborn to exhaust its accumulated karma. The problem is the moment the subtle body is associated with a new gross body, the vasanas compel this 'new' jiva to perform more actions, accumulating yet more karma, requiring them to assume yet another body. And so the wheel of samsara keeps turning.

In the final chapter of the Gita, Krishna says, "By my maya, I cause all beings to revolve as if mounted on a wheel."

In other words, Ishvara is causing the jivas to dance like puppets on a string, pushed and pulled by their likes and dislikes in the form of the vasanas.

Vidyaranya Swami clarifies that, "'Mounted on a wheel' means that jivas think they are doers. 'Revolve' means that, impelled by their vasanas, they do the same good and bad deeds over and over."

A Futile Game

Samsara is a cycle of perpetual frustration and suffering. The jiva is driven to keep performing the actions he or she thinks will bring happiness and wholeness. Unfortunately, as we've seen, nothing in this world is capable of delivering lasting happiness. Even the attainment of desire is only a short fix, because, given that everything in maya is in constant flux, objects are incapable of providing lasting happiness.

Yet the compulsion to keep chasing is hard-wired in the form of the jiva's vasanas, forcing the jiva to take body after body in an attempt to exhaust their accumulated karma.

The way out of this is revealed in the above quote by Vidyaranya Swami. What keeps the jiva on the wheel of samsara is the belief that "I am the doer".

The belief that "I am the one doing" and that "the results of my actions belong to me" is the fundamental error based on ignorance of one's nature.

The Self, as we explored in chapter two, is by nature actionless. Appearances notwithstanding, you are the Self. What else could you be? As the Self is everything everywhere—and being limitless, by definition it has to be—there's nothing you could be but the Self. If the Self is actionless, and you are the Self, then you must be actionless.

Swami Dayananda says:

> If you know you are actionless, how can you perform action and how can the results ever come to you? When one appreciates that one's nature is actionless, all karma standing in one's 'account' is written off, for there is no

longer a doer to reap those results. There is no rebirth for the wise person, for there is no karma to inherit, and therefore no cause for taking a body.

The way out of samsara doesn't lie in trying to master the game. There are no winners in a zero sum game. For the samsari, 'happiness' means having more fulfilled desires than unfulfilled. But even if this is the case, the basic problem of desire remains. There's no end to the raging inferno of desire. The more you feed it, the more it consumes and the more it reinforces the vasanas. To paraphrase an old saying, even if you win the samsara race, you're still a samsari.

That's why action isn't the way out of samsara. Samsara is emotional dependence on external factors. Here, Krishna says that Self-knowledge is the greatest secret. It's the greatest secret because, owing to the concealing power of maya and the extroversion of the mind, no one realises that what they seek is already within them.

The great tragedy of the human race is that we spend lifetimes chasing rainbows; looking for happiness and security in objects incapable of delivering it.

What we're really seeking is our own Self; the nature of which is wholeness, peace and contentment. The irony is that we were the Self all along. What else could we be? Our problem was only ever one of ignorance.

As Krishna says here, "The one who knows Me as his own divine Self overcomes bodily identification and attachment and is not reborn into this world." The key to liberation is, therefore, knowledge of the Self.

You Are the Love and Happiness You Seek

Vedanta describes the Self as *sat chit ananda*; meaning that its nature is existence, consciousness and bliss.

But, you might argue, if bliss is our nature why would we need to seek it?

We seek it like the absent-minded professor desperately searching for his hat, when all along the hat was exactly where he put it—on top of his head.

The search for what is already there can only be motivated by ignorance. Because we're unaware that wholeness is our nature, we seek it in the external world. When we encounter an object that aligns with our likes and dislikes, that particular object seems to deliver happiness. Or getting rid of a certain object might remove unhappiness.

But it's never the object itself that brings happiness. It's the value we place upon the object which determines our response to it. When we get what we want, our desire is temporarily abated. Freed from the pull of this desire (desire itself being suffering; a sense of lack and limitation), we temporarily taste the bliss of the Self reflected in a tranquil, desire-free mind. Similarly, when we get rid of an object we dislike, we are temporarily freed of fear or anger, and we again experience the fullness of our own Self.

The Self is our source of love, even if we're not consciously aware of it. We all want to live, to protect ourselves and experience happiness because we love ourselves. If we didn't love ourselves, we wouldn't seek happiness in any way, shape or form.

Even suicidal people love themselves. If they truly hated themselves, they'd be glad to continue suffering. But they want to free themselves of suffering because they love themselves and don't want to suffer. When someone claims to hate themselves, what they really hate are the thoughts they're thinking about themselves, and these are based on ignorance.

The Brihadaranyaka Upanishad makes it clear that whatever we love, we love not for its own sake, but for the sake of the Self, which is our ultimate love:

> A wife loves her husband not for the husband's sake, but for the sake of the Self.
> A husband loves his wife not for the wife's sake, but for the sake of the Self.

Parents love their children not for the children's sake, but for the sake of the Self.
People love wealth not for its sake, but for the sake of the Self.
The gods, the worlds, the beings in the world and everything else—they are not loved for their sake, but for the sake of the Self.

If you loved an object for its own sake, then as long as that object was present, your love would remain. However, the moment your husband, wife, friends, children, job, or any worldly object ceases to bring you the happiness it once did, your love begins to dry up. The honeymoon ends. Like a once-cherished car that begins falling apart, that object becomes problematic and you may even want to get rid of it. Therefore, you loved the object not for its sake but for the bliss it brought you. When the bliss stops flowing, your love will soon stop flowing too.

This proves that the love is not in the objects themselves, but is in, and for, our own Self. Everything that you do, everything that you seek to have, become, or experience is all to align you with the bliss of the Self.

Unfortunately, as long as you're unaware of the Self as your ultimate source of bliss, your attention won't be upon it. Rather, your focus will remain fixed upon the world of objects.

A Misdirected Search

Because most people are completely unaware of the Self as the source of their happiness, they remain emotionally dependent on objects. These objects become the focus of their worship.

Those who seek happiness through wealth and material goods worship money. This worship may take the form of working overtime, doing whatever they can for a promotion, or even taking on an extra job. Others may seek happiness through physical beauty and having the perfect Instagram-friendly body. Their worship will likely take the form of elaborate skincare regimens or pumping iron at the gym.

"People seek me [the Self] in many ways," Krishna says. "In whatever way they approach Me, I bless them accordingly."

If you worship money and work hard and often enough, you'll get money. If you worship abs and break enough of a sweat at the gym, you'll get your abs.

However, if your ultimate goal is to attain the fullness and bliss of the Self, seeking it in worldly objects wastes a lot of unnecessary time and energy.

The pursuit of object-happiness is a precarious endeavour because at any moment the object you work so hard to attain can be lost. When you become rich, you then get anxious about losing your money. When you're finally happy with your body, you then have to work hard to maintain it. In both instances, the initial joy is short-lived.

A life spent pursuing nothing but worldly gains is a life squandered. Even if you do attain some measure of worldly success, certain failures are inevitable, and when you reach the end of your life, it all begins anew at the next birth.

Alas, there's no solution in samsara. Action based on the desire to be free—the compulsion to seek, acquire and attain objects—can never lead to freedom. It simply leads to yet more action; action that will continue throughout successive lifetimes, all the while reinforcing the false notion of doership.

The only solution to samsara is to get off the wheel.

Anatomy of a Jiva

Arguably the main theme of this chapter is the nature of action and doership. Courtesy of self-ignorance, people generally assume themselves to be the doer of action and the enjoyer of the results of action. Addressing this mistaken notion is crucial to liberation.

Krishna admits that it's a topic which confuses "even the wisest of men." That's why it's helpful to start at the beginning and examine the very anatomy of the jiva.

A jiva consists of three interfunctioning instruments: a gross (physical) body, a subtle body (comprising the mind, intellect and ego) and the causal body (unconscious), all of which are enlivened by the reflected light of awareness/consciousness, which is our innermost essence and true nature. Let's explore each in turn.

1. Physical Body and Senses

First of all, it goes without saying that all human beings and animals have a gross or physical body comprised of the five elements.

Functioning through this body are the sense organs, of which there are five perceptive organs (sight, sound, touch, taste and smell) and five active organs (relating to speech, manipulating objects, movement, sex and excretion).

These senses allow us to perceive and interact with our environment. They function automatically, connecting to their respective sense objects without any effort on our part. For instance, when you wake up in the morning, you don't have to switch on your eyes in order to see, or switch on your hearing in order to hear. In this respect, the senses are like open gates.

2. The Subtle Body

I. Mind. According to the Upanishads, above the senses, is the mind. The mind, as a component of the subtle body, manages the five streams of sensory data coming through the perceptive senses and arranges them into one cogent experience.

The senses register around eleven million bits of data per second, yet we can only consciously deal with around forty bits per second. The mind must determine which bits are relevant and which to filter out.

The second function of the mind is to doubt and determine. It must question the information being relayed by the senses.

Let's say you're wandering through the jungle alone. Although the senses objectively relay your surroundings to you, you have to make sense of and interpret what you are perceiving. The jungle might look safe, but the mind is hard-wired to doubt; to question things. After all, who knows what might be lurking unseen in the shadows? This doubting function helps you navigate your environment and avoid dangers and threats.

The mind also emotes. All behaviour is driven by emotion. Emotion is what compels us to act. If the mind determines that you are in danger, it generates the appropriate emotion—in this case fear—which activates the organs of action, allowing you to respond appropriately—ie., run!

The mind is amorphous by nature. Constantly modifying to sensory data, it takes the shape of each and every thought you think. The *yoga sutras* refer to thoughts as *vrittis*, which means 'modifications of the mind'. The mind constantly changes configuration according to these vrittis. These, in turn, are largely determined by the vasanas and the interplay of the *gunas*, the three qualities of matter which determine the makeup of the entire universe (rest assured, much more will be said of the gunas in subsequent chapters.)

II. Ego. Another component of the subtle body is the *ahamkara*. The word ahamkara literally means "I-maker", and is our sense of ego; of "I-ness". In Vedanta, terms are used with exacting precision to avoid potential confusion. The word 'ego' has different meanings depending upon context. In this instance, ego is the "I-sense"; the agent that takes ownership of the mind's thoughts and interpretations and acts them out accordingly.

James Swartz explains:

> [Ego] identifies with the body-mind-sense complex. The ears listen but they do not say, "I am listening." The one who says, "I am listening," is the ego (ahamkara), the part of the subtle body that owns action.

It's necessary for the mind to create a sense of ownership in order to initiate and perform action. This, however, is simply another modification of the mind. Ego is based upon the thought, "I am seeing/listening/hearing/thinking/acting." What was hitherto simply an impersonal set of mechanisms is now given the stamp of "me-ness". Things become personal!

The ahamkara is both a blessing and potentially a curse. Because of the problem of self-misidentification, this simple mechanism has the potential to create worlds of suffering for the jiva.

III. Intellect. There's still another faculty of the subtle body, even subtler than the senses, mind and ego: the intellect. The intellect is the part of you capable of weighing up what you sense, think and experience. Having considered all the variables, the intellect will then determine the appropriate course of action.

The intellect might be seen as part of a checks and balances system. Instead of blinding acting on emotion, as many people are prone to do, the intellect helps you respond to life in a more mature fashion. Capable of seeing the bigger picture, it's the part of you that's able to learn from past experience and help you navigate life with greater intelligence, skill and reason.

Like a muscle, it atrophies if not exercised. If someone goes through life acting on impulse and emotion alone, their intellect is most likely undeveloped, and their life riddled with chaos and stress.

While New Age-type spirituality tends to denigrate the mind and intellect as somehow 'unspiritual', Vedanta maintains that the intellect is crucial to helping us discriminate the true from the false. Without discrimination, you'll continue blindly acting out your vasanas, forever binding you to samsara.

Ideally, once the intellect has made sense of the data relayed by the senses and resolved the mind's doubt, it then relays instructions to the ahamkara. The ego, by assuming ownership of the thoughts, feelings and actions, then carries out the appropriate action.

3. The Causal Body

We've already spoken about vasanas, the unconscious imprints created in the mind whenever we perform action, and which make us likely to repeat or avoid that action in the future.

These psychological tendencies, which are our likes and dislikes in hard form, are stored in what we call the causal body. The closest parallel in modern terms might be the unconscious mind. It's sometimes called the unmanifest 'seed state' because it contains the self-replicating 'seeds' sown by our past thoughts and actions. These seeds later germinate in the subtle body as certain thoughts and impulses, predisposing us to act in certain ways.

The vasanas of the causal body can be either positive or negative and binding or non-binding. Positive vasanas include thoughts and actions that are in harmony with our nature and beneficial to our well-being, such as the habit of eating healthily, exercising and meditating every day. Negative habits create corresponding negative vasanas, continually compelling us to do things that may not be beneficial for us, such as overeating, smoking, drinking, procrastinating or thinking negatively.

A non-binding vasana expresses as a preference or predilection, whereas a binding vasana becomes an unstoppable compulsion or addiction.

It's impossible to enjoy psychological freedom as long as your mind is continually pushed and pulled by binding vasanas. They agitate and distort the mind, and may compel you to violate dharma left, right and centre in order to get what you crave. That's why it's necessary to convert all binding vasanas to the non-binding variety by the steady practice of karma yoga.

The Lightbulb Metaphor

There is, of course, one final factor in the equation—the most important of all, and the very means by which the jiva apparatus functions.

We have just discussed the body-mind-sense complex, consisting of the gross, subtle and causal bodies. As perceivable objects, these occupy the category of mithya, meaning they have no independent existence of their own. They rely upon another factor for their existence. Mithya, the dependent effect, can never exist without satya, the independent cause—which is the Self, or awareness/consciousness.

Matter alone, whether gross or subtle, is inert and insentient. What brings it to life is the light of the Self. Awareness blesses these objects with sentience, much as the sun blesses the moon with its reflected light. The body and mind function, therefore, with the reflected consciousness of the Self.

Swami Paramarthananda uses the analogy of a lightbulb. Let's imagine that the bulb and filament represent the jiva's gross and subtle bodies. By themselves, these components are inert and incapable of producing light. Another factor is required; the invisible principle by which the bulb becomes a source of light: electricity.

Like electricity, there is an independent factor pervading the otherwise inert body-mind-sense complex, granting it life. Just as electricity continues even if the bulb is broken, so is this animating principle unaffected by the condition of or loss of the body. The body may be gone, but the Self cannot go anywhere. It is, as we have established, without limit and without beginning or end.

Although there may be millions of lightbulbs, electricity is one. Similarly, although there are billions of jivas, the Self pervading, illumining and granting them life is also one.

One of the key points of this chapter is that the Self is free of doership. It is all-pervasive, like space. That which is all-pervasive cannot perform action. Action necessitates movement, whether physical or mental; a progression from one state to another. Space is actionless because it can't move from one place to another. It's already everywhere. While it's possible for air, fire, water and even earth to move, space cannot.

The Self, like space, pervades all things. There is nowhere and nothing it is not. That's why the Self is ever free from action. As the Self, it's impossible for you to give up or renounce action, because action never actually belonged to you in the first place.

The Three Orders of Reality

If the Self doesn't act, and you are the Self, then how does action happen? From the perspective of the jiva, it certainly seems as though you're acting. Everyday you perform numerous actions, from brushing your teeth first thing in the morning, to driving to work, eating, making decisions and implementing various goals and projects.

In order to understand the nature of action and actionlessness, it's necessary to consider what Vedanta calls the three orders reality. Most of the confusion around the topic of doership comes from confusing these levels.

These three orders of reality are the absolute, the objective and the subjective.

1. The Absolute Order of Reality (*Paramartika*)

The absolute reality, *paramartika*, is Brahman, the Self. It is free of attribute, limitless, divisionless and beyond birth and death. As the very ground of existence, nothing can exist without it, including the other two orders of reality. The absolute alone is satya, while all else is mithya. When we speak about the Self, we're referring to this absolute order of reality.

2. The Objective/Empirical Order of Reality (*Vyavaharika*)

Courtesy of maya, within the absolute we experience the objective, empirical universe; the world of form and experience. This order of reality, *vyavaharika*, includes all the elements, the stars, galaxies, worlds, objects, all the jivas, and anything perceivable to the senses.

The objects of the empirical order of reality, maya, clearly exist, otherwise we wouldn't be able to experience them. However, they cannot be considered absolutely 'real', because, as we've demonstrated, they are finite and have no independent existence of their own, just as pots do not exist independently of the clay. As an effect, the objective reality is always entirely dependent upon its cause—which is pure awareness, the Self, or the absolute order of reality.

3. The Subjective Order of Reality (*Pratibhasika*)

Within the objective order of reality appears a third order of reality, called the subjective or *pratibhasika* world.

This is the private world of the jiva's imagination, projections and dreams. In our dreams at night we experience all kinds of things that have no empirical existence. However, they do exist at a personal, subjective level, because we clearly experience them.

It's not only in sleep that we experience this imagined world. We also experience it throughout the day. Whenever you find yourself daydreaming, imagining or fantasising, you're inhabiting pratibhasika, the jiva's subjective order of reality; a place accessible and known only to you.

Fears, projections, and mistaken notions are also pratibhasika. Vedanta famously uses the metaphor of the snake and the rope. One night, a weary traveller reaches the outskirts of a village and stops by a well. He's about to quench his thirst when he seizes up in terror, having caught sight of a snake by the side of the well, its head upraised and poised to strike. It's not until another man approaches with a lantern that the traveller realises it isn't a snake at all. It's simply a length of rope coiled by the side of a bucket.

When it comes to pratibashika, what you see is not actually there. It's an error of perception; a projection caused by the mind. But, real or not, you still see and experience it, so in that moment, it does inhabit a certain, subjective, order of reality.

Confusing the Orders of Reality

Throughout our day, we flit between these latter two orders of reality; interacting with the objective reality, and creating all kinds of subjective interpretations and alternative realities out of our judgements, ignorance and projections.

The subjective order of reality is a creation of the jiva's mind. It's a private world, experienceable only by that particular jiva. The objective order of reality is Ishvara's creation, arising from this innate cosmic intelligence. It's not a private reality, for it is experienced by all jivas. Both these orders of reality are, however, mithya. They borrow their existence from the absolute order of reality, which is satya.

Perhaps the most helpful way of understanding the difference between these levels of reality is to again consider dreaming. Your dreams occupy one level of reality, in which you can experience all kinds of wondrous and terrifying things. Upon waking, however, you find yourself completely unchanged by whatever happened in this dream. In your dream you may have murdered someone, but upon waking, you don't go and hand and yourself in to the nearest authorities.

That's because what happens in one order of reality is particular to that order. There's no overlap. Your dreams won't suddenly spill into your waking reality. And neither your dreams or your waking reality in any way affect the absolute reality; the changeless ground of existence which is pure, undifferentiated awareness/consciousness.

Sticking with the dream analogy, you can't say that your dream didn't exist, for you clearly experienced it. But knowledge negates the dream as nothing but a projection in consciousness, from which it borrowed its limited existence.

In terms of doership, the dream occurred because of you, but you cannot say that you were the doer of the dream. There was no doership involved. The dream was simply an appearance in consciousness; its form and content determined by factors outside your conscious control.

To summarise the three orders of reality: the jiva's subjective world of thoughts, interpretations and dreams is superimposed upon Ishvara's objective/empirical world. In fact, the jiva itself is a product of and is non-separate from Ishvara. Both these orders of reality take place within the underlying absolute reality that is the Self—the substratum from which all things derive their existence.

How Action Happens

You might be wondering how this talk of orders of reality relates to action and actionlessness. In short, at the absolute order of reality, the Self is actionless. Courtesy of maya, however, action occurs at the objective order of reality; the world of form and differentiation.

In much the same way as the sun enables all life to exist without doing anything itself other than shining, the Self is the principle by which all the creation is made possible, while itself remaining actionless.

While the Self is motionless, everything in the material creation exists in a state of perpetual motion. Even things that appear to be inert, such as rocks, are bursting with activity at the subatomic level: a frenetic dance of electrons, protons and neutrons, all driven by the innate organising intelligence of Ishvara.

While the jiva is quick to claim ownership of its actions, all action ultimately belongs to Ishvara, as we shall see. After all, Ishvara set up the entire mechanism by which the jiva functions.

In order for the jiva to perform any action, five factors must be in place: the physical body, the subtle body, the physiological system, the ego, and, of course, Ishvara.

The physical body and the senses of perception and action are obviously essential to the performance of any action. As, of course, are the physiological systems (such as respiration, circulation and digestion) necessary for the body and mind to function. Also involved is the subtle body, which includes the mind, intellect and ego.

To recap, our senses relay information to the mind, which then filters, questions and interprets the data. The intellect then weighs up our options and, using past knowledge and experience (and, indeed, impelled by the causal body's vasanas), decides on an appropriate response. The mind then emotes, and this emotion compels action. Finally, the ahamkara, or the ego/ doer function, then performs the action using the organs of action.

It's important to note that although the ego thinks of itself as a lone authority and the sole agent of action, it's actually only one factor among many.

The ego is our sense of autonomous being; of being the one that initiates actions and takes responsibility for the results. While a vital component of the subtle body, the ego nevertheless has an overinflated sense of its own importance. It puts its stamp on everything, retrospectively 'owning' every thought and feeling, when, in fact, it's only the tip of a very large iceberg.

Ishvara is the Doer

While the ego sees itself as the sole agent of action, its agency is limited. After all, the jiva doesn't even have control of the thoughts and feelings arising in its own mind. These appear in the subtle body automatically, arising from the causal body, the unconscious, which is Ishvara.

Avidya (self-ignorance) causes the jiva to identify with these thoughts and feelings. The ego invests them with "I"-ness, and they become *my* thoughts and feelings. Taking appearance to be real, the jiva believes itself to be a limited entity at the mercy of a separate and disconnected universe.

From ignorance, a world of desires and fears is born, pre-disposing the jiva to act. With each and every action, the vasa-nas grow stronger, compelling the jiva to keep acting again and again, all the while becoming ever-more entangled in the net of samsara.

The jiva's mistake is taking ownership of what ultimately doesn't belong to it. In actual fact, the jiva isn't the doer. It has a sense of doership, of agency, but everything in the objective realm, in maya, belongs to Ishvara.

The entirety of the creation is Ishvara—the whole manifest-ed universe. While the ego considers itself to be the sole author of its actions, it's impossible to discount Ishvara. Ishvara is the environment in which the action takes place, and the force that, in the form of vasanas, generates the action in the first place.

In spite of what most personal development and motiva-tional programs might have us believe, the jiva is not captain of the ship. Ishvara created the jiva's gross and subtle bodies and the causal body. Furthermore, the entire creation is controlled by Ishvara's laws. Everything happens according to these laws, including the jiva's thoughts and feelings, as determined by the gunas and vasanas.

The ego doesn't like to hear this. It doesn't want to be out of a job, after all, or to suffer a humiliating demotion. Its job is to take ownership of all its thoughts and actions, and it fundamentally believes itself to be responsible for doing them.

This notion of doership is a hardwired illusion, however. In order for the jiva to be the doer, the sole agent of action, it would have to be aware of and in control of all the factors that generate and influence action. Clearly, this is not possible.

As Carl Sagan once said, "If you wish to create an apple pie from scratch, you must first create the whole universe."

Because Ishvara created the whole universe and the laws that run the universe, including all the jivas, the ultimate doer is Ishvara.

The Issue of Free Will

Does this mean that free will doesn't exist?

It's hard to give a simple yes or no to this question. From the perspective of the Self, there's no free will, because the Self has no will at all. It has no will because there's nothing other than it. What could the Self possibly want when it is already everything everywhere?

The question of free will with regards to Ishvara and the objective order of reality is also irrelevant. Ishvara operates according to universal laws, of which it is both the author and the implementer. This is a lawful universe and those laws remain constant.

As wielder of maya, Ishvara has all-power and all-knowledge, so it is conceivable that Ishvara could exercise will to change the rules of the game. But this is an impersonal, objective creation. Changing even one aspect—say, making fire cold instead of hot—would disrupt the entire creation and upset the dharma field. Ishvara's will is dharma. By living in alignment with dharma, the jiva is living in alignment with God.

When it comes to the jiva, there is an apparent free will. Unlike plants and animals, which live entirely according to their nature, human beings have the ability to exercise a degree of choice. Although we have no direct say over the body we're given, we can choose whether we eat and live healthily, how we style our hair, and what kind of clothes we wear. Similarly, we may have little control over the external world, but with luck we can decide where we want to live, who we want to be around, and what kind of environment we create around us. We can choose whether we have tea or coffee, an apple or an orange. Heck, now you can even choose your gender if you're not happy with the sex you were born with!

Of course, any objective analysis of human experience will conclude that most of the choices we make are pre-determined rather than volitional. Our behaviour and choices are largely determined by our environment, and our conditioning in the form of the vasanas and gunas. That's why it's accurate to say that it's really Ishvara running this whole show.

However, the apparent free will of the jiva is an essential component of our makeup. Rather than adopting a fatalistic attitude and refusing to budge from the couch, it's imperative that we exercise this capacity. Life is a dance, a show, and it's important that we 'get with' the show.

For the jiva, one choice is always preferable to another. Following dharma is unquestionably the best option, because adharma comes rife with adverse consequences.

Of course, a person's nature or upbringing may incline them to perform adharmic action. That's why the intellect should always be employed to determine whether our actions are right and appropriate.

In short, we must live consciously rather than unconsciously; our actions guided by a discriminating intellect rather than the blind reactivity of emotion and impulse.

The complimentary principles of dharma and karma yoga provide a solid template for our interactions with the world. This not only ensures that our actions are in harmony with Ishvara, but effortlessly relieves the stress caused by our burden of apparent doership.

For the jnani, whose mind is blessed by the light of integrated Self-knowledge, the sense of doership has been completely negated. Doership and will are seen as belonging only to mithya; the empirical world of the senses. The Self, as satya, remains ever free even as the phenomenal universe continues its eternal dance.

Deleting the Karma Account

"The wise see actionlessness in action" means that even in the midst of action, the jnani is aware that the Self is not the doer. The Self is that by which action happens, while itself remaining free of action.

If you really were the doer, there'd be no escaping samsara, because the very basis of samsara is attachment to action and its results. The only way out of it is by examining and negating the whole notion of doership.

Swami Dayananda notes:

> The destruction of something belonging to a given order of reality can only be brought about by shifting to a higher order of reality. For example, when the dreamer wakes up, everything that was done in the dream is destroyed. Therefore, destruction can only take place by falsification. To falsify what is false is knowledge.

When all notions of doership as seen as belonging to mithya and not satya; to the empirical reality and not the absolute, the notion of the Self as a doer is negated.

The ego is an obstacle to Self-knowledge because it places a stamp of "I-ness" on anything it touches. An imposter self subverting your self-identification, it keeps you bound to the notion that you are a limited, time-bound entity.

Contrary to what some spiritual teachings assert, the ego cannot be destroyed, nor need to be. It simply needs to be understood for what it is. The ego is not the Self, although it believes that it is. As an observable component of the subtle body, it is mithya and is dependent on the Self, consciousness, for its existence.

While action is continuously happening in the domain of maya, this action is specific to the empirical order of reality. The Self, the absolute, remains free of all action.

Even if you still take yourself to be a jiva, the above analysis makes it clear that doership belongs to Ishvara and neither the jiva nor the Self. Either way, you are off the hook—for you are free of doership. If karma doesn't belong to you, then the results of karma don't belong to you either. Action and its results belong to Ishvara alone.

When you no longer identify as a jiva, there's no longer anyone to claim ownership of the results of karma. Your 'karma account' is deleted from the system, so to speak.

While *prarabdha karma*—the karma fructifying in this particular lifetime—still has to play itself out, Self-knowledge as good as neutralises it. As a jnani, a liberated soul, you are insulated from this karma because your mind remains alike in both favourable or unfavourable conditions. No new karma can be accrued because there is no longer an 'addressee' on file.

Unencumbered by the ego's delusions of doership and false self-identification, you come to know yourself as whole, complete, and endlessly content in yourself alone. You no longer need to manipulate the outer world and chase after objects in order to be happy. Why would you when you have an unlimited source of happiness within you?

Action for the Enlightened

The knower of the Self attains life's highest goal and has nothing more to seek in the world. For the ignorant, action arises out of the need to 'become somebody'; to attain fullness, happiness and wholeness. But knowing oneself to be already whole, the jnani has nothing to gain or to prove. Their actions spontaneously align with dharma because they have no reason to violate it.

An enlightened mind no longer takes itself to be a finite entity appearing in and subject to the limitations of a hostile external world. Everything is seen as the Self. The jnani views the entire world as an appearance in awareness just as the dream-world appears in consciousness at night.

No longer lost in endless self-rumination, nor gripped by compulsive desires and fevered projections about the past and future, the liberated live in the present moment, enjoying life for what it is, free of the need to grasp and control.

While the samsari performs action *for* happiness, the jnani performs action *from* happiness. Whereas the samsari works *for* fulfilment, the jnani works *with* fulfilment. Whatever the samsari is seeking, the jnani has already found.

Devoid of egoistic desire or will, the liberated act to bless the world rather than to take from the world.

Vedanta defines success as the ability to manage both the successes and failures of life with equal grace. It is, after all, impossible to experience one without the other. Alike in both good fortune and bad, and free of emotional dependence on objects, only the jnani is able to truly enjoy the game of life. Such souls view life as *lila*; as a game or sport.

Self-knowledge shifts the locus of our identity from jiva to the Self; from mithya to satya. Of course, the body, mind, intellect and ego remain for their allotted lifespan. Life continues its merry dance. The jiva still has to get up in the morning, make the bed and go about its day. Action, therefore, continues as before according to our karma.

The wise do not, therefore, renounce action by abstaining from action—which is, after all, an impossible task. Instead, they renounce action through knowledge. They continue to act, but no longer identify themselves as the doer of those actions.

Swami Paramarthananda likens this to selling a house but continuing to live in it. Everything might seem the same and life goes on as before, but the deeds have been handed over to Ishvara (who, in actual fact, owned everything all along). Instead of living with a sense of ownership and entitlement, the wise live as trustees, with the knowledge that everything in this world is on temporary loan from Ishvara.

As that which manufactures and maintains the entire creation, Ishvara has provided the house—specifically, our body and environment—and takes care of most of its upkeep. In exchange for rent, we are expected to follow dharma and keep everything healthy, clean, and in order. While ultimate responsibility belongs to the landlord, we still have to take good care of the landlord's property. After all, any tenant causing too many problems for the landlord runs the risk of eviction!

Life as an Offering

It's only appropriate to live with gratitude and devotion. Krishna talks about living a prayerful life; a life of devotion and sacrifice. We've been given everything by Ishvara, and therefore we have a debt to repay.

Krishna outlines different ways we can give *yajnas*, or sacrificial offerings. This includes helping others, whether in terms of our time, effort, or money, practicing moderation in diet and lifestyle, and performing yoga to purify the body and mind.

The highest form of offering, however, is the pursuit and practice of Self-knowledge, which liberates the jiva from bondage to action and samsara. That's why Krishna recommends finding a qualified teacher who can unfold the vision of Vedanta and resolve any doubts or confusion that might arise.

In order for the teaching to work, you must ensure that you are a suitably qualified student. Therefore, you must cultivate an abiding, tranquil mind; one that's capable of listening to and reflecting on the teaching with single-pointed devotion. You need both faith in the teaching and the teacher, and the sincerity and commitment to see it through. Discipline of the senses is also important, otherwise you'll find your mind galloping here, there, and everywhere like a wild horse.

The greatest obstacles to knowledge are ignorance, lack of faith, and doubt. The solution is to practice karma yoga in order to neutralise the mind's extroversion and entrenched likes and dislikes. Only then are you fit for jnana yoga, the yoga of Self-knowledge.

This Self-knowledge destroys the notion of doership. It does so by providing what Shankara calls 'clear vision', which is steadfast discrimination between satya and mithya, the real and unreal. All action, including the agent of action, the purpose and means of action, and the action itself, are understood to be mithya—only apparently real.

As sorrow, delusion and suffering dissolve in the light of Truth, you attain the absolute peace of your own nature as the ever free, ever shining Self.

Renunciation

¹ Arjuna remained confused. "Krishna, you have recommended both the performance of action and the renunciation of action. Tell me definitely which is the better."

² Krishna said, "Both renunciation of action and the performance of action as karma yoga eventually lead to liberation. But of the two, the path of action is better suited to most aspirants.

³ "The person who neither hates nor longs for anything is known as a renunciate. Such a soul, free from any sense of duality and devoid of personal likes and dislikes, achieves effortless liberation from bondage.

⁴⁻⁵ "The ignorant believe there is a difference between the path of knowledge and the path of karma yoga. But the person who is established in one path will attain the fruits of both. Both eventually lead to the same result, so the wise view the path of knowledge and the path of yoga as one.

⁶ "Renunciation of action is difficult without first mastering karma yoga. But the one who is committed to a life of yoga, with a purified and discriminating mind, will quickly realise Brahman (the Self).

⁷ "Having mastered the body and the sense organs, and realising that they are the Self in all beings, they are untouched even as they perform action.

⁸⁻⁹ "The knower of truth understands, "I am not the doer". Even while seeing, hearing, touching, smelling, eating, walking, sleeping, breathing, talking, releasing, grasping and opening or closing the eyes, they understand that these are only the actions of the sense organs engaged with their respective objects.

¹⁰⁻¹¹ "The one who acts without attachment and who offers the action to Brahman is unaffected by karma, just as the lotus leaf remains dry even when in water. No longer driven by egoic

desire or attachment to results, the karma yogi's only aim in performing action is purification of the mind.

12 "The karma yogi, having given up attachment to the results of his or her actions, cultivates a peaceful, composed mind, free of agitation. Those who fail to practice karma yoga, whose actions are driven by desire and attachment to results, remain bound by action and suffer accordingly.

13 "Those who are self-controlled and renounce actions mentally by virtue of knowledge, live happily in the body, neither driven to act, nor desiring to cause others to act.

14-15 "The Self creates neither the sense of doership nor action, nor the cause and effect resulting from action. These arise from one's own nature as part of the field. The Self remains untouched by the merit or demerit caused by action. Because knowledge of the Self and the nature of reality is obscured by ignorance, people take themselves to be the doer of action.

16 "Ignorance, however, is destroyed by Self-knowledge. The light of this knowledge, shining like the sun, reveals the nature of Brahman as the Self in all beings.

17 "Those whose intellects are illumined by truth, remaining absorbed in the Self and committed to integrating Self-knowledge, are cleansed of impurity and are no longer reborn into the world of multiplicity.

18 "They see the Self in all beings, from the greatest spiritual master to an elephant, cow or dog.

19-21 "Such souls have broken the cycle of birth and death. They abide in the Self as the Self, which is limitless, changeless and free of defects. They neither rejoice in worldly gain, nor do they resent loss. Unattached to external supports and secure with steadfast Self-knowledge, they gain limitless peace.

22 "Worldly pleasures have a beginning and end and inevitably cause pain. Therefore, the wise do not seek happiness in them.

23-24 "But those who master the impulses of lust and anger before release from the body attain happiness. Revelling in the light of the Self, they find fulfilment within and gain the freedom which is the Eternal Self.

25-26 "With a pure mind devoid of inner conflict, the wise, having achieved self-mastery, and working for the good of all beings, attain freedom. A mind free of craving and resentment is liberated both here and hereafter.

27-28 "Closing the eyes, keeping the external objects external, steadying the breath, and focusing their attention upon awareness, the contemplative person masters their senses through meditation. Their ultimate goal is liberation. Knowing me as the imperishable Self; the Lord of all worlds, he or she attains eternal peace."

COMMENTARY

Chapter five opens on a note of déjà vu. Still confused about the path of action and the path of renunciation, Arjuna once again asks Krishna to clarify which is the better path.

In response, Krishna summaries the teaching of the past three chapters. Therefore, chapter five is something of a 'greatest hits' of the first section of the Gita. The closing verses then introduce the topic of meditation, which the next chapter wilcover in greater depth.

Clarifying Action and Renunciation

Krishna first answers Arjuna's query by re-clarifying the difference between the path of action (karma) and the path of renunciation (sannyasa). Indeed, the Gita spends considerable time addressing this topic.

The Vedas prescribe two types of lifestyle. The first, *pravritti*, is an active life of work and family in society, and the second, *nivritti*, is a life of seclusion and withdrawal from society. Vedic culture recognises the latter, the path of sannyasa, as the final ashrama, or stage of life. When worldly duties conclude, a person can retire from work and social life, devoting their final years to the pursuit of Self-knowledge and moksha.

Those with a naturally contemplative disposition, having little desire for worldly attainments, have the option to forgo the householder stage altogether and become a sannyasi at a younger age. In doing so, they relinquish all social and family obligations and devote their entire life to the pursuit of enlightenment. The closest historical parallel in Western society is to opt for a life of monasticism.

In actual fact, relatively few people took sannyasa, even in ancient India. Although held as life's highest goal, only a small minority have ever pursued moksha with any serious intent. Why would this be the case? After all, Vedanta reveals that all our goals in life are driven by the underlying desire to be free of limitation, and only moksha provides lasting freedom.

Alas, the allure of worldly life is simply too great for most. Owing to the natural extroversion of the mind and senses, and the concealing and veiling power of maya, human beings are hard-wired to seek happiness in the world of objects alone.

The psychological pressures of the vasanas, manifesting as our seemingly intractable desires and aversions, keep us locked in the cycle of samsara. Worldly entanglement self-perpetuates as long as we takes ourselves to be the doer and the enjoyer of our actions. For most people, the gravity of their karma is so strong that they have no interest in spiritual matters at all.

The desire for spiritual liberation isn't something that can be manufactured. For most worldly people, it's the very last thing on their minds.

Even many seekers who believe themselves to be 'spiritual' are simply samsaris whose desire for material gratification is wrapped in spiritual clothing. Such people, often followers of the law of attraction and suchlike, seek to manipulate the universe into giving them what they want. In this way, they're no different to worldly people; their lives still driven by their likes and dislikes, and their happiness completely reliant on the fulfilment of their desires.

For such a mind, moksha is unattainable. Samsara can be defined as dependence on objects for happiness, and moksha is freedom from such dependence.

A genuine interest in spirituality; a yearning to understand the truth about life, about oneself and God, and the burning desire to break free from samsara, is the result of good karma from meritorious action. A crack appears in the facade of the ego, and through that crack shines a light that cannot long be ignored.

The more you purify your mind through dharmic living, karma yoga and upasana yoga (which will be explained in the middle section of the Gita), the stronger the spiritual impulse becomes until, eventually, it becomes the driving force in your life. The mind shifts from extroversion to introversion. Instead of seeking happiness in what you *have*, you realise that happiness comes from what you *are*. Only then is spiritual progress possible, and liberation through Self-knowledge attainable.

The majority of people, whether seekers or otherwise, are not yet at that point. They aren't natural sannyasis, for they still have significant karma in the world. Countless vasanas—deep compulsions, desires, and aversions—bind them to action and its results.

All but the most accomplished yogis, those who have taken considerable time and effort to purify their minds, bodies, and lifestyles, will find themselves bound to the world of karma to a greater or lesser degree.

Arjuna is one such man; neither a sannyasi by temperament nor by duty. That's why Krishna discourages him from absconding from battle and going off to become a monk in the forest.

First of all, it would be against his dharma. Secondly, his mind is not suited to such a lifestyle. Until the mind is sufficiently purified by neutralising the binding vasanas, true renunciation is impossible. In fact, far from leading to moksha, renunciation for a worldly person would be a form of torture.

Maturity Can't Be Forced

A contemplative temperament must be cultivated. Swami Dayananda makes an important distinction between giving things up and growing out of things. When you were a child, there were certain things you loved and couldn't live without, such as teddy bears, action figures, Barbie dolls, or Saturday morning cartoons. Fast forward a few years, and what once meant the world to you is likely of no interest at all. It's not that you gave it up; you simply outgrew it.

When you give something up, an attachment remains. As long as you still value a particular thing, you retain a desire for it.

It's easy to give something up when you have no value for it, such as last week's garbage. The moment the garbage is collected, you never think about it again, because it has no value to you. It's much harder to try to give up the things you love and value, such as money, status, relationships, cars, or holidays. As Swami Dayananda says:

As long as there are things without which you cannot live, you cannot call yourself a sannyasi, because there are things that bind you and upon which you depend on for your well-being.

That's why you can't rush headlong into renunciation. As long as you depend upon anything worldly for your happiness, you remain bound by it. No matter where you go, you can be sure that your vasanas will be there with you. Before you can progress on your path, you must first learn to tame and manage the mind, and that requires maturity.

What makes the Gita particularly important in Vedantic literature is that it is addressed to a general audience; those who still have karma in the world and who either aren't suited or ready for a lifestyle of renunciation.

The Upanishads generally seem to favour, and indeed, glorify the path of the ascetic. They are aimed at highly mature souls whose minds have been purified and prepared for knowledge.

This has led many to assume that moksha is solely the province of sannyasis, and that one could only hope to attain liberation by renouncing all action and becoming an ascetic. Krishna says this is not so. He advocates the path of action in the world as the better option for most seekers, including Arjuna.

The two paths, the path of karma yoga and the path of jnana yoga, lead to the same destination: liberation through Self-knowledge. Whereas sannyasis are ready to plunge straight into jnana yoga, karma yogis must take the longer route, for they must first refine the mind, rendering it fit for inquiry.

Only jnana yoga, Self-knowledge, leads to liberation. Karma yoga doesn't directly lead to liberation, but essentially prepares the mind for jnana yoga. Therefore, it may be the longer route, but until one's mind is freed from the pull of binding likes and dislikes, karma yoga is a necessary prerequisite and cannot be skipped.

The Karma Yogi

As a karma yogi, you aren't called upon to renounce all worldly and materialistic pursuits. Indeed, such pursuits will likely be necessary and appropriate for your stage of life. What changes is your attitude with regard to them.

Worldly goals are no longer an end in themselves. You no longer seek wealth for the sake of wealth, pleasure for the sake of pleasure, or virtue for the sake of virtue.

In other words, you are no longer a samsari; someone who seeks happiness in worldly objects. Your goal is now the same as that of the renunciate: freedom through Self-knowledge. When your goal is moksha, you become what we call a *mumukshu*; a seeker of liberation.

As a karma yogi, it's not so much your actions that change as your attitude toward action, and this is where the spiritual journey really begins.

A pure mind is the primary aim of karma yoga. According to the Gita, the impurities of mind all boil down to *raga-dvesas*; your likes and dislikes. When the Gita talks about likes and dislikes, it doesn't mean whether you prefer tea or coffee. Raga-dvesas are the binding desires and aversions that filter your entire experience of life and compel you to perform actions that may or may not be in harmony in dharma.

These binding likes and dislikes appear in the form of vasanas, the strings by which the jiva is made to dance. This conditioning dictates every aspect of a person's life, and, until it is neutralised, the mind remains in bondage.

You might think of the vasanas as the cogs that keep the wheel of samsara in motion. They bind the jiva to action and its results, keeping the mind fixed on mithya and dependent on objects as a source of happiness.

A mind thus agitated is unfit for inquiry. Therefore, until the vasanas have been managed, the pursuit of Self-knowledge will fail to have the desired effect.

Even from a pragmatic point of view, it makes sense to master your desires and aversions rather than be controlled by them. If you had the omniscience of Ishvara, it wouldn't be a problem. You'd have the power to ensure that all your likes were attained and all your dislikes were avoided. As a jiva, however, you lack this ability, so, unfortunately, a lot of the time your likes and dislikes will not be met. Whenever this happens, you suffer.

A life driven by your desires and aversions is a life of constant ups and downs, and it comes with endless frustration, anger, and sorrow. The problem with desire-based living is that behind every desire is an expectation and attachment to gaining a certain result.

Krishna makes it clear that unfulfilled expectation and attachment leads to anger. Anger is a mental disturbance which distorts and deludes the mind. Lost in a realm of projection and subjectivity, it becomes impossible to think and act objectively, much less to practice self-inquiry. Such a conflict-ridden mind becomes ever more enmeshed in samsara.

That's why the entire psychology of the Gita focuses on the management of your likes and dislikes, which are seen as the root of all psychological disturbances. The management of these psychological compulsions is not a one-time affair. As Swami Chinmayananda often said, "eternal vigilance is the price of freedom."

Karma yoga helps you manage your likes and dislikes until, little by little, the mind becomes steady, stable, and fit for inquiry.

As object-dependency diminishes, you find that grief over the past and anxiety about the future begins melting away. Living a life of karma yoga, you take what happens as prasada, as a divine gift. A situation may or may not bring the result you hoped, but because your action is no longer motivated by your likes and dislikes, you can accept it. After all, your primary intent as a mumukshu is to cultivate a peaceful and pure mind.

You now trust Ishvara to dispense the appropriate result according to the greater good of the whole. Your previously narrow view of life shifts from complete subjectivity to objectivity. You also find your mind automatically becomes more discriminating and dispassionate; the two key qualifications necessary for self-inquiry to bear fruit.

Dharma Is Ishvara

In order for karma yoga to work, it's necessary to approach life with a devotional mindset. Rather than pursuing action solely for the sake of gratifying your likes and dislikes, every action is undertaken as an offering to Ishvara.

Obviously, you will only want to offer actions that are worthy of Ishvara, and this is done by living with strict adherence to dharma. You won't, for instance, go about robbing banks and mugging old ladies and claim that you're doing it for Ishvara!

Rather than a chore or inconvenience, dharma is actually your greatest friend. In fact, the scriptures call it a 'protector'. This is a lawful universe, a dharma field, and by living in harmony with those laws, you are living in harmony with Ishvara.

In fact, the karma yogi understands that dharma is Ishvara. Ishvara, wielding maya, is the principle that determines, sets, and maintains the universal laws of creation.

When you play by the rules and follow the appropriate dharma with regards to your body, mind, and environment, you generally get positive results. Life flows, you avoid too much calamity, and you cultivate the peaceful and abiding mind necessary for successful self-inquiry. Your life becomes a dance of dharma, and, as such, every action becomes an act of devotion to Ishvara.

Swami Dayananda says:

> When you are impelled by likes and dislikes, you are performing action for your own sake. Whereas, if you sacrifice your likes and dislikes and perform action with the awareness of dharma, then you are doing it for the sake of Ishvara.

Of course, this is easy when the dharma of a situation happens to be aligned with your desires. However, when it conflicts with your likes and dislikes, you might find yourself less inclined to act. If you happen to be an immature, desire-oriented person, you may decide to violate dharma in order to get what you want, regardless of the consequences.

Violating dharma, even in the subtlest and most seemingly insignificant ways, creates ripples. It agitates the mind, not least because you feel a pang of guilt, and also because you instinctively know that when you rub against Ishvara, Ishvara will rub against you. You'll find yourself constantly looking over your shoulder and fretting about when your indiscretion will catch up with you.

As a karma yogi, you always conform to dharma, even if the action isn't to your liking.

We all have to do things in life that we don't necessarily like or enjoy, but we do them because we know that we have to. In this way, actions are done for Ishvara, for the totality, rather than our own personal preferences.

As long as your actions are motivated by your own self-interest, attachment remains in the form of expectations, frustration, anger, and sorrow. But when your action is motivated by dharma, you remain in harmony with Ishvara.

As Swami Dayananda explains:

> [This] is why there is always a sense of relief when you do something that is right. There is a satisfaction because you are not rubbing against the law. There is no conflict. The absence of conflict is *shanti* (peace).

Although the Self is actionless, the jiva, as part of the creation, is compelled by its very nature to act, and is expected to contribute to the creation in some way. A certain degree of participation is mandatory. That's why we've been given not only organs of perception, but also organs of action. This participation takes the form of doing what is to be done when it is to be done—in other words, following dharma.

Skipping to the End Doesn't Work

Modern spiritual teachers tend to skip the part on preparatory work. You'll find little to no talk of dharma or karma yoga in most spiritual literature because it isn't exactly an enticing notion to the average seeker.

Accordingly, wily spiritual entrepreneurs package only the juiciest elements of the teaching in order to sell their books and workshops. People generally don't want to hear that qualifications are necessary and that they have to put in some hard graft in order for the teaching to work. In today's society, we all want and expect instant gratification.

Unfortunately, skipping to the end doesn't work with Vedanta. It might if one's mind is extremely pure to begin with, but such a soul is uncommon. Almost anyone living in today's confused and confusing world, with its endless distractions, iPhones, gadgets, social media, Netflix and porn, can safely assume that they don't yet have the tranquil, refined mind of a yogi.

That's why everyone should start at the beginning, by adopting the karma yoga mindset and following dharma in order to neutralise the mind's extroverting vasanas.

How will you know when karma yoga is working? As with everything in life, the proof is in the pudding. You'll know when karma yoga is working because you'll begin to enjoy an increasingly contemplative mind, which, as Krishna states, "neither hates nor longs for anything."

Swami Chinmayananda says:

> When the mind is swept clean of its desire-waves, it must, necessarily, become more and more quiet and peaceful. When the intellect is purified (meaning rendered immune to desire-disturbances), the mind, which reflects the condition of the intellect, cannot have any disturbances. The sentimental and emotional life of one who has controlled the floodgates of desires automatically becomes tame and equanimous.

The impurities of desire and aversion melt away when you commit to a life of self-mastery and devotion. Through karma yoga, your actions are consecrated to Ishvara and performed for dharma, for the good of the total, rather than for personal gain. You accept whatever results Ishvara dispenses with equanimity, because your true goal is the cultivation of a peaceful and pure mind.

Such a mind, when illumined by the alchemy of Self-knowledge, shifts from dependence on the worldly objects for happiness, to true Self-dependence, as you come to know your self as one with the entire creation.

A Shift in Perspective

Krishna again makes reference to the illusion of doership. As he tells Arjuna:

> The Self creates neither the sense of doership nor action, nor the cause and effect resulting from action. These arise from the nature of the field.

In other words, action belongs to the field of matter, or what the Gita calls *prakriti* (a term from Samkhya philosophy that will be explained in chapter seven). In the previous chapter's commentary, we explored in great detail how, in spite of the sense of agency and doership imposed by the ahamkara ('I-notion', or ego), neither the jiva nor the Self is actually the doer of action.

Action happens as a result of a combination of factors, all pertaining to the material world. Although you are not actually the doer, action appears to be taking place in and around you. Under the spell of ignorance, the ego superimposes an erroneous sense of doership by claiming ownership of the action.

Swami Chinmayananda used an analogy to illustrate this. Imagine yourself standing perfectly still on a riverbank. Although you aren't moving, if the water is disturbed, your reflection will appear to move; to shake and quiver. If you know that this is only a reflection, you realise that the appearance of movement is but an illusion caused by the reflecting medium, and you are unaffected by it.

In the same way, when you know that you are the Self, you know that action doesn't belong to you, and therefore the results of action don't belong to you either.

That's why the jnani, the liberated person, lives happily in the material world, while remaining unattached and unperturbed by anything in that world. While mind and matter are subject to change and modification, the Self remains changeless.

Like the river and the reflections in it, the body-mind apparatus is merely a reflecting medium for consciousness. The Self enlivens the otherwise inert gross and subtle bodies, yet remains independent of them. Because the Self is limitless and all-pervading like space, it's impossible for it to perform action. Action, after all, requires limitation and movement.

By shifting your identification from the body-mind-ego to the Self, or awareness, you come to know yourself as a non-doer; as the actionless light in which all things happen. The ahamkara, the sense of being a separate, autonomous ego, is no longer the entire basis of your identity, but just another object appearing in awareness.

In the words of Swami Chinmayananda again:

> Just as the ocean, were it conscious, could watch and observe its own waves rising and subsiding upon its surface, declaring its own glory, so too, from the infinite depths of his own personality, the jnani watches the actions performed by the various layers of matter in him.

This simple yet radical shift in perspective changes your entire experience of life in an instant. When your sense of identification moves from the ego to the Self, problems that previously seemed insurmountable—such as ageing, sickness, and relationship or monetary problems—now seem insignificant, much as a nightmare fades into inconsequence upon waking up.

At the root level, all of your problems are caused by ignorance of your true nature. This can be solved by shifting your identification from mithya to satya. While this doesn't mean that your material problems will necessarily go away, it does rob them of their all-consuming significance.

By assuming an objective view of life, you become emotionally independent from the world of objects. Therein lies the fruit of moksha: the ability to weather life's inevitable storms, and to be happy regardless of whether or not the world conforms to the mind's expectations and demands.

Happiness In the Self Alone

Knowing the Self to be the essence of wholeness, the jnani no longer seeks fulfilment in the ever shifting world of objects. To do so would be foolish, because object-based happiness is always fraught with peril.

Because mithya is a dance of perpetual motion, worldly pleasures are by their very nature finite. All such pleasures, Krishna warns, "have a beginning and end and inevitably cause pain." Like the rose, worldly joys may entice you with their beauty, but they always come with thorns.

The joy of object-happiness is offset by three types of pain: the pain of acquiring the object, the pain of having to then preserve it, and the eventual pain of losing it. Each pain is worse than the last, rendering all worldly joys bittersweet at best. Temporary happiness, or happiness offset by sorrow, is not true happiness at all.

Knowing that objects bring as much pain as they do joy, some people attempt to withdraw from objects altogether. But this can bring its own kind of suffering. Deliberately avoiding relationships, for instance, might prevent the pain of attachment and heartbreak, but such avoidance can lead to other kinds of pain, such as loneliness, regret, and depression.

There's no getting around the fact that life is a zero sum game. Seeking happiness in the inherently insecure and unpredictable world of duality is clearly an unwise strategy.

The solution, then, is to find happiness and wholeness in your own Self; which is without limit, without taint, ever free, and ever secure.

When you know yourself to be whole and complete, you need no longer depend on the world of objects to make you full any more than the ocean looks to rivers for its fullness. Rivers can only supply water that belonged to the ocean in the first place, and whether they flow or not, the ocean remains full. Similarly, although worldly experiences come and go, the essential wholeness of the Self cannot be diminished.

With a discriminating mind, you understand the limitations of object happiness, and therefore seek the happiness that does not wane.

By mastering the mind, you come to realise the fullness that is the nature of the Self. Only in the Self do you find infinite wholeness; a bliss, or complete satisfaction, that has no beginning nor end. Thus, moving from object-happiness to Self-happiness, you attain freedom from dependence on the world of form.

The Self is Everything

Until Self-knowledge is fully assimilated, your sense of identification remains fixed to the world of form; erroneously pinned to the body, mind, intellect, as well your memories, thoughts, desires, fears, nationality, age, gender, sexuality, wealth, education, and any number of other factors.

These become you. You create a narrative about who you think you are; an ad-hoc assemblage of personas; a parade of often-conflicting identities, strung together by wants, desires, fears, and goals, all competing for mental bandwidth. When I ask who you are, you tell me, "I'm a straight, middle-aged Republican doctor from Utah."

A mind fixed on mithya is always burdened by a sense of insufficiency, lack, and limitation. This 'I' has limited itself by identifying with form and thought, and a limited self is never acceptable to us.

At our core, we feel a deep, burning desire to be whole; to be complete, to be validated, to be acceptable to others and thereby acceptable to ourselves. This is the fundamental 'itch' of samsara, caused by ignorance of the fact that we are already whole and full, and completely acceptable exactly as we are.

Digging around in maya, scrambling for wealth, security, and pleasure, can never provide a lasting sense of wholeness because, as we have seen, object-happiness is inherently tainted by dissatisfaction and pain.

Only knowledge of who we truly are can bring lasting wholeness and peace. This isn't a case of adding anything to ourselves, either. Anything that can be added can then be taken away again.

Freedom is the recognition of the wholeness and happiness that was always there, as our innermost nature, but which was previously obscured from us by ignorance.

Swami Dayandana says, "For the wise, there is no goal other than Brahman (the Self), which they already are."

The wise attain liberation, not by manipulating the maya world to their liking, but by shifting their self-identification from the limited jiva to the limitless Self. While such a soul still lives and functions in the world, duality is destroyed by negation; by knowledge.

The jnani knows that everything in existence is the Self—consciousness alone. They see the Self everywhere, in all things; as That which is immaculately pure, eternally shining, and untouched by anything in this world.

It's worth noting that, although the wise see the Self in all, they do not treat all equally. In his classic text, *Aparokshanubhuti*, Shankara says that the wise see no difference between a lump of gold and the excreta of a crow. Both are objects appearing in consciousness, and both derive their existence from the Self. That doesn't mean, however, that a jnani would treat both objects the same way. An enlightened person wouldn't take a lump of crow poop to the bank and try to exchange it for currency. Clearly, only a fool would do that!

The jnani doesn't lose the ability to transact with the material world. As long as their body remains, they still have to play by the rules of the empirical reality. Like everyone, they must eat, sleep, sustain the body, and perhaps work or take care of various worldly duties.

They know, however, that action is apparent only. Although, courtesy of maya, appearing as a universe of seemingly separate forms, the Self is free from limitation. Being of a different order of reality, the Self is unaffected by the world of matter and the subtle forces that drive action and experience.

Divested of the samsari's sense of doership and ownership, the enlightened know that karma and its results pertain only to the mind and body, and never the Self.

The jnani, by owning this knowledge, and seeing him or herself in all beings, is freed from limitation. Even amid the world of multiplicity, they see nothing but the one universal consciousness.

Released from identification with form, there is ultimately no jiva at all, only the Self, and this is the highest liberation. Just as the wave is liberated by knowing that it is none other than the mighty ocean, the jiva is freed by the knowledge *aham Brahmasmi:* "I am the deathless, eternal Self".

CHAPTER SIX

Meditation

1-2 "The karma yogi performs action with no expectation of reward," Krishna continued. "Those who profess renunciation yet are still driven by desire for results are neither renunciates nor karma yogis.

3-4 "The practice of yoga brings the contemplative disposition necessary for meditation and the assimilation of Self-knowledge. The one who is attached to neither sense objects, nor to the results of action, easily attains liberation.

5-7 "To succeed, you must lift yourself up by yourself. The mind alone can be your greatest asset or your worst enemy. By cultivating self-mastery, you ensure that your mind works for and not against you. Such a mind remains tranquil and composed in both pleasure and pain, light and dark, and praise and criticism. For the one who lacks self-mastery, the mind remains a great enemy.

8-9 "One whose mind rests contented in the knowledge of the Self, who retains equanimity in all circumstances, who has mastered the senses, and for whom a clump of earth, a stone and gold are the same, can be called a yogi. Such a person sees all beings as the Self, whether they are a friend, an enemy, an acquaintance, a saint or a sinner.

10 "The meditator, whose body and mind are relaxed, and who is free from longing and attachment, should sit in a quiet place and constantly unite his or her mind with the object of meditation.

11-12 "Sitting alone, they should be one-pointed in their focus, restraining mind and senses, relinquishing attachment to material possessions; using meditation as a tool for purifying the mind.

¹³⁻¹⁴ "One's posture should be upright; the body, neck and head not rigid, but held in a straight line. The eyes should be gently focused as if gazing at the tip of the nose. With a tranquil mind and open heart, the meditator contemplates the Self, having That as the ultimate goal, while withdrawing the mind from all else.

¹⁵ "Continually connecting the mind in this manner, the meditator gains peace as his mind is absorbed in Me. This is the ultimate liberation.

¹⁶ "Meditation is not for those who fail to exercise restraint and moderation in daily living. It will not benefit gluttons or those who starve themselves. Nor will it help those who sleep all day or those who deprive themselves of sleep.

¹⁷ "For those capable of living mindfully and with moderation, meditation will cure the greatest sorrow and suffering.

¹⁸ "When the mind is composed, and remains happily focused on the Self, and when one is free from longing with reference to sense objects, then one has accomplished the goal of meditation.

¹⁹ "Just as a candle sheltered from the wind does not flicker, so too does the mind of the accomplished mediator remain still and unmoving.

²⁰⁻²³ "A mind tamed by meditation to abide in the Self, and to rejoice in the Self alone, finds absolute contentment; a happiness beyond the mind and senses. Being rooted there, one never loses the liberating light of Self-knowledge. Having attained the goal of all goals, those established in the Self as the Self are unshaken by worldly fortune or by sorrow.

²⁴⁻²⁶ "Relinquishing all desire and withdrawing the senses from the sense objects, with great resolve one continues to unite one's mind with the Self. The mind, abiding in the Self alone, is free of all other thoughts. Whenever the mind wanders, one simply brings it back to rest in the Self.

²⁷ "Abiding joy is experienced by the meditator whose mind is tranquil, free from self-effacing thoughts, and who, through the assimilation of knowledge, realises his or her unity with Brahman.

28-29 "The joy of this realisation illumines the minds of those who have released the conflicts born of improper thought and conduct, and who continuously contemplate their nature as Brahman. With a vision of unity, they see the Self in all beings and all beings in the Self.

30-32 "I am ever-present to those who see My radiance in all things. Seeing all existence as a manifestation of My being, the yogi abides in Me always, and all their actions proceed from Me. Seeing all things through the eyes of equanimity, pleasure and pain are the same whether experienced by oneself or another."

33-34 Arjuna shook his head. He said, "Krishna, this talk of divine unity is beyond my ability to comprehend. My mind is restless and agitated; an entrenched tyrant. I can no more control the turbulence of my mind than I can control the wind."

35-36 Krishna said, "Without doubt, the mind is by nature restless and difficult to tame. But it can be mastered through constant practice and objectivity. Along with self-control, practice and objectivity are essential to one's progress."

37-39 Arjuna had another question. "What happens to those who have faith in the teaching but lack effort and self-control—and who stray from the path of Self-realisation? If an aspirant falls under the spell of delusion and loses his way, what becomes of him? When he dies, does his effort die with him like a cloud scattered across the heavens? No one other than you can remove this doubt of mine."

40 Krishna answered, "Arjuna, no one who performs good actions ever reaches a bad end. Such people will go on to enjoy other realms, where they may dwell for countless years. They will then be reborn, by merit of their previous efforts, into a family that is pure, prosperous and committed to dharma.

42-45 "Or they will be born into a family of wise yogis. A noble birth such as this is difficult to attain in this world. But such a soul will enjoy life circumstances conducive to their spiritual progression. The wisdom acquired in previous births will awaken and reignite their quest for Self-realisation. Through continued effort over many lifetimes, one purifies the obstructions of mind and heart—and, in time, attains freedom.

46-47 "The yogi, who integrates spiritual knowledge through a life of meditation, is considered superior to mere scholars or those who perform action alone. Therefore, be a yogi, Arjuna! The one who has faith and whose mind is absorbed in Me is the most exalted of yogis. This is my vision."

COMMENTARY

Meditation is a topic needing little introduction. In fact, what was once the province of monks, yogis, and spiritual seekers is now mainstreamed as a billion-dollar industry, with scientists, doctors and psychologists all extolling its many benefits.

Countless studies have demonstrated that meditation reduces stress and anxiety, decreases blood pressure, improves memory and emotional well-being, manages pain, boosts cognitive functioning, and even slows ageing. Accordingly, the majority of meditators use it purely for these physical and mental/emotional benefits.

Interestingly, it's not until halfway through the Gita that Krishna explores the topic. His initial advice to Arjuna isn't to sit down, close his eyes and meditate. As we shall see, certain lifestyle factors must be in place in order for meditation to yield fruit. This fruit, as we shall see, extends far beyond simple physiological benefits.

Lift Yourself Up By Yourself

Before diving into the topic of meditation, this chapter first reiterates the necessity and benefits of karma yoga. As a seeker of liberation, your goal is not simply a healthier body and a calmer mind—your goal is nothing less than liberation from samsara.

Human nature being what it is, we're quick to point to others, circumstances, the state of the world, or even the hand of fate as the source of our problems, when, in truth, the enemy always lies closer to home.

Although we might assume that our problems are out there in the world, samsara is not an external struggle. Krishna makes it clear that the battlefield is the human mind, and it's a war against ignorance: "The mind can be your greatest asset or your worst enemy."

That's why the key to freedom lies in mastery of the mind. It's essential that you learn to make your mind work for rather than against you. To do this, you must, in Krishna's words, "Lift yourself up by yourself."

Some spiritual seekers have the unfortunate tendency to look to others for their liberation, perhaps in the form of a charismatic guru or evangelist, or maybe conspiracy theories, a church, community, or even a cult.

Prone to laziness and magical thinking, many seekers don't want to have to get down in the trenches and put in the hard graft necessary to overcome lifetimes of ignorant thinking. In fact, they don't want to have to think and discriminate for themselves at all.

Such a person will look for someone else to think for them (anyone confident and charismatic enough will do) and, like a baby secure in its mother's arms, will depend entirely on that person for their sustenance and liberation.

This never leads liberation, however; only greater bondage. No one else can set you free. Krishna makes it clear that you alone must take responsibility for your own liberation. If you fail to gain mastery of your body/mind/ego, you forever remain its hostage. The real enemy is within, and until the untamed mind is conquered, moksha is impossible.

Karma Yoga is the Foundation

The first step to liberation is ensuring that you have an appropriately qualified mind. The primary means of achieving this is karma yoga. It's no use sitting down to meditate once or twice a day in the vain hope of getting free. Your entire life must be reoriented, and karma yoga is the means of doing that.

For the samsari, who seeks happiness in external objects and experiences, action is determined by his or her likes and dislikes, and performed with attachment to the results. The karma yogi, on the other hand, is no longer driven by the desire to achieve specific material ends.

As a karma yogi, your primary goal is moksha; freedom from emotional dependency on objects. You act not according to your likes and dislikes but according to dharma. You do what is to be done when it is to be done, offering every action to Ishvara with gratitude and devotion. Recognising Ishvara as the giver of the results of action, you then accept whatever results come as legitimate and proper; taking every outcome as prasada, a divine gift.

When performed in conjunction, dharma and karma yoga relieve stress like nothing else. Grief over the past and anxiety about the future melt away when you cease living your life solely for yourself, but as an offering to Ishvara.

As a seeker of liberation, this is your primary *sadhana* (spiritual practice). Performing action in accordance with dharma and with the karma yoga mindset gradually renders the vasanas non-binding. This purifies the mind, making it fit for liberation through the application of Self-knowledge.

Self-Insufficiency

It pays to remember that action itself isn't what binds you. What hooks you into samsara is the notion of doership, and the need to compensate for what you perceive as a lacking, limited sense of self.

As a result of self-ignorance, you experience a fundamental sense of lack. You believe that in order to feel good about yourself, and to be whole and secure, you must pursue various objects and worldly ends.

This sense of self-insufficiency can always be traced back to early childhood. As an infant, when you first become self-aware, you experience yourself as the epicentre of the universe—as whole, unconstrained and entirely sufficient as you are. For most parents, a little baby can do no wrong. Every last smile, coo or burp elicits adoration.

As you grow up, however, things begin to change. It becomes clear, often with great indignity and humiliation, that you aren't the centre of the universe after all. With horror, you realise that you aren't the only ego in existence, and that you must contend with the egos of others. The unconditional love you lapped up as a baby is now replaced by an altogether more conditional love. You learn that there are rules, and you have to follow these rules in order to receive love and validation.

You experience a growing sense of self-limitation when you come to realise that you aren't the smartest in class, or the most popular, that you don't live in the biggest house or have the most toys.

As you move through life, you find yourself criticised and condemned in a thousand subtle and not so subtle ways—first at school, then at work, in the family, and perhaps in society at large.

All your pursuits and actions are driven by the need to overcome this sense of limitation. Even boastful, arrogant people are simply trying to compensate for a sense of self-insufficiency in their own eyes and the eyes of others.

The Tao Te Ching observes that, "The more you care about the opinion of others, the more you become their prisoner." It's a fact that you never really know what other people think of you. Most people are actually too busy worrying about themselves to spare much of a thought for you or anyone else. Yet how often do you allow yourself to be controlled by the tyranny of 'what others think'?

Swami Dayananda points out:

> Seeking acceptability from others is nothing but self-acceptance through others. Why should anyone accept you? So that you can accept yourself. Therefore, seeking the acceptance of others can always be reduced to self-acceptance.

The real problem is not what others think about you. The problem is what you think about yourself. That is what must be addressed.

Samsara has its basis in this sense of self-limitation and insufficiency. It's a disease caused by an erroneous self-concept. In spite of its pandemic proportions and difficulty to resolve, it is curable. The sad part is that almost no one is interested in the cure.

Owing to the extroversion of our mind and senses, we only tend to seek solutions in external objects and conditions. But the solution isn't trying to get the world to conform to our likes and whims; a futile endeavour if ever there was. This inner lack, limitation and self-condemnation is the true malady, and that is what must be cured.

The Value of Values

The value of values cannot be understated. Lack of clarity with regard to your values inevitably leads to muddled or improper priorities—one of the greatest impediments to enlightenment.

Unless you hold moksha, your ticket to freedom, as the highest of all values, it'll never be much more than an afterthought or side interest. Instead, you'll continue devoting your time and energy to pursuing happiness and security through samsaric worldly endeavours.

Swami Dayananda says:

> To have been born a samsari itself is destructive. If your mind is not in order, if your value structure is confused, then your entire life and the lives of those around you will be confused.

In unquestioningly accepting the cultural conditioning imposed on you from almost the moment you were born, you adopt a false set of values. You place undue importance on worldly success, money, power, prestige and control of others. You perhaps see yourself as a consumer first and foremost; someone who has to amass as much wealth as possible in order to acquire the goods and objects you believe necessary for your happiness and well-being.

A warped value system leads to similarly warped desires, goals and actions. If you value wealth above all else, you'll spend your entire life relentlessly pursuing money; only to find that enough is never enough. Your quest for fortune, fame and power may also lead you to violate dharma in order to get what you want.

Anyone with such a value system will have little interest in meditation, karma yoga, or spiritual liberation.

It's only when you objectively analyse the limitations of object-based happiness that you come to realise that whatever joy objects bring is fleeting in nature and always offset by pain and frustration. You realise that you've spent a lifetime seeking happiness from objects incapable of delivering it. What a self-inflicted misery!

A person only values what they believe will bring them happiness. The moment you realise that money, power and possessions can deliver only limited, temporary happiness, your value system will naturally realign.

You come to see that what you've really been seeking all along is freedom from limitation. Courtesy of Vedanta, you learn that moksha is the only pursuit capable of delivering lasting freedom and happiness.

When your values change, your priorities change. Only then will you find the necessary drive and determination to whole-heartedly commit to your spiritual path. Understanding the importance of a pure, dispassionate and discriminating mind, you begin to practice karma yoga, dharma, and Vedantic study in earnest. By fully committing yourself to moksha, you finally become your own best friend rather than your own worst enemy.

The Art of Discipline

Self-mastery necessitates discipline of the mind and senses, something the Gita makes repeated reference to. Vedanta highlights four types of discipline:

1. Physical Discipline

People often have a stereotype of yogis as extreme ascetics who ignore or intentionally damage their bodies—and, indeed, some do. The Gita, however, rebukes this type of self-flagellation, making it clear that moderation should be practiced at all times with regard to all things.

As the physical body is your primary instrument for transacting with the world, it must be kept healthy and in good condition. Poor health may hinder your ability to effectively inquire and contemplate, so dharma should always be followed with regard to the body's needs and requirements.

That said, you should avoid pandering to the body's appetites. In this chapter, Krishna makes it clear that moderation and restraint are essential for the inquirer. He recommends a disciplined approach to eating, in terms of both the quantity and quality of food you eat, and also with regard to sleep. Lack of sleep has an adverse effect on the body and mind; as does too much sleep. A judicious balance between activity and rest should therefore be maintained.

2. Verbal Discipline

Nowadays, people often consider it a virtue to be upfront and "tell it like it is". However, being vocal and opinionated is less a virtue than simply fuel for the ego and lower nature. Like young children unable to restrain themselves, people blurt out ill-considered opinions, comments, and 'advice', and then have to deal with the bad karma resulting from such a loose tongue.

That's why Krishna prescribes verbal discipline for the inquirer. You should always think before you speak, and anything you do say should first pass through the 'three gates of speech':

Is it true? Is it kind? Is it necessary?

If the answer to any of these questions is no, you would do best to keep quiet.

Unnecessary arguments should be avoided, as should idle chatter and gossip. This saves a lot of time and energy which can then be devoted to study, inquiry and meditation.

Excessive talk about the past and future can pull you into pointless rumination, leading to much stress and unhappiness. As a karma yogi, you surrender the past to Ishvara by acknowledging the laws of karma. You learn to accept the past upon realising that all experience, whether bitter or sweet, is an opportunity to facilitate inner growth. One of the greatest tragedies in life is dwelling too much upon the past or the future, thereby robbing yourself of the ability to fully appreciate the present.

3. Discipline of the Senses

As you may recall, the Katha Upanishad likens the body-mind-sense complex to a chariot, with the senses as horses. Unless you stay in control of your chariot, the horses are liable to bolt. When you lose control of them, you'll find it impossible to get where you want to go, and your destiny will no longer be your own.

The senses are, by nature, hungry for experience. Like a blazing inferno, they never reach a point where they declare, 'enough!' As we all know, experience can be highly addictive. It is, therefore, up to you to manage your senses; to restrain tendencies toward excess, and, in so doing, protect your mind from unnecessary agitation and extroversion.

A person who lacks even basic sensory discipline will find meditation impossible. They'll be unable to sit for more than a few minutes without being compelled by the psychological pressure of the vasanas to feed the senses. Like the monstrous plant in 'Little Shop of Horrors', their senses will be continually crying out, "Feed me!"

4. Mental Discipline

The final and perhaps the most important quality to cultivate is mental discipline. With your mind, you experience the world— and from your mind come the thoughts, words, desires, and actions that determine your life and destiny.

The crux of Vedanta is shifting your identification from the body, mind and senses, to the awareness by which they are experienced. This necessitates a tranquil and abiding mind; a mind tempered by discipline and discrimination. As we have well established, an agitated, extroverted and desire-ridden mind is an infertile ground for the seeds of Self-knowledge to flourish.

Living a life of dharma and karma yoga creates a mature, refined and dispassionate mind. Such a mind has the ability to focus, discriminate and devote itself to the attainment and full realisation of Self-knowledge.

A properly cultivated mind is a powerful tool, with three significant powers:

1. The power to think, imagine, to know, and remember.
2. The power to desire and will.
3. The power to act, to make, or do.

Some spiritual teachings purport enlightenment to be a state of thoughtlessness; of having a blank and empty mind. Such a state, *samadhi*, can be achieved through consistent meditation and yoga, and is certainly beneficial for purifying the mind and burning out vasanas. But enlightenment is not the absence of thought. Thought is not the enemy. The enemy is self-ignorance and its corresponding sense of lack and limitation.

Emptying the mind of thought is like trying to empty the ocean of water. It's the nature of the mind to think. All that needs to change are the errors of thinking that have caused a world of suffering and limitation for the jiva.

Enlightenment is simply the negation and de-conditioning of layers upon layers of ignorance. Vedanta doesn't seek to eradicate the mind and thought. Indeed, it uses them to replace thoughts of ignorance with thoughts of Truth. A mind oriented to the pursuit and actualisation of Self-knowledge is your vehicle to freedom.

The second power of a cultivated mind is the ability to desire and will. This may cause some confusion, because desire is often considered the spiritual seeker's deadliest foe.

Desire itself is only good or bad in relation to the quality of that desire. In terms of quality, we have higher desires and lower desires. The scriptures caution us about the latter; those relentless cravings for sense gratification that so easily escalate into obsession and addiction, and which rob the mind of its ability to reason and discriminate.

Speaking as the Self, Krishna says, "I am the desire that is not opposed to dharma." In other words, when lower desires are sublimated into the desire for liberation through Self-realisation, this potent force becomes an invaluable aid along your path.

In fact, without the desire to be free, you wouldn't have the necessary motivation to pursue moksha. Desire prompts action, so it's not until desire for passing worldly pleasures is sublimated into an all-encompassing desire for freedom that enlightenment becomes possible.

What Meditation Isn't For

We're all familiar with the physical and psychological benefits of meditation. In terms of moksha, the parameters differ somewhat. In order to understand what meditation is, it's helpful to first consider what it is not.

Firstly, meditation is not a means of liberation. Some schools of yoga and Buddhism believe that meditation is the key to liberation and that, if you sit long enough, you can achieve enlightenment by attaining successively higher states of consciousness.

Vedanta does not concur with this. First of all, liberation is not something that can be attained by action. Liberation is your very nature. The Self is already there, fully existent. It's not something new, nor is it something that can be added to you in some way. Like the absent-minded professor searching everywhere for the hat that's already on his head, try though you might, action can't create something that is already there.

Let's say you woke up one day and for some reason started to believe that you didn't have a nose. You might pray to Ishvara with all your mind and might to give you a nose. But even though Ishvara, as the all-powerful force that creates entire worlds, galaxies, and universes, can do anything—Ishvara cannot give you a nose. It's impossible to give you something that you already have.

The Self can't be added to you, because it's already an accomplished fact. All that's missing is correct knowledge of the Self, and this can only be attained by the removal of ignorance.

That leads us to the second point. Meditation by itself won't give you knowledge of the Self. The Self is not opposed to ignorance. Awareness shines upon an ignorant mind just as happily as it shines upon an enlightened mind. Meditation has many benefits, but it is not a means of knowledge, otherwise anyone who meditates would be enlightened, which is clearly not the case.

Finally, meditation is not intended as a vehicle for mystical experience. It's true that as the mind becomes more tranquil and refined, the meditator may experience different states of consciousness and perhaps even mystical visions and cosmic epiphanies.

For a seeker of liberation, however, these experiences can be as much a hindrance as anything. Meditators often become thirsty for such experiences, which then become the goal of meditation rather than a pleasing byproduct.

Such experiences, no matter how profound or blissful, should always be viewed with dispassion and discrimination. All experiences, whether gross, worldly experience or the subtlest states of samadhi—including *nirvikalpa samadhi* (a state of no thought or sensation)—belong to the objective field. Even the greatest spiritual vision is still just an object in consciousness. It belongs to mithya, and, like all things phenomenal, has a beginning, a middle and an inevitable end.

Therefore, heightened states of consciousness and spiritual visions should never be pursued as ends in themselves. Chasing spiritual experiences keeps the mind fixed on the world of form and experience (maya) rather than on the eternal subject, the Self.

Experience and Knowledge

The distinction between knowledge and experience is an important understanding for all inquirers. The Self is limitless. Limitlessness cannot be attained by a limited action—and all actions are by their very nature limited. A finite action can never yield an infinite result.

James Swartz writes:

> The idea that enlightenment can be gained through action—the experiential notion of enlightenment—does not work, because it is contrary to the irrefutable nondual nature of reality. It is based on the appearance of things, not the reality of things. And appearances are not permanent, so an enlightenment that I may gain through action will not last.

Owing to avidya (self-ignorance), human beings are predisposed to seek wholeness and fulfilment in external objects and experiences. That's why spiritual seekers tend to believe that enlightenment is about chasing the ultimate experience; which they imagine as some kind of endless cosmic bliss.

The Self, however, is not an object of experience. Any object of experience is finite and subject to time. In short, if it can be gained, it can and, in time, will be lost. Even the greatest cosmic rapture can be shattered by something as simple as a fly landing on your nose.

The Self, far from an object of experience, is the ever-present subject of all experience. It cannot be gained, and it cannot be lost. All that's missing is knowledge of this Self. Knowledge doesn't add anything to what's already there. It's simply the removal of ignorance. That's why, as an inquirer, you should be clear that what you are seeking is knowledge. Experience binds, whereas knowledge liberates.

Experience in itself is not reliable as a means of knowledge, because experience can be deceptive. Every day I see the sun rise in the East and cross the sky. Based on experience alone, I might conclude that the sun orbits a stationary Earth. Knowledge, however, puts my experience into context, and thus I know that actually the Earth orbits the sun.

Of course, it's not so easy to discount the role of experience in human life. The mind is driven by experience, and in our hunger for bigger, better and more satisfying experiences, we pursue certain ends and goals which undoubtedly bring moments of joy, happiness and fullness.

That might lead some to conclude that the secret to happiness and freedom is simply generating as many positive experiences as possible. After all, we naturally assume that happiness is linked to certain objects and experiences, because when we have them, we experience joy.

What actually happens when you achieve the object of your heart's desire, is that your previous sense of want and lack temporarily abates, and you taste the freedom and bliss inherent to your very nature as limitless awareness.

The problem with relying on objects, goals and experiences for happiness, however, is the fact they are all finite and subject to time. Owing to the pain you feel when it goes, temporary happiness is in some ways worse than no happiness at all.

What's more, no matter how pleasing your experience, experiences alone are unlikely to bring you the knowledge that your nature is pure awareness.

Swami Dayananda explains:

> The fullness that obtains in that experience is not due to any object or situation; it is yourself, free of the taxing, demanding, desiring and willing mind. Unfortunately, you do not recognise that fullness is your very nature. Experience does not give you knowledge; it only gives you a height at which you want to abide, and you cannot settle for anything less. To know that fullness is yourself, you require knowledge, and for gaining that knowledge, teaching is necessary.

What Meditation Is For

Meditation has two important functions in Vedanta. The first is for preparation and purification of the mind, and the second is to enable full assimilation of the teaching.

If karma yoga is the external means for purifying the mind, meditation is the internal means. It is practiced to tame the restless, desire-driven mind and to create the dispassionate, equanimous mind necessary for Self-inquiry.

Vedanta teaches us to switch our attention from the mind, body, and senses to the changeless awareness pervading and illuminating them. Our focus moves from mithya to satya; from the fleeting world of phenomenal objects to the eternal, changeless Self.

This is only possible with a calm and stable mind. This shift of identity from the world of objects to the Self is the key to moksha.

The Practice of Meditation

Krishna provides clear and concise instructions for meditation. He first emphasises the importance of a steady and dispassionate mind, free from longing and attachment. Such a mind doesn't just happen, but is crafted by the steady and consistent practice of karma yoga. It's for this reason the Gita introduces karma yoga before it discusses meditation.

The main points of meditation as prescribed by the Gita are:

1. Find a suitable environment. The place in which you meditate should be clean, quiet and secluded to avoid interruption. Ideally it should evoke spiritual thoughts and a feeling of tranquility. An altar of some kind may be helpful in this regard, but is not essential.

2. Meditate at the appropriate time. Meditate at a time you're unlikely to be disturbed, and when your mind is reasonably calm and capable of withdrawing from worldly affairs for a while. Early morning upon rising is often a good time to meditate.

3. Sit properly. Find a seat that's comfortable, supportive, and which allows for a stable, upright, yet not rigid posture. Sitting with such poise helps you to stay relaxed yet alert. Make sure your body is relaxed by perhaps taking a moment to release any tension or tightness in the muscles.

4. Withdraw the sense organs. Begin to withdraw your attention from the world of the senses. Krishna suggests your eyes should be gently focused "as if gazing at the tip of the nose". This simply means that rather than looking around in different directions, your focus should be gently directed to a single point.

5. Allow the breath to settle. An even, steady breath is balancing to both body and mind, and brings a sense of restful stability and harmony. It can be helpful to begin your meditation by spending some time focusing on the breath. Instead of trying to control the breath, simply observe each inhalation and exhalation. To deepen your practice, direct your attention to not only the rise and fall of the breath, but also the subtle spaces or pauses between each breath.

6. Mental focus. Allow the mind to settle. Allow all concerns, goals, desires, fears and troubles fall away as you withdraw your attention from the material world. Whenever you observe the mind grasping at things—whether in the form of passing thoughts, memories, feelings, etc—simply let go of this tendency to grasp, and return your focus to the present moment and the steady inflow and outflow of your own breath.

7. Connect the mind with the Self. These preparatory steps will create a quietened, peaceful and reflective state of mind. There are two ways to proceed with your meditation now. You can either bask in the inner silence, or you can consciously direct your mind to thoughts of the Self.

The silence you experience in meditation is actually the light of the Self as it shines upon the reflecting medium of a tranquil, *sattvic* mind. As the mind becomes subtler and more serene, you enjoy an ever deeper sense of stillness. In this expanse of silence, you can let go of the need to be, have, or do anything. You simply allow yourself to rest in awareness as awareness.

Krishna makes it clear that the meditator's only goal is to continually connect the mind with the Self. Every time your mind starts to wander, simply pull your attention back to contemplation of your nature as pure consciousness/awareness, or allow it to rest in the silence.

The three movements of meditation, as detailed in Patanjali's Yoga Sutras, are firstly, turning the mind away from the external world; secondly, fixing the mind upon the object of meditation; and thirdly, steady absorption in the object of meditation.

As Krishna says to Arjuna:

> Continually connecting the mind in this manner, the meditator gains peace as his mind is absorbed in Me. This is the ultimate liberation.

Meditating on the Self

All day long we meditate upon the self—or rather the jiva, which, until the advent of knowledge, we take to be our self. We're constantly preoccupied by the jiva's wants, needs, opinions, projections and assumptions. The whole of Vedanta is simply shifting our attention from this phantom, pseudo-self to the real Self, the eternal substratum of existence; the consciousness principle that illumines all perceptions and experiences.

Vedantic meditation is the art of reconditioning the mind to identify with the true Self—pure awareness or consciousness. By keeping our attention fixed upon our nature as awareness, we effortlessly reorient the mind to its natural state of peace and wholeness.

In Panchadasi, Vidyaranya Swami says:

> One should repeatedly meditate on the idea, "I am awareness".

In concurrence, the Yoga Vasistha states:

> This is the supreme meditation, the supreme worship; the continuous and unbroken awareness of the indwelling presence, inner light, or consciousness.

Visualisation and Mantra

Bringing your attention to your own awareness and holding it there requires a very subtle and refined mind. While the Self, as Krishna has stated, is formless, limitless and without attribute, for the purpose of meditation, the inquirer may find it initially easier to focus on a symbol of the Self.

That's why it can be helpful to visualise a personal deity, such as Krishna, Shiva, Ganesha, Parvati, or any number of other symbols for the divine. You should, however, reflect on the knowledge that you are not separate from this deity. Both you, the devotee, and the object of devotion are united as the one, limitless Self, just as all waves are united as the same ocean.

Another technique for keeping your mind fixed on the Self is the use of a *mantra*. Mantra is an excellent tool for meditation, for it occupies the mind, preventing your thoughts from wandering, and each mantra itself represents the universal consciousness that is the Self.

The scriptures offer a range of mantras, from the *Omkara* (the repetition of Aum), to *Om Namah Shivaya, Om Namo Narayana,* the *Gayatri* mantra, *Mahamantra*, and countless others. Find a mantra that appeals to you, and be sure to look up the translation so you can be clear about the meaning of the words.

You may find it helpful to use a mala or prayer beads as you recite your mantra, focusing not only on the sound and rhythm of the words, but also contemplating their meaning. While you chant, gradually increase the space between each repetition. As the space between syllables increases, allow your mind to rest in this silence.

Another way of keeping your mind fixed on the Self is to reflect upon key statements from the Gita or Upanishads. The *mahavakyas* ('great sayings') are what we call identity mantras; statements of Truth about who you are.

Two of the best for meditation are *Tat tvam asi,* and *Aham Brahmasmi. Tat tvam asi* means 'That thou art'; 'That' referring to the limitless Self and 'thou' referring to the limited self, the jiva. *Aham Brahmasmi* is even more direct. It literally means 'I am Brahman (the Self)'.

The Three Stages of the Teaching

Vedanta is essentially a tool for acquiring and assimilating the knowledge, "I am awareness." It works in a systematic three stage process. There's no skipping any of these stages and each must be taken in sequential order.

1. Listening (*Shravana*)

The first stage is called *shravana*, which means 'hearing'. Having taken steps to qualify your mind through the practice of karma yoga, your next step is to find a qualified Vedanta teacher and consistently expose your mind to the knowledge. You do this by clearing your mind of preconception and prejudice, and simply listening to the teacher as he or she unfolds the teaching from beginning to end.

2. Reflection (*Manana*)

It's not enough to simply hear the teaching. Even a parrot can listen to and repeat words. For Vedanta to work, you must fully understand and integrate the teaching on all levels. This necessitates working through any doubts, confusion or areas of misunderstanding that might arise, with the help of the teacher.

3. Integration (*Nididhyasana*)

Stage one begins with words. Stage two converts those words to knowledge. Stage three converts that knowledge to conviction. *Nididhyasana* takes the form of sustained contemplation and reflection upon the teaching. For Self-knowledge to translate to moksha, you must *own* who you are by fully assimilating the knowledge, "I am awareness".

That's the purpose of Vedantic meditation, and why Krishna repeatedly states that the true object of meditation is to keep the mind fixed on the Self.

While you can gain an intellectual understanding of the teaching during the first stage by simply listening to the teacher, there's a difference between mere understanding and assimilated knowledge. It's insufficient simply knowing about the Self. Until this knowledge is integrated into every aspect of the psyche, your previous emotional and psychological problems will remain.

The fruits of Self-Knowledge rarely ripen immediately. After all, you're dealing with a mind subject to decades and, indeed, lifetimes of ignorance.

The effects of this ignorance—which manifest as your thoughts of self-limitation and self-rejection, as well as desire, anger, frustration and grief—will not disappear overnight. Until the knowledge that you are the Self is fully integrated, until it becomes a living, breathing reality for you, these 'knots of the heart' remain.

Therefore, in order to enjoy the benefits of Self-Knowledge—specifically a sense of freedom, peace and happiness independent of the world of objects—you must commit to nididhyasana through sustained meditation upon your nature as the Self.

The Man Who Thought He Was a Worm

There's a story which perfectly illustrates the importance of nididhyasana. It's about the man that thought he was a worm!

This otherwise ordinary fellow went through life believing himself to be inferior to everyone else. The idea that he was a wriggling worm not only caused terrible self-esteem problems, but also gave him an overwhelming fear of birds. Birds, after all, eat worms. Whenever he stepped outside, the mere hint of a bird twittering was enough to strike mortal dread into his heart.

One day, a concerned friend decided that enough was enough. He told the man that he couldn't go on like this, and that he had to get help. His friend made some phone calls, pulled a few strings, and got the man booked into a renowned mental health institution.

There, the man received excellent care. Every day he met with a skilled psychologist who eventually managed to convince him that he wasn't a worm—but was, in fact, a human being like everybody else.

It took some time for the man to accept this. After all, he'd spent a lifetime labouring under his delusion. But as the truth began to sink in, he found himself overcome by a tremendous sense of relief and liberation. If he really was a human being like everyone else, then he had nothing to worry about, and he could actually enjoy his life!

The last morning of his stay, he thanked his doctor profusely, a tear of gratitude in his eyes. He then discharged himself and stepped outside, ready to take on the world. Until, that was, he caught sight of a bird sitting in a nearby tree—a big black crow, silently eyeing him.

Overcome by panic, he dashed back into the hospital and raced all the way to his psychologists's office. He shouted as he banged at the door, his heart racing and his skin covered in a cold sweat. The doctor came out, astonished. "Whatever is the matter?"

"There's a bird out there!" The man cried, his entire body trembling. "It—it was looking at me!"

The doctor frowned. "But we've been through this again and again. You don't have to worry about birds now. You're not a worm—you're a human!"

"*You* know that," the man said, "and *I* know that—but the bird doesn't know that!"

The moral of the story is simple. When you've spent a lifetime thinking of yourself a certain way, it's going to take time and effort to shift out of that way of thinking. Habitual patterns of thought rarely change overnight. Even once you've seen an illusion for what it is, the aftereffects of fear and suffering may remain for some time.

Here's another analogy. Imagine a beggar finds a lottery ticket in the trash and, to his astonishment, learns that he has the winning numbers. He may have been living on the streets for years, but he suddenly has enough money to afford a big house, a fancy car, and every luxury he could dare to dream of.

Although his outer circumstances have changed, it may still take him some time to overcome his old ways of thinking. Inwardly, he may still see himself as a beggar; as someone who has to worry about where the next meal is coming from.

To overcome this sense of limitation, he must own his new status by meditating on himself as a rich man and not a beggar.

The same is true when it comes to Self-knowledge. Unless your mind is highly qualified prior to the first stage of teaching, you won't immediately enjoy the full benefits of Self-knowledge. In all likelihood, you'll still have certain blocks and obstructions preventing you from enjoying your nature as limitless, ever-free awareness. Owing to your past thinking, you may still feel beggarly when, in fact, Self-Knowledge reveals you to be the king of all kings or queen of all queens.

How to Practise Nididhyasana

For this reason, nididhyasana is a vital step that cannot be skipped. While the first two stages of teaching may last a certain duration, either months or years depending on the student, the final stage, assimilating and integrating the teaching, has no set timespan. In fact, nididhyasana should be practised for the rest of your life. This prevents old habitual thought patterns from reasserting themselves and obscuring the knowledge that you are *sat-chit-ananda*: existence, consciousness and bliss.

A key aspect of nididhyasana involves learning to evaluate your life in the light of Self-knowledge. Your old habits, thought patterns, values, relationships, activities, and ways of relating to others and the world must be re-evaluated in the light of Truth. Anything that no longer serves you or which is incongruous with your identity as the Self—including adharmic habits that cause unnecessary agitation to your mind, body, or senses—should be weeded out.

The way that you live should be as close a reflection of who you truly are as possible. When you realise your identity as the Self, you may notice that a lot of what was previously important to you—prior ambitions, goals, and the compulsive need to attain and acquire—simply falls away of its own accord. Why would you continue seeking fullness in the world when you have finally found fullness in yourself? An enlightened person feels happy in him or herself, and not because of external factors, but rather in spite of them.

The second component of nididhyasna is practicing Vedantic meditation, which is the subject of this chapter. Swami Paramarthananda calls this 'self-opinion revision meditation.'

You came to Vedanta feeling like a lowly jiva subject to the compulsions and sufferings of samsara. Vedanta reveals this to be but a superimposition; an erroneous assumption caused by maya, which masks your true identity as the Self. Over time, you experience a shift of identity. Whereas before you identified with the body-mind-ego, now you know yourself to be pure awareness; eternal and ever free from the limitations of name and form.

As we've established, however, it will likely take time until this reorientation of your identity becomes as natural to you as rattling off your name when someone asks who you are. Until it does, you must consciously apply self-inquiry to any self-limiting thought, negative self-opinion or misplaced identification as and when it arises in the mind.

Whenever you find yourself identifying as a jiva, as a wanting, grasping ego, you must get to the root of that ignorance and substitute it with a thought of truth; a thought of the Self.

Vedantic meditation focuses your attention on the object of meditation—your own Self. You fix your mind on the teaching over and over again until Self-knowledge becomes firm conviction. Continued and sustained reflection on your identity as the Self, as the awareness in which all objects and experiences arise, gradually shifts your identity from the finite jiva to the infinite Self.

The Benefits of Meditation

Krishna tells Arjuna:

> When the mind, tamed by the practice of meditation, abides in the Self, rejoicing in the Self and the Self alone, it finds absolute contentment; a happiness beyond the mind and senses... Having attained the goal of all goals, those established in the Self as the Self are unshaken by worldly fortune or by sorrow.

A mind absorbed in the Self loses all sense of separation and, along with it, all sense of longing. Desire, after all, stems from not knowing your innate wholeness. Just as there's no point adding water to an already full ocean, there's nothing you can add to your Self. Therefore, a mind united with the Self has neither attachment nor longing.

As Swami Dayananda puts it:

> The truth of oneself is absolute happiness, ananda, whereas all other happiness always depends upon a mental condition. Ordinary enjoyments depend upon one's external and mental condition. Some external object must be available in a situation and in a form that is desirable.

Self-knowledge frees you from the need to have external objects and circumstances be a certain way in order for you to be happy. By continuously contemplating your nature as the Self, you develop what Krishna calls the "vision of unity".

With the eyes of sameness, you see yourself in all beings and all beings in yourself. Name and form are negated by understanding that although clay pots and gold ornaments are many in number, the clay and the gold is the same in all these forms. Similarly, the enlightened understand that all names and forms in the material world are but the effects of a singular cause: the Self.

"I am ever-present to those who see My radiance in all things," Krishna says.

That's why the wise see the Self wherever they look. The Self is in everyone and everything, pervading all bodies, minds and forms, much as space pervades the universe. This vision of sameness, seeing the Self in all things and all things in the Self, is both the highest wisdom and the greatest devotion.

Swami Chinmayananda summarises:

> To contact the Infinite in us is to contact the Eternal everywhere. The yogi recognises the Divine Presence immanent in everything. For them, there is no experience but of the Divine.

The Entrenched Tyrant

Arjuna, however, isn't satisfied with Krishna's words. Such talk is all very good and well, he says, but what use is it to a mind that is turbulent and out of control; an "entrenched tyrant" as he calls it?

Krishna agrees that taming the mind is no easy task. It is, however, an essential one, because as Vidyaranya Swami says in Panchadasi: "Knowledge of one's self as awareness does not happen for those whose minds are fickle and agitated."

If you observe your mind, you'll notice that it tends to be in constant motion, continuously moving from one thing to the next. This is actually a good thing. If it wasn't continuously modifying to new input it would be forever stuck on the same thought.

The mind naturally gravitates to objects of love or objects of pain. The former entices the mind, and the latter creates agitation. Because your attention generally seesaws between the two, between desire and fear, true peace of mind can be difficult to attain.

Krishna has a two-fold solution: practice and objectivity.

The past five chapters of the Gita have dealt with practice, presenting karma yoga as a means of neutralising binding likes and dislikes. This also has the effect of managing the vasanas, which otherwise compel the mind to dance like a crazed puppet. This chapter, of course, prescribes meditation as a practice for reorienting the mind to appreciation of its ultimate nature as awareness. The remaining chapters present *upasana yoga* and management of the gunas as other key tools for cultivating a calm and abiding mind. Once the mind is fit for inquiry, your primary practice will be applying Self-Knowledge to the mind, cutting ignorance at its root.

The Power of Objectivity

Krishna's second recommendation, objectivity, is particularly helpful for dealing with attachment to objects of pleasure.

Why is it we seek objects to make us happy in the first place?

Objects themselves have no inherent value. They have only the value we ascribe to them. By superimposing certain qualities and values onto worldly objects, we then believe they can give us something more than they're capable of giving. We think that by acquiring this or that we'll somehow be happier, more secure—and that we'll finally 'become somebody'!

These superimpositions rarely happen at a conscious level. From a young age we adopt the values, assumptions and judgements of the culture in which we find ourselves. That's why our sense of what is important and desirable is largely conditioned into us by the social order.

Money being the god of the modern age, it's likely that you grew up believing your worth to be determined by your bank balance or social standing. If you happen to see wealth, a big house or marriage and children as your ticket to lasting happiness, what you're actually doing is superimposing the quality of happiness onto those objects.

The more that you focus on an object, the more your desire grows and the stronger your attachment becomes. The problem is your vision is clouded by subjectivity. You're not seeing the object itself—you're seeing only what you're projecting onto it.

Objectivity is simply the ability to set aside your subjective impressions and reduce an object to its own status.

To overcome problematic attachment to objects, particularly objects of love and desire, Shankara suggests reflecting deeply on the inherent limitations of those objects. It pays to recall that everything in duality has an upside and a downside. Nothing in the phenomenal world is capable of delivering lasting pleasure and fullness. To expect otherwise is to invite a lifetime of frustration and sorrow.

Therefore, attachment can be neutralised by continuously contemplating the downside of that particular object. By practising objectivity, you see the object as it actually is; neither fully good nor fully bad. After piercing the bubble of subjectivity through which you view the world, you'll find the world ceases to have the same hold over you.

It's important to realise that it's never actually the object of your desire that you're really after. Whatever you love, you love not for its sake, but for your sake. You don't love pizza for the pizza's sake. You love pizza because you believe it brings you happiness.

As we've established, happiness is never in the objects in themselves. It's in you. All objects are merely proxies. It feels good when we fulfil a desire not because of the object of desire itself, but because its attainment temporarily frees the mind from the desire, which itself is a form of pain.

A desireless mind is a tranquil mind, and a tranquil mind enables us to enjoy the bliss of our own limitless nature. As James Swartz puts it, "Happiness is the Self experiencing itself."

In Panchasdasi, Vidyaranya Swami states:

> The love for the Self is infinite. Love for an object always changes because an object can only deliver happiness for a limited period, after which a new object is required to apparently produce happiness.

Given that the happiness we derive from objects is finite and subject to change and loss, and that the Self is infinite and unchanging, true and lasting happiness can only be found by fixing your mind and heart on the Self.

No Effort is Wasted

The chapter closes with Arjuna still in a pessimistic mood. What if, he asks, in spite of our best efforts, we fail to attain liberation in this lifetime? Is all this effort in vain?

Krishna assures him that no such efforts are wasted. A lifetime is but a flicker in the grand span of eternity, and whatever progress one makes toward liberation will be carried forward to the next birth.

Nothing is ever lost. Even death, which is seen by most as the ultimate end, is but the shedding of a particular gross body. The subtle body, composed of finer elements, does not die along with it. Comprising the assorted vasanas that make up the individual's temperament, desires and fears, the subtle body simply associates itself with a new gross body, and the grand play continues.

Whatever strides you make spirituality; whatever practices you do and whatever knowledge you gain changes the very structure of the subtle body. Karma yoga and meditation neutralise worldly vasanas and the alchemical power of Self-knowledge gradually reorients your entire sense of identity.

Any progress that is made will never be in vain. Krishna even goes so far as to say that even if you don't attain moksha in this life, upon rebirth, you will find yourself in circumstances conducive to the continued pursuit of liberation.

Vedanta generally de-emphasises the topic of rebirth, however. What matters is doing your best in this life; committing to a lifestyle of self-inquiry, and making the pursuit of moksha your highest value. Krishna assures us that for those whose vision is clear and whose mind and heart are fixed on the Self, freedom can be attained in this life.

Direct and Indirect Knowledge

1 "Arjuna," Krishna said, "In order to know Me totally and beyond all doubt, keep your mind on Me and take refuge in yoga.

2 "I will teach you both indirect and direct knowledge. In light of this knowledge, nothing else remains to be known.

3 "Among many thousands of people, rare is the soul who seeks liberation through enlightenment. Even among those seekers, only a precious few attain the goal and come to know Me in reality.

4 "This *prakriti* of Mine, the phenomenal universe, is divided eightfold into earth, water, fire, space, mind, intellect and ego (the sense of doership).

5 "Beyond this lower prakriti is the higher prakriti, which is the essential nature of the individual; the source and support of this entire universe.

6-7 "The union of these two aspects of My nature is the womb of all creation. I am the One from whom this phenomenal universe is born, and into Me it resolves. There is no source other than Me and nothing separate from Me. All worlds are woven in Me like pearls in a necklace.

8-9 "I am the taste of pure water; I am the light of the sun and moon; I am the sacred word of the Vedas; I am the sound vibrating through space and the innermost strength of all human beings. I am the sweet fragrance in the earth and the brilliance and heat in fire. I am the very life in all beings and the spiritual impulse of the devoted seeker.

10-11 "Understand me, Arjuna, as the eternal seed in all beings. I am the intelligence in a discerning intellect and the brilliance in a brilliant mind. In those who are strong, I am the strength that is free from desire and attachment. In all beings, I am the desire that is not opposed to dharma.

¹² "The shifting qualities of *sattva, rajas* and *tamas* shape the things of this world, but I remain unconditioned by them. These qualities of creation exist in Me, but I am not in them.

¹³⁻¹⁴ "These three *gunas* delude the entire world. Unable to perceive beyond the world of changing appearance, people fail to see Me as the Changeless Essence. Indeed, this maya, which belongs to Me and which is the modification of these changing qualities, is difficult to traverse. Only those who seek refuge in Me find their way to freedom.

¹⁵ "Helplessly deluded by maya, those who commit woeful actions are low in spiritual stature and have no impulse to seek Me. Having lost the capacity for discrimination, such souls follow only the base impulses of their lower nature.

¹⁶ "Those who worship Me do so for different reasons. Some are suffering and seek an end to their distress. Some seek Me as a means of attaining security and pleasure in this world or beyond. Others seek to know Me and understand the purpose of life. And a few have already realised My nature.

¹⁷⁻¹⁸ "Among these, the jnani, the knower of the Self, is most distinguished. Such souls are unwavering in their devotion and are always united with Me in mind and heart. All are exalted, but the jnani, being absorbed in Me, is non-separate from Me and has attained the highest goal of life, beyond which nothing more is to be gained.

¹⁹ "Though it takes many births, the one liberated through Self-knowledge sees Me in all things and attains unity with Me. Such a soul is rare.

²⁰⁻²² "Those whose discrimination is obscured by their lower nature are driven by their binding desires to worship other gods, including money, status or sense pleasure. In whatever form you worship Me and through whatever actions, I fulfil your prayers and strengthen your faith. The person whose faith and determination is unwavering will gain the object of his or her devotion, but it is through Me alone that every desire is fulfilled.

²³⁻²⁴ "Those with limited understanding fixate on worldly and material goals, while those who seek the bliss of eternity come

to Me. It is through lack of understanding that the undiscriminating, being unaware of My nature as limitless and unmanifest, believe that I am manifest in a certain form.

25 "Few are able to pierce the veil of maya and realise the true nature of existence. Deluded by the world of phenomenal appearance, people fail to apprehend Me as the unborn, changeless and imperishable source and essence of existence.

26 "I alone know all that has happened, all that is happening and all that will happen in the future. But almost no one knows Me.

27 "Driven by the forces of duality, and of desire and aversion, all beings are born into delusion, Arjuna.

28-29 "But those who free themselves of wrongdoing and overcome their binding desires, become firm in their commitment to seek liberation through Me. Taking refuge in Me, they transcend the limitations of form and time and come understand the nature of action by knowing themselves to be Brahman, the imperishable Self.

30 "Those who see me as manifest in the physical world, in nature and the cosmos, by keeping their minds absorbed in Me, even at the time of death, also come to know Me."

COMMENTARY

At the beginning of this chapter, having established that Arjuna's goal is to know the Self and keep his mind fixed on the Self through yoga, Krishna promises to teach Arjuna both indirect and direct knowledge. "In light of this knowledge," Krishna says, "nothing else remains to be known."

The Difference Between Direct and Indirect Knowledge

The first stage of the teaching provides indirect knowledge. You learn about the nature of the Self as the very basis and substratum of existence; as That which pervades all things and by which they exist. There's a dichotomy at this stage, however; an apparent duality between the knower and the object of knowledge; between you and the Self.

In order to attain moksha, this indirect knowledge must be converted to direct knowledge. By assimilating the knowledge *Tat tvam asi* (That I am), you come to realise that you are the Self. The Self is no longer an object of knowledge to you, but is claimed as the very essence of your being.

The Gita presents both indirect and direct knowledge, often side by side, which can be confusing unless properly understood.

Chapter seven marks a shift in topic as Krishna moves from the finite to the infinite; from the nature of the jiva to the nature of Ishvara as the cause of creation. This is primarily indirect knowledge, and there's a particular emphasis on *bhakti*, or devotion to the Lord, inherent in which we find an apparent duality (ie., the devotee and object of devotion).

Yet even as Krishna talks of His divine glory, He also offers statements such as, "Those whose minds are fit for inquiry, come to realise themselves as non-separate from Me."

Thus, the final part of the equation is converting indirect knowledge to direct knowledge. It's not enough to know that the Self exists. You must claim your identity *as* the Self.

To Know Your Self is to Know Everything

The word 'Vedanta' is derived from the Sanskrit words *Veda* and *anta*, which together mean the 'end of knowledge'. Vedanta is the knowledge which ends the need for all further knowledge, revealing that by which all things are known.

According to Swami Dayandana, "There is no other knowledge that can make this claim. Every other form of knowledge is only of a given thing, which is mithya."

If you think about it, you don't need to know all the rivers, lakes, puddles and drops of rain in the world in order to know what water is. Similarly, you don't need to know every object in existence in order to know the essence of those objects.

This is made clear in the Chandogya Upanishad:

> As by knowing one lump of clay, dear one,
> We come to know all things made out of clay:
> That they differ only in name and form,
> While the stuff of which all are made is clay;
> As by knowing one gold nugget, dear one,
> We come to know all things made out of gold:
> That they differ only in name and form,
> While the stuff of which all are made is gold.

Knowledge of the phenomenal world is mithya knowledge. There's no end to such knowledge because the mithya world contains countless objects.

But in order to know all things, you simply need to inquire into the essence of those things. A potter can create many pots, but the clay from which they are made is the same. Therefore, if you examine one lump of clay, you then know the essence of all the pots.

Recall that mithya is a dependent effect derived from satya, the independent cause. Satya is the intrinsic and all-pervading substratum of existence from which all phenomenal objects borrow their limited existence. Satya, or *sat* ('being') is the fundamental nature of the Self, which—courtesy of the power of maya—lends existence to the universe of form.

All forms borrow their existence from the Self, just as all clay pots borrow their existence from the clay, and all waves derive their existence from the ocean. By knowing satya (the cause), you know the entirety of mithya (the effect) in essence.

You Are the Entire Universe

The Puranas of India have a wonderful story to illustrate this. In Puranic mythology, Lord Ganesha and his brother Subrahmanya are the sons of Lord Shiva and Parvati. To settle some brotherly bickering, Shiva set the boys a test. He told them to circle the entire universe and whoever made it back first would be crowned the winner.

Subrahmanya was certain he would win the contest. After all, he was strong and athletic, and his vehicle was a glorious peacock, whereas all that chubby Ganesha had was a little mouse on which to travel.

Confident and determined, Subrahmanya set off, traveling the entire universe and speeding back to his divine parents. Upon his return, he was dismayed to find Ganesha had beaten him to it and was standing victoriously by Shiva and Parvati.

"How did he finish before me?" Subrahmanya cried.

Shiva smiled. "I asked you boys to circle the entire universe. Ganesha did this. He circled Myself and Parvati."

Subrahmanya was speechless. A humbled Ganesha lowered his head and said, "You told me to go around the entire universe, father. But I know that you are the entire universe."

You don't need to travel from one side of the cosmos to the other to know the nature of all things. If you know the source and essence of all form—which is the Self—then you know everything in the creation.

One Self, Many Faces

You may recall that in chapter two, Krishna described the Self as eternal, infinite and without form or limitation. This Self does not create. How can it, when it is the actionless, changeless

Absolute? Action requires form, movement and time. These are limitations that do not apply to pure awareness.

However, although the Self does not create, it is that by which the creation happens. By its power of maya, it enables the universe of form to arise, be sustained, and to eventually resolve back into the unmanifest. As an upadhi, a limiting adjunct, maya allows the Self, pure awareness, to apparently assume the qualities of form and multiplicity. Thus, the One appears to become many, while actually remaining unchanged.

The Shvetashvatara Upanishad says:

> From His divine power comes forth all this
> Magical show of name and form, of you
> And me, which casts the spell of pain and pleasure.
> Only when we pierce through this magic veil
> Do we see the One who appears as many.

Although maya appears in the Self, the Self remains free of the creation. You might say that the Self and the creation occupy different orders of reality, just as the waker and the dreamer inhabit different orders of reality.

Yet the presence of upadhis makes the Self appear to be other than it is. To identify with any form is avidya, self-ignorance; and, owing to the immersive power of maya, this ignorance is near universal.

Awareness identified with the upadhi of a particular body and mind is called a jiva, an individual. Awareness associated with all the bodies and minds, and the totality of creation at the macrocosmic level, we call Ishvara, or God.

The key is to remember that neither Ishvara nor the jiva exist independently of the Self. Both depend entirely upon the Self for their existence, much as the pot depends upon the clay, and the ring depends upon the gold.

This means that both Ishvara and the jiva are mithya. God doesn't exist independently of the Self, and neither does the individual. Both are just the Self appearing, via maya, as separate names and forms. Understanding this is the key to liberation.

All objects in the phenomenal reality—all the bodies, minds, plants, animals, planets, stars and galaxies—are mithya. They enjoy only a limited, time-bound existence, and are entirely dependent upon the substance and intelligence that created them. After all, an effect can never be separate or independent of its cause.

Ultimately, the Self alone is satya; real. Everything else is just appearance; a configuration of name and form superimposed upon the Self. Existence belongs to the Self alone, and you are that Self.

The Marriage of Consciousness and Matter

In this chapter, Krishna explains the maya creation in terms of the union of two types of *prakriti*. The term prakriti comes from Samkhya, one of India's oldest schools of philosophy. Samkhya, from which the Gita borrows certain key concepts, sees the universe as a combination of two factors: *prakriti* and *purusha*.

Prakriti is sometimes translated as 'nature' and refers to the level of matter or matter in its seed form. This prakriti is the product of maya and is composed of the three gunas—sattva, rajas and tamas; the powers of intelligence, dynamism and solidity. Much more will said about the gunas in chapter fourteen onward.

Krishna defines this prakriti as the gross and subtle elements that constitute the jiva; specifically the mind, intellect, and ego. Therefore, prakriti, here called the 'lower prakriti', is the matter principle. Matter itself is inert. It requires another principle in order to function, just a lightbulb requires electricity.

Krishna calls the second principle the 'higher prakriti', or purusha. Purusha is the principle of consciousness or sentience, which is the essential nature of the Self. While matter, being a product of maya, depends upon the Self for its existence, consciousness exists independently. It cannot be created or destroyed, and, unlike anything belonging to the material realm, cannot be known as an object.

Some people think of the Self as pure energy. Energy, however, is also a product of maya and, like matter, is subject to change and modification. Matter, whether gross or subtle, is always in motion and subject to change. The Self, however, being divisionless and formless, neither moves nor changes.

Without purusha, or consciousness, prakriti would remain latent and inert. It is only by virtue of consciousness that the field of matter is granted life, motion and sentience via the reflected light of the Self. Purusha, then, is the 'electricity' that powers the material creation.

From this marriage of purusha and prakriti, consciousness and matter, comes Ishvara—the substance and the support of the entire creation. As the intelligent and efficient cause of creation, Ishvara wields maya to create a universe of seeming multiplicity. Much as our dreaming mind moulds a dream-world out of consciousness alone, Ishvara (the Self identified with the entire field of maya) creates a universe of gross and subtle forms.

Within this field of creation appears billions of jivas (a jiva being the Self identified with a particular gross/subtle form).

Although the Self pervades the creation as threads pervade a tapestry, the concealing power of maya obscures it, and jivas are thus subject to the self-ignorance of avidya. Unable to apprehend the Self as your innermost being, you become helplessly fooled by the magic show of maya. The indivisible, all-pervading awareness that you are mistakes itself as a limited, finite entity; one amid billions, each seemingly separate and subject to the ravages of time and fate.

The Spell of Maya

By taking yourself to be a finite entity, a meagre conglomeration of gross and subtle matter, you suffer all the pain associated with such limitation. This fundamental self-misapprehension, caused by taking appearance to be reality, forms the basis of samsara.

James Swartz explains:

> It creates a major problem; this belief that objects exist independently of the self and that they contain happiness. It causes individuals to pursue objects to complete themselves when they are already complete. It creates

bondage to objects. Unless [this ignorance] is removed, samsara continues.

In spite of the universal nature of this problem, Krishna laments that those who seek true freedom are rare. Even among those rare seekers, rarer still are those who actually attain liberation. The sad fact is that most beings fall too deeply under the spell of maya.

The building blocks of maya are the three gunas of prakriti, which will be addressed in great detail in later chapters. Speaking of the creation of the material universe, Krishna says:

> The shifting qualities of sattva, rajas and tamas shape the things of this world, but I remain unconditioned by them. These qualities of creation exist in Me, but I am not in them.

Because all things in maya are born of the Self and derive their existence from the Self, the world of objects is utterly dependent upon the Self for its existence. If you take away the cause, the effect disappears along with it. The Self, however, limitless and eternal, and the source of all things, depends on nothing else. Although maya makes it appear otherwise, the Self is the One without a second; indivisible and whole; self-existent and self-sustaining.

Unfortunately for us, maya acts like a blinder, obscuring our vision. We can no longer apprehend our true nature as the Self—and so, as Krishna says, the entire world is deluded by the play of the gunas. Swami Dayananda adds: "In their delusion, people are busy trying to fulfil their desires, all the while complaining about their inadequacy."

Samsara is a case of false expectation and misplaced seeking. People naturally seek security, permanence, fulfilment and happiness. The problem arises when we seek them in the world of the perishable, not realising they belong to the Self alone. The samsari thus seeks permanence in the world of the impermanent, fulfilment from the finite, and happiness from that which can only ever deliver it with an equal measure of sorrow.

Krishna admits that the spell of maya is hard to break. There's no solution to maya within maya, because anything within maya is limited to maya. Therefore, the only solution is to seek the Self, the underlying essence of reality, which remains ever untouched by the world of ignorance and plurality.

Mohini, the Deluder

Indian mythology symbolises maya as the goddess Mohini, whose very name means 'the one who enchants and deludes', thus luring us from our purpose.

In Puranic lore, Lord Shiva found himself the target of Bhasmasura, an *asura*, or demon, determined to destroy him. This asura had previously tricked Shiva into giving him the power to reduce anyone to ashes by merely touching their head.

Now realising that his life was in danger, Shiva regretted granting the asura such a power! He fled for his life, traveling across the universe from place to place, before eventually seeking the help of Lord Vishnu, known to help people in tough situations.

Vishnu agreed to intervene by assuming the form of Mohini, the enchanting goddess whose beauty bedazzled all who laid eyes upon her. This illusion, representing the magic show of maya, was so tantalising that, upon encountering her, Bhasmasura stopped in his tracks. Forgetting all about Shiva, the lovestruck demon pleaded with Mohini to become his wife. Mohini agreed, but only on the condition that Bhasmasura followed her and copied her divine dance, move for move.

Mohini danced across the cosmos, and Bhasmasura followed, mirroring her every movement. Eventually, as part of the dance, Mohini put her hand to her head, tricking the asura into touching his own head. Because his mere touch turned a person to ashes, the demon combusted into flames and was reduced to fiery ash.

Like all the Puranic tales, it's a story loaded with symbolism. The asura represents the impure seeker who initially wants to pursue God, in this case Shiva. However, the illusion of maya lures him from his path, keeping him entranced and deluded, and making him forget all about his original goal. In fact, by falling for the spell of Mohini, he forgets everything, including his own power, which ultimately destroys him.

Mohini, the ultimate seductress and deluder, appears in a variety of forms in life, including the allure of money, power, fame and lust—all of which are capable of diverting us from our true goal of freedom.

Disposition of the Asura

Those helplessly deluded by maya, Krishna warns, are liable to commit 'woeful actions'. Such people are "low in spiritual stature and have no impulse to seek Me."

The Gita uses the term *asura* to describe such souls. While asura is generally taken as a term for 'demon', the word literally means 'sunless'; specifically, those with a dark-minded disposition who have turned away from the light; ie., what is good. Without the light, we become blind; another synonym for ignorance.

An asura, caught in the spell of maya, is someone who has lost their ability to discriminate. They live only to satisfy the desires and whims of their lower nature and remain blind to truth of their higher nature. As Swami Chinmayananda writes:

> Identifying with maya, the ego, in its preoccupations with the outer world and with its idle imaginings, finds itself incapable of knowing its own true nature, misunderstanding oneself to be only a mass of flesh and continuously panting for self-gratification through the senses.

This core delusion impels a person to commit adharma and all manner of self-insulting actions.

Shankara identifies three basic types of human being: the exalted, the average, and the lowly. The asura is the lowliest of people; those who live only to gratify their senses, desires and greed, irrespective of the cost to themselves and others. Such behaviour isn't necessarily indicative of an inherently bad person. It arises from lack of knowledge and discrimination, both of which are robbed from them by the alluring enchantment of maya.

Such people blindly grope in the dark of their own ignorance, bound by their mind's desires and aversions, further entrenching them in their own private world of delusion. Life becomes an exercise in manipulating reality to conform to their likes and dislikes.

These likes and dislikes are always changing, yet are powerful enough to totally distort a person's mind and intellect. The spiritually blind lose touch with objective reality, and become immersed in a mind- created subjective world—a kind of a mental overlay superimposed upon the objective world and mistaken for reality. Overcome by a veil of delusion, such an incapacitated mind is only concerned with what it wants, irrespective of right and wrong. That's what the Gita means when it talks of an asuric disposition.

This all stems from a basic misapprehension of identity. Even though the Self is always there, as that by which all experience is known, the deluded fail to recognise this Self for what it is.

The knowledge 'I am' is, after all, self-evident; we all know that we are. The error arises from attaching the knowledge of 'I am' to what I am not. By falsely identifying with the adjuncts of body, mind and ego, we create an enormous amount of suffering based on erroneous self-assumptions. Unable to see anything clearly, we end up digging an ever deeper hole for ourselves, because until the 'original sin' (self- ignorance) is resolved, the subsequent sins will be never-ending.

A Devotional Mindset

Krishna sums up maya by saying:

> Deluded by the world of phenomenal appearance, people fail to apprehend Me as the unborn, changeless and imperishable source and essence of existence.

The solution, Krishna says, is to seek Him—which means to seek the Self; the truth, essence and totality of all existence.

This portion of the Gita often adopts the language and style of the *bhakta*, or devotee of God. Alternating between talk of discriminative Self-knowledge (knowing oneself as God) and talk of devotion (worshipping God) can create confusion. That's why the topic of *bhakti*, or devotion, must be understood in its proper context.

These middle chapters of the Gita unfold the nature of the Self as the cosmic force that creates and sustains the universe. A strictly superficial, exoteric interpretation of these verses might lead one to conclude that Krishna, the person, is proclaiming himself alone as the 'one true God'. Such a dualistic interpretation would negate much of the rest of the Gita, however, which began by emphasising the non-dual nature of the Self and reality.

Religions generally establish a central God figure who must be worshipped above all else, and this worship alone is seen as the means to salvation. This applies to certain branches of Hinduism, such as Vaishnavism, which views Krishna as the 'supreme personality of the Godhead'. This devotional-based tradition is based on a dualistic interpretation of the scriptures and doesn't recognise moksha as a possibility during one's lifetime. Vaishnavists believe that the best we can hope for is to worship Krishna and generate the meritorious karma needed to get to heaven. There, they believe, the soul is free to sport with Krishna for eternity and will eventually attain liberation there.

One has to question, however, how it's possible to escape maya by means of maya? Even the subtlest of heavenly realms are still mithya and thus subject to its limitations. If our efforts to attain liberation from maya are dependent on maya, then where is the possibility of crossing maya?

Vedanta makes it clear that moksha is attainable in life through Self-knowledge. Moksha, in fact, isn't the attainment of anything as such. It is the recognition that we have always been free, for freedom is our very nature.

Vedanta embraces the bhakti approach, emphasising the benefits of a devotional mindset for cultivating the pure and refined mind required for the assimilation of Self-knowledge. However, without the proper understanding, the belief that the devotee and the object of devotion are separate and distinct creates a false duality, rendering moksha impossible. That's why bhakti is an aid to but not a substitute for knowledge. (Chapter twelve's commentary explores this in more detail.)

Moksha is the realisation of the non-dual nature of reality. The entire essence of the Vedas is encapsulated in three words: *Tat tvam asi*—'That I am'. The problem with devotion divorced from knowledge is that the devotee focuses on the 'That' and the 'I', while overlooking the all-important 'am' bridging the two.

Desire-Based Devotion

According to Krishna, people come to God for different reasons. The first type of devotee is one who prays only in times of crisis or distress. These tend to be materialistic people with no real interest in spiritual matters. It's not until something goes terribly wrong that they turn to God, usually only as a last resort when they've tried everything else. Such a person will usually forget about the Lord almost immediately after—until the next big crisis, that is.

The second type of devotee is the one who seeks some form of material gain. It might be wealth, power, security, fame, or the attainment of any number of desires. The desire-based seeker is again a staunch materialist, but at least they recognise there is an extra factor over which they have no control.

In an attempt to increase their leverage, they may turn to prayer, ritual or meditation. A great deal of Western spiritual literature is marketed to the spiritual materialist, with books about the 'law of attraction' and 'cosmic ordering' often topping the new age bestseller list.

These first two types of devotion fall into the category of *sakama bhakti,* which means desire-based devotion. The sakama bhakta is always oriented to a material end. They either want to get something—or to get rid of something.

The downside of seeking happiness via material pursuits is threefold. First of all, object-based happiness always involves pain. There's the initial pain and sacrifice involved in trying to acquire an object, followed by the struggle of then having to maintain it, and then the pain and sorrow of eventually losing it. Each pain is greater than the last.

Furthermore, because every worldly object and attainment happens to be finite and limited in nature, no such end is capable of delivering lasting happiness.

Finally, the pursuit of worldly objects, even when successful, tends to keep us locked in the cycle of lack and desire that is samsara. As long as our mind is lost in the distractions of maya, we are prone to delusion, making spiritual liberation impossible.

In spite of these downsides, the Vedas do sanction desire-based devotion for those in the initial stages of the spiritual path. After all, if you have worldly karma, it's only right to want to do as well as you can and to attain success. It's also believed that in the fullness of time, sakama bhakti will eventually lead to *nishkama bhakti*, a higher form of devotion not limited to material ends.

Selfless Devotion

Nishkama bhakti literally means 'desireless devotion', which may be a little misleading. It is still motivated by desire, but it's a spiritual desire rather than a materialistic one. Krishna calls it "the desire that is not opposed to dharma."

The third type of devotee mentioned by Krishna is the one who desires to know God; to know the Truth. Such a devotee doesn't view Ishvara as just an invisible wealth-dispenser, but as the very object of devotion itself.

The basic principle of devotion is that what you worship you eventually attain. People worship money not for money's sake, but in order to get money. A worldly person can worship any number of objects in mithya, but no matter what they attain, it's still just mithya.

Those who desire liberation aren't satisfied by worldly ends alone. They seek the Self through enlightenment. Fortunately, like all worshippers, worshippers of the Self eventually gain the object of their devotion.

There's another type of devotee, and that is the jnani; the one who has already realised his or her identity as the Self. This devotee doesn't see God as either a means or an end, for they have already realised their essential oneness with the divine. This non-dual devotion is considered the highest form of devotion because, in this case, the devotee and the object of devotion are known to be non-separate.

The Tenth Man

In terms of enlightenment, the goal is never separate from the seeker. The Self isn't something that can be added to you by ritual, prayer or practice. You can't been given what you already have, nor can you become what you already are. All that's lacking is the direct knowledge that you are the limitless Self; you are That in which the worlds of form arise and subside like ephemeral clouds in an eternal sky.

Vedanta uses an old story to illustrate this fundamental point. One day, a group of ten young men staying at their master's ashram in the forest decided to go back to the village to attend a festival. The guru put one of the men in charge, telling him to keep count and make sure that none of the party get lost.

As they journeyed through the forest, they eventually came to a wide river. Though the crossing was precarious, one by one, they carefully made it to the other side. The man in charge immediately lined everyone up to check that everyone was present and correct. He counted everyone; all the way from one to nine. Where was the tenth? Confused, he did a recount. Again, he could only count nine men!

He began to panic. Surely one of them must have fallen into the river and drowned—? His heart began racing as he counted again and again, and could only find nine of them. What would he tell his guru?

A wise old woman happened to be sitting nearby, watching the whole episode with a smile on her face. She got up and ventured, "Here, let me—I can produce the tenth man."

"But there's clearly only nine of us. I've counted again and again."

"Trust me," the old woman said with a twinkle in her eye.

She got the young men to stand in a line, and placed her hand on the shoulder of each as she counted. "One, two, three, four, five, six, seven, eight, nine..." She then came to the man responsible for keeping count and placed her hand on his shoulder. "Ten."

The man let out a cry of relief. The tenth man hadn't drowned in the river after all. "I am the tenth man!"

Seeking What Was Always There

Although the Self is always present, for those of us who lack discrimination, worldly allure proves too much. The mind gets lost in the world of form and differentiation and we are unable to apprehend our own self. Or, as Swami Dayananda puts it:

> One has nectar in one's hand and gives it up and extends the other hand for some gruel. The Self is already available without any effort. One has only to claim it, nothing else. Only a single effort is involved here, knowledge.

Those who seek the Self directly attain liberation through Self-knowledge. The worldly, however, who look upon the pursuit of wealth, security and desire as the only legitimate means to happiness, gain only the limited ends they seek, and to those they remain bound.

According to Vedanta, the world is neither the cause of your sorrow nor of your happiness. Sorrow is the result of self-ignorance; failure to know your own Self. Happiness, on the other hand, is born of Self-knowledge. This happiness comes from the realisation that you are already whole and free from all lack. One of the words Vedanta uses to describe the Self is *purnam*, which means fullness.

Regardless of what you think you're after in life, whether it's fame, fortune or fast cars, what you really seek is the fullness of your own nature. Nothing in this world is capable of delivering fullness because all objects in maya are limited and time-bound. Even those things that seem relatively eternal, such as the stars and galaxies, are subject to a slow spiral of decay and death.

A life spent seeking wholeness and permanence in a world that's incapable of delivering it is a lifetime wasted. The sorrows of life are endless for the self-deluded ego. It's only when you seek the highest truth—liberation through Self-knowledge—that, like the confused tenth man, the realisation dawns that what you were seeking was never lacking to begin with.

CHAPTER EIGHT

The Eternal Self

1-2 Arjuna had many questions. "Krishna, what is Brahman? What is the nature of the Self and the individual? What is karma and how does it relate to the Self? What of the higher realms? For whom is action and ritual performed in this world? And how are you known at the time of death to those of steady mind?"

3 Krishna answered, "Brahman is that which is limitless, imperishable and unchanging. It is That which gives all beings existence, residing within as their innermost essence. When associated with a body and mind, it appears as an individual person, called a jiva. Karma, action within the field of existence, is the cosmic force that brings physical forms into being.

4 "All that exists in the world of gross objects is subject to change and decline. The higher worlds are relatively eternal, but the Self alone outlasts all things. Here in this world, actions and rituals are performed for My sake, whether this is known to the individual or not.

5-6 "At the time of death, if a person keeps their mind on Me alone, they will gain My nature. Whatever the mind is focused on at the time of death will determine one's destination.

7-8 "Therefore, remember Me at all times and fight! Keep your mind and heart fixed on Me alone, you will indeed be united with Me. Of this there is no doubt. With a mind fortified by the practice of yoga, liberated by the light of Self-knowledge and one-pointed in its focus, you will realise the self-effulgence of your own limitless nature.

9-10 "Contemplate upon the nature of the Self; That which is all-knowing, all-pervading, timeless, the cause and ordainer of all things, beyond form, radiant as the sun, beyond knowing and unknowing. At the time of death, with a mind made steady by yoga and devotion, fix your concentration upon the centre of spiritual awareness between the eyebrows and you will indeed realise the Ultimate.

11 "I will tell you briefly about the eternal Self; That which does not decline, of which the wise talk, and which is realised by self-controlled, disciplined and sincere seekers of truth.

12-13 "In meditation, remove your attention from the gates of the senses, withdraw the mind into the heart, and bring the breath and attention to the head. Hold it there while chanting the syllable Om, which is the sound of Brahman. Then, whether you remain in the body or not, you will inevitably realise the eternal Self.

14-16 "For the one whose mind sees no other, and who remembers Me constantly, I am easily gained. Such a person is a true yogi. Having realised Me, they have attained the ultimate goal of life and are freed from the shackles of mortality. All beings in all the worlds are subject to return. But, having realised Me, Arjuna, there is no further rebirth.

17-19 "Those who understand the cosmic cycle of existence know that a Day of Brahma consists of one thousand yugas and a Night of Brahma also lasts one thousand yugas. At the beginning of the Cosmic Day, all manifestation arises from the unmanifest. When Day turns to Night, these forms again resolve into the formless unmanifest. The same beings, as expressions of universal consciousness, repeatedly come into being at Day, and then dissolve again when Night comes.

20-21 "But beyond the manifest and the unmanifest is another Unmanifest: the imperishable Self. It is neither created nor destroyed when the cosmos rises and falls like a wave in the ocean of infinity. This Unmanifest, being beyond creation and destruction, is the highest end. Upon realising this truth, a soul attains the highest and is never again subject to separate existence.

22 "The limitless Self is the root of Being and That which pervades all things. Realisation of this Self can be gained by a devoted heart which knows no otherness.

23 "Arjuna, there are two paths a soul may take. One leads to further rebirth and the other leads to liberation, after which no rebirth is necessary.

24-25 "The path of light, of fire and day, leads northward, to the good fortune of a pure mind and heart. This path leads knowers of Brahman to the abode of the Self. The path of dark, of cloud and of night, leads southward into smoke and obscurity, keeping the soul locked in the cycle of rebirth.

26-28 "These two paths, the light and the dark, are eternal, leading some to liberation and others to rebirth. Knowing these two paths, the yogi chooses his course carefully and is not deluded. At all times, Arjuna, the choice is yours and liberation is attainable. Knowledge leads to freedom. Beyond the teachings and injunctions of the scripture, and beyond the performance of ritual and charity, it is through the practice of Self-knowledge that you attain the highest goal of liberation."

COMMENTARY

Arjuna begins the chapter by firing off a number of questions, each of which Krishna succinctly answers. Although most of the answers had already been provided in the previous chapters, repetition is an essential part of the teaching process. After all, until all doubts have been completely resolved, it's impossible to convert knowledge into conviction.

At this point, Arjuna is still flitting between the first and second stages of Vedanta: shravana and manana—listening to the teaching and reflecting upon it until it makes complete sense. This chapter also touches upon the third and final stage: nididhyasana, or sustained contemplation upon the knowledge. Nididhyasana is the key to reorienting our identity from the finite to the infinite; which is to say, from the jiva to the Self.

Krishna also delves into some weighty theological and cosmological topics. He describes what happens to the jiva after death, how liberation is to be attained, and on a grander note, examines the nature of cosmic time and the cyclic birth and death the universe.

The Only Factor in Existence

The fundamental principle of Vedanta is that there's only one factor in existence: Brahman, or the Self—That which is eternal, divisionless, and beyond time and form.

The nature of the Self is described as *sat chit ananda*, meaning existence, consciousness, and bliss. The term 'consciousness' refers to pure, unconditioned consciousness. This consciousness is synonymous with awareness; the light by which all objects are perceived and experienced; a light forever present, yet always untouched by all objects of perception.

This isn't some kind of exalted or 'special' awareness that you can only acquire by practising advanced yoga and meditation for years on end. Awareness is already present as the very essence of what you are; as the ever-present screen upon which the gross objects of the physical world and the subtle objects of your inner mental world appear to you. It's that perfectly ordinary, everyday awareness present throughout your entire existence, but of which most people are rarely, if ever, conscious.

The use of the word ananda, or 'bliss', often causes confusion. This bliss doesn't refer to a particular mood or feeling state, all of which are caused by the gunas and therefore subject to change. It's the bliss inherent in the recognition of your own limitless nature.

Chapter two explored the nature of this all-pervading Self at some length. Because the Self is limitless, reality can only be non-dual in nature. After all, limitless is a strict definition. It means there can't be anything other than the Self, so the appearance of duality is just that—an appearance and not an actuality. Recall that maya is that which makes the impossible possible; the factor by which the one changeless Self appears as a universe of distinct and changing forms. The very word maya means illusion; that which appears to be real, but isn't.

While it might sound like splitting hairs, it's incorrect to say 'the Self exists'. Rather, the Self *is* existence—the eternal substratum of all both manifest and unmanifest. Anything in the creation can only be said to exist because it borrows its existence from the Self, much as the wave borrows its existence from the ocean and the pot borrows its existence from the clay.

The Relationship Between Jiva, Ishvara and the Self

To re-summarise, Brahman, the limitless, non-dual Self, is the only factor in existence. This pure consciousness/awareness is the very ground of existence, yet itself has no form or differentiation. We call this Nirguna Brahman, which means the Self without form or attribute.

Maya, a power within awareness, projects a universe of form and duality. This creation appears within the Self much as a dream-world appears in the mind of the dreamer. When the Self, courtesy of maya, appears as the world of form, we call it Saguna Brahman. It's still the same Self, plus maya. Another word for Saguna Brahman is Ishvara, or God.

Therefore, because of maya's creative power, we now have two orders of reality. We have the absolute order of reality (*paramartika satyam*), which is the one formless Self—pure consciousness without boundary or differentiation. Within that appears the objective order of reality (*vyavahrika satyam*)—the world of form, time and space created by Ishvara.

This entire universe of matter and form is Ishvara. Ishvara is both the intelligence that shapes the world and the very substance of which it is created. Again, Ishvara is not separate from the Self—Ishvara is the Self plus maya.

Maya is best understood as an upadhi; something which apparently transfers its qualities to something else. The classic Vedanta example is of a clear crystal held in proximity to a red rose. If you aren't aware of the rose behind the crystal, you might assume that the crystal is red. In actual fact, the rose is an upadhi, lending its quality of redness to the transparent crystal In the same way, maya acts as an upadhi, making the formless, limitless Self appear as Ishvara; as a universe of name and form.

Within this creation, awareness associated with an individual gross and subtle body is called a jiva. Because maya casts a spell of ignorance, pure awareness, which is formless, genderless, and free of attribute, apparently becomes a person with a particular body and mind—one among billions.

Again, this is simply the work of an upadhi. Just as the crystal remains free of colour even though it appears to borrow the red of the rose, the Self remains limitless and non-dual, even though it appears to be a limited form subject to birth, death and duality.

Immersed in the spell of maya, the human ego takes itself to be an actual, independently existent entity, when it is, in fact, only an appearance in awareness, afflicted by a mind conditioned by ignorance.

Because of this ignorance—the inability to apprehend the true nature of reality—the jiva sees itself as separate from others, from the world and from Ishvara. Subject to maya's concealing and projecting power, the jiva creates a whole subjective reality (*pratibhasika satyam*) based on ignorance, which is then superimposed onto the objective reality of Ishvara.

In actuality, as an object of creation, the jiva is non-separate from Ishvara. As already stated, everything in the creation is Ishvara, for Ishvara is both the creative intelligence and the very substance of the material universe.

Again, appearances notwithstanding, the Self is the only factor in existence. Whether it's the Self associated with the upadhi of the total creation (Ishvara) or identified with the upadhi of a particular body and mind (jiva), everything is only the Self, as every river and ocean is only water.

Any apparent difference is down to our point of reference. From the perspective of a man's wife, he is a husband. From the perspective of his father, he is a son. From the perspective of his sister, he is a brother. It's the same man in all cases. Only the point of reference makes him appear to be different things.

Karma and Rebirth

Although the first section of the Gita dealt extensively with the topic of karma, chapter seven again sees Arjuna seeking clarification about the nature of action and its relation to the Self.

Karma refers to both action and its corresponding result or reaction. Keeping the jiva bound to samsara is the compulsive need to keep performing action in order to produce beneficial results. This desire is rooted in ignorance; specifically, failing to understand that, as the Self, you are by nature actionless, whole and complete.

Because the Self is beyond doership, and the jiva is actually the Self, action belongs solely to Ishvara; to the world of mithya. As satya, the Self is That by which action happens—much as the sun is that by which plants, trees and beings live and grow—while itself remaining actionless.

The notion of doership and ownership—that belief that your action and its results belong to you—is what keeps you entangled in karma. As long as you identify with the ego, all your actions, whether they produce good or bad karma, merit or demerit, are credited to your 'karmic account'.

This karma, stored in subtle form as your vasanas and samskaras (the psychological impetus to repeat or avoid past actions), can only be exhausted by assuming physical form. Thus, innumerable bodies are created out of karma for the purpose of exhausting karma (while unfortunately accruing new karma in the process). This is why Krishna describes karma as "the cosmic force that brings physical forms into being."

As long as self-ignorance remains, the drive of past karma will impel your subtle body to keep assuming new gross bodies. This is what Krishna means by 'returning': rebirth for the purpose of resolving past karma. Karma is the irresistible 'itch' that keeps the subtle body reincarnating. After all, you can't scratch an itch unless you first have a body!

Death and Heaven

By now, it should be clear that even although the physical body dies, the subtle body remains—as, indeed, does the causal body. The causal body is, as its name suggests, the unmanifest seed state from which all outer manifestations sprout. You might think of it as the repository or storehouse for all karma, which later manifests via in the subtle and gross bodies.

Some may wonder what happens to the jiva after the death of the gross body. Krishna makes references to life in the higher worlds, which, he says, are 'relatively eternal' compared to Earthly existence.

The Vedas speak of eight levels of heaven, each successively more refined and pleasurable. By accruing enough meritorious karma during your lifetime through dharmic living, the subtle body, following the death of the gross body, is then said to reside in the loka, or realm, corresponding to its karma.

Like Earthly life, this is not a one-way ticket. Whether your stay in the higher lokas is a long or short one, when your meritorious karma is exhausted, you again find yourself drawn back to the material world and assuming another gross body in order to work out the rest of your karma.

That's why Vedanta doesn't see the attainment of heaven as an end in itself. Even the highest lokas are but temporary experiences. Anything experienceable to the senses, whether gross or subtle, belongs to maya and, as such, is bound by the limitations of maya. The attainment of heaven, therefore, is not moksha. It's an experience like any other—and, like any form, is time-bound and impermanent.

Moksha means freedom. If you depend on anything for your freedom—including heavenly experiences—then you're not really free, because freedom is the absence of dependence on any form or factor outside of yourself.

As the Self, you are eternal and free from limitation. While all things in maya, including any higher worlds, are finite and perishable by nature, the Self is the infinite and imperishable essence of existence. Shankara calls it, "the principle that graces all bodies as their essential self." This isn't something that needs to be attained through some special state of consciousness or some exalted loka. It's already an accomplished fact. All that's required is knowledge of this fact.

Through righteous and dharmic action, a person might strive to attain heaven, but the Self needs no attainment. As Swami Dayananda states, "If the Self is whole, it cannot be separate from you. If it is separate from you, it becomes finite, not whole."

Therefore, the Self is attained by realising that it was never not attained, but simply veiled by the ignorance of maya. Because freedom is the nature of the Self, the recognition that you are the Self is the gateway to liberation. Freedom is already yours. The entirety of the spiritual path is simply realising this fact and then claiming that freedom as yours.

Your Focus Determines Your Fate

According to Krishna, those who keep their mind fixed on the Self at the time of their death attain unity with the Self.

The idea that our last thought at the time of death determines the trajectory of the soul is an ancient one dating back to Vedic times. This might sound like an inane superstition to some, but it actually points to one of life's greatest psychological truths: as a person thinks, so does he or she become.

Krishna's statement that whatever the mind is focused on at the time of death will determine the soul's destination can be taken literally or metaphorically, and it applies equally to life and death.

Thought is a creative force, and the engine driving your life. Your thoughts determine your values, which in turn determine your desires and actions, shaping the trajectory of your present and future lives. Your thoughts have such power that they can, in the words of John Milton, "create a heaven of hell or a hell of heaven."

Indeed, the Brihadaranyaka Upanishad states:

> You are what your deep, driving desire is.
> As your desire is, so is your will.
> As your will is, so is your deed.
> As your deed is, so is your destiny.

The thoughts you think today are generally determined by the momentum of your past thoughts and actions. Each thought modification leaves a trace in the malleable, shapeless mind; a subtle imprint in the form of vasanas and samskaras.

Vasanas might be thought of as self-replicating grooves in consciousness. The more you think a thought, the more you strengthen its imprint, and the more likely the mind will keep repeating that same thought. Every time it does, that particular vasana grows stronger. Clusters of vasanas eventually combine to form *samskaras*, which manifest as deep-rooted personality complexes.

It's for this reason that Krishna continually stresses the importance of mastering the mind. Until you learn to take the reins, you'll find your mind, actions and entire life driven by the unconscious tendencies of your vasanas.

The mind naturally gravitates to what it loves and values. Therefore, if your highest value is for worldly objects and material pursuits, your mind will continuously focus upon those. When the mind dwells upon an object, desire is born, action is initiated to acquire the object—and the byproduct is the creation of a vasana. It's the vasanas, the deeply imprinted volitions of the psyche, that compel rebirth into the world of form.

The Brihadaranyaka Upanishad states, however, that those who are free from such desires:

> ...are free because all their desires have found fulfilment in the Self. They do not die like others. Instead, realising Brahman, they merge in Brahman.

Always Be Clear About Your Goal

Some might wonder if it's possible to cheat the system by living a life of licentious sense-gratification and at the time of death simply turning their attention to the Self and achieving liberation that way. Swami Dayananda explains why this doesn't work:

> The problem is, after living such a life, you will not think of the Self at the time of death. Whatever thought has dominated throughout your life, that alone will come to the forefront at the time of death. The thought patterns are conditioned.

A person's last thought at death is a fair indicator of the way they have lived their life. A lifetime spent chasing material objects and sense indulgence creates deeply ingrained vasanas—which, after decades of reinforcement, intensify rather than diminish with age. The soul is then compelled to again take on form in order to satiate its desires, attachments and cravings.

That's why Krishna implores Arjuna to:

> Remember Me at all times […]! Keep your mind and heart fixed on Me alone, you will indeed be united with Me. Of this, there is no doubt.

The mind is conditioned and moulded by every thought that you entertain and every action you undertake. As a seeker of liberation, you must always be clear with regard to your values, goals and priorities. If moksha is your true goal, then it's imperative that your mind be conditioned with spiritual, beneficial vasanas rather than worldly desires and addictions.

Swami Paramarthananda urges us to "create Godly vasanas"; to reprogram the mind with thoughts of Truth. This is done by by shepherding the mind and only exposing it to stimulus and input which inspires and elevates.

The company you keep always has an enormous effect on your state of mind. While it's true that you should love all people as embodiments of the divine, you would be well advised to keep a distance from those with asuric tendencies. By osmosis, we tend to become like those we spend our time with. That's why spending too much time around materialistic, desire-driven, egocentric personalities can be deleterious to your spiritual aspirations. It's all too easy to unwittingly internalise such people's warped values, desires, and outlook.

As a seeker of liberation, you must keep your goal in mind at all times. For the discerning, the Self alone is the primary goal of life. For the undiscerning, the goal will be pretty much anything other than the Self.

Self-Remembering is the Highest Devotion

The human mind is indeed the greatest of all battlefields. That's why Krishna repeatedly urges us to master the mind with discernment and self-control, and to sublimate the desire for perishable objects into a burning desire for the imperishable Self.

Krishna assures us:

> I am easily attainable to the yogi who constantly and continuously remembers Me always with an undistracted mind.

A mind devoted to the Self to the exclusion of all else cannot help but 'attain unity' with the Self through Self-knowledge. Vedantic meditation, nididhyasana, is the art of training the mind to rest in its own nature as pure consciousness.

The actualisation of Self-knowledge is achieved by fixing the mind on thoughts of Truth and reflecting deeply upon one's nature as the eternal, deathless Self.

Of this, Swami Dayananda says:

> The object of meditation produces a samskara in the mind, and with repeated meditation, the samskara deepens. For a seeker of liberation, the only object of meditation is the Self.

The highest devotion is the absorption of the mind on the Self. Krishna offers some practises for attaining this, including the chanting of the syllable Om, which, according to the Upanishads is the primordial sound of the Self as manifest in the creation. Such techniques are helpful for bringing the mind to a state of stillness, enabling you to reflect upon your nature as the Self.

By continually exposing your mind to the knowledge "I am awareness", false identification with body and mind gradually dissolves and, with the entirety of your being, you come to realise your identity as the Self.

No longer bound by the painful limitations inherent in form, you begin to taste the joy of *tripti*—the perfect satisfaction of knowing yourself to be ever whole and free.

With this knowledge, you have, as Krishna says, "attained the ultimate goal of life and are freed from the shackles of mortality and the suffering inherent in this finite existence."

Krishna further clarifies that for such a soul, having attained union with the Self, there is no further rebirth into the worlds of form. As long as ignorance binds you to the chains of karma, desire and attachment, the subtle body must continually assume new bodies for the outworking of its karma.

For the liberated soul, freed from the spell of self-ignorance, no further rebirth is needed. The subtle body resolves into the causal body much as the wave resolves into the ocean. Realising yourself to be non-separate from the totality, all separation is gone. The wave isn't lost as it folds back into the ocean. It simply returns to the greater reality of which it was always a part.

The Birth and Death of the Universe

Midway through the chapter, Krishna steers the discussion to more cosmological matters, examining the nature of Ishvara and the material creation.

Vedic cosmology speaks of a cyclic creation with neither beginning nor end. These cycles of creation are initiated by Brahma, representing Ishvara as the Creative Principle, whose divine breath essentially 'breathes' the entire cosmos in and out of manifestation.

When the Day of Brahma dawns, the entire creation arises from the unmanifest causal body, and the stars, galaxies, universes and all the lokas, or dimensions of experience, are born. This cycle of manifestation lasts for a thousand *yugas* (epochs lasting billions of years) and, much like a single lifetime, passes through successive stages of birth, growth, maturity, decline and eventual death.

This death, however, is simply a return to the causal seed state. The term for this is *pralaya*; the dissolution of the universe. Nothing is actually destroyed, because, as physics tells us, matter can be neither created or destroyed. It can change state, however. Water appears as visible liquid, but when boiled, changes into invisible vapour. The same is true of the universe. When the Night of Brahma falls, the world of prakriti resolves into its unmanifest seed state, where it exists in potential form only.

Then, following another thousand yugas of 'deep sleep', Brahma again awakens and the world of form again comes back into existence. All the universes, worlds and lokas are born again, and all the jivas too.

Although clothing themselves in successive bodies and forms, no new jivas are actually created. What appears are the same jivas with the same set of karmas responsible for the continued creation of the universe. Therefore, the same "multitude of beings return in spite of themselves". This means, according to Swami Chinmayananda, that:

> ...the very same bundles of thought-impressions (an individual being nothing other than the thoughts that he entertains) arrive at different fields of activity and states of consciousness in order to exhaust themselves. 'In spite of themselves' is a powerful expression indicating the incapacity of an individual to disinherit himself from his past. The past always faithfully follows us like our shadow—darkening our path when we turn our back to the light of knowledge.

Therefore, until a person attains liberation through Self-knowledge, burning their karma to ashes, there's no escaping the ever-turning of wheel of samsara. The jiva, strapped to this wheel by a misplaced sense of identity and erroneous notion of doership, is subject to the same old game throughout eternity.

The only solution is to recognise the truth of our nature as the actionless, eternal Self—as That which remains ever unaffected by the grinding dance of the material creation. This is what Krishna is referring to when he speaks of the 'greater Unmanifest'. Impervious to the changing world of forms, the Self is the unchanging substratum of existence: "It is neither created nor destroyed when the cosmos rises and falls like waves in the ocean of infinity."

The realisation of this Self as the Truth of our being is the "highest end." With this knowledge, the liberated soul is never again subject to separate existence. Like the wave merging back into the ocean, complete wholeness is attained. Krishna promises this union (which is but the realisation of non-separation) can be attained by a mind which remains fixed in contemplation of its nature as the Self.

The Two Paths

Krishna ends the chapter by outlining the two basic paths available to every human being (these two paths will be elaborated upon in chapter sixteen). As the terminology he uses is some-what esoteric and archaic, I have stripped it back for ease of un-derstanding. Basically, the two directions available to the soul are the path of north, which leads to light, and the path of south, which leads to darkness.

'North' and 'south' refer to the path of the sun. The sun moves northward in the sky after the winter solstice, leading to brighter days, and moves southward following the summer solstice, heralding darker days. The northern path is thus the path of light, leading to liberation from rebirth.

Those who venture down the southern path, however, travel ever deeper into the darkness of ignorance—into immersion in the material world of desires, compulsions, pleasures and pain, leading to further karma and rebirth.

This analogy echoes the words of the Chandogya Upanishad:

> A hundred and one subtle tracks lead from the heart.
> One of these goes upward to the crown of the head.
> Going up by it, he goes to eternal life.
> Others depart in various directions.

These 'various directions' are the result of ignorance and are driven by the person's vasanas and accumulated karma. Fooled by maya and gripped by the experience-hungry senses, the ig-norant vainly seek lasting happiness, security and gratification in the world of the finite, even though each fleeting moment of happiness is inevitably offset by sorrow.

The wise, however, heed Krishna's words. Committing themselves to the path of light, they set their sights on the at-tainment of liberation through Self-knowledge. While the igno-rant pursue endless material goals, seekers of liberation have only a single goal in mind: the realisation of their true nature as pure awareness.

Swami Paramarthananda notes:

> As a seeker of liberation, you are not against the world, or people, or possessions. These are all gifts from God. Use

them, but do not depend on these ephemeral things for your security, peace and happiness. Hold onto the Self alone.

It's essential that you choose your path wisely. Your focus determines your fate. So what do you want? Do you want the limited and finite, and continued entanglement in samsara, or do you want the freedom and liberation of the infinite? The choice is yours. Krishna promises that, for the devoted seeker, liberation is at all times attainable, and the key to this liberation is Self-Knowledge.

CHAPTER NINE

Royal Wisdom and the King of Secrets

1-3 "Now," Krishna declared, "because you are of pure heart and devoted spirit, I will reveal the secret knowledge that will release you from all doubt and suffering. This royal knowledge, the king of secrets, is the greatest purifier. When directly appreciated, it is easy to accomplish, in line with dharma and imperishable. Those who lack faith in this knowledge do not find Me, Arjuna. They remain entangled in samsara, passing from death to death.

4-6 "Although my form cannot be objectified, I pervade this entire universe. All beings have their existence in Me, yet I am free from all form. The world of the manifest appears to exist in Me. By my nature I bring forth and sustain all beings, yet I am not confined by them. They move in Me as the wind moves through space.

7-9 "At the end of the creation cycle, all forms are withdrawn to My unmanifest seed state. At the beginning of the next cycle, I once again breathe them into life. Controlling the eternal dance of prakriti, I bring forth these same beings over and over, where they are subject to the laws of prakriti. No karmas bind me, Arjuna, for I am unattached and unaffected by the play of form.

10 "My light shines through the creation, setting the worlds in motion, enlivening beings and causing perpetual movement and change.

11-12 "The deluded fail to recognise My presence, never realising My limitless nature as the Lord of all creation. Devoid of wisdom, of vain hopes and fruitless action, their lives are fraught with calamity and suffering.

¹³ "Those of noble heart, however, gifted with a spiritual disposition, know the Self as the imperishable cause of all creation and seek Me with one-pointed devotion.

¹⁴⁻¹⁵ "With worshipful appreciation, effort and commitment, they keep their mind and hearts on Me always. Others worship Me through Knowledge, knowing Me as the source and substance of all forms and all beings. Where others see multiplicity, the wise see only the One indivisible Self, appearing in all faces and all forms.

¹⁶⁻¹⁷ "I am the ritual of the devotee and I am the worship of the worshipper. I am the offerings given and I am the sacred mantras. I am he who performs the ritual and He to whom it is offered. I am the Father and Mother of the universe; I am its entire support. I am the uncaused cause. I am what is to be known. I am the purifier, the syllable Om, and the wisdom of the Vedas.

¹⁸ "I am the nourisher and sustainer of all things; the goal of all actions; the eternal Witness; the abode, refuge and timeless friend of all beings. It is from Me the entire creation has arisen; it is in Me that is sustained, and in Me that it is again resolved. I am the eternal and imperishable womb of creation; That in whom all people and all things have their Being.

¹⁹ "I am the heat of the sun and I am the nourishment of the rain. I am immortality and I am also death. I am both cause and effect, Arjuna!

²⁰⁻²¹ "Those who follow the injunctions of the scriptures free themselves of accumulated *papam* (demerit) and after death attain the celestial realms where they enjoy heavenly pleasures as a result of their meritorious deeds. When their *punyam* (merit) is exhausted, these souls again return to the world of mortals. Though observing Vedic rituals, they remain in samsara's cycle of repeated death and rebirth.

²² "But those whose minds are fit for inquiry come to realise themselves as non-separate from Me. For those who remember and meditate on Me always, I take care of all their needs.

²³⁻²⁴ "Those who worship other gods with faith are worshipping only Me, although they know it not. I am the object of all

rituals and all seeking, but those who fail to realise my nature again succumb to samsara.

25 "Those who worship the gods will gain the world of the gods. Those who worship the ancestors will gain the plane of the ancestors. Those who worship the spirits will gain the realm of the spirits. Those who worship Me, however, will reach Me.

26-27 "Whatever is offered to Me with devotion—whether a leaf, a flower, fruit, or even a drop of water—I gladly accept. Whatever you do, make it an offering to Me, Arjuna.

28 "In this way, you are released from the bondage of karma, whether that karma takes the form of desirable or undesirable results. With a mind made pure by renunciation and karma yoga, you will come to Me, attaining liberation.

29-31 "I am the same in all beings. I see all with equal vision; there are none that I dislike and none I personally favour. But those who seek Me with devotion are united with Me in mind and heart. Even someone who has committed highly improper acts can seek Me with a clear mind and will come to know himself as non-separate from Me. With this non-dual understanding, his mind will quickly conform to dharma and he will gain eternal peace. Never forget, Arjuna, that anyone sincerely devoted to Me will never come to harm.

32-33 "Anyone who takes refuge in Me, whatever their birth, race, sex or social standing, can attain the ultimate goal of freedom through Self-realisation. Those with fortunate births, the wealthy and successful, having gained this world and finding it to be ephemeral and devoid of lasting happiness, may also seek Me.

34 "May you devote yourself to realising Me. Fix your mind and heart on Me, offer your actions to Me, and surrender all results to Me. By knowing in your heart that Self-realisation is the ultimate goal, and pursuing it with all your heart, you will be united with Me."

COMMENTARY

This chapter again deals with the topic of Self-knowledge, which Krishna refers to as *raja vidya*—the king of knowledge and greatest of all secrets.

Self-knowledge is the king of knowledge because, like a king, it shines by itself and is the highest authority in the land. By knowing the true nature of the Self, you not only know the essence of all things, but are freed from the endless sorrows of samsara.

No other type of knowledge can make such a claim. All other types of knowledge pertain only to the world of mithya. In mithya, one's knowledge will always be incomplete—firstly, because of the inherent divide between the subject and the object of knowledge, and secondly, because there's no end to mithya knowledge. No matter how much you learn about the objective world, and how many advanced degrees you take, what you know will always be far outweighed by what you don't know. While Ishvara has knowledge of the totality of mithya, the jiva's knowledge will only ever be partial.

When it comes to satya, however, there are no parts at all, for the Self is a partless whole. That's why it's impossible to have only partial knowledge of the Self. You either know the Self, or you don't. Once you do, and have a clear understanding of satya and mithya—the real and the apparent—you gain knowledge of everything, because everything has its being in the Self alone.

Why Vedanta is the World's Best Kept Secret

You might wonder why this knowledge is considered such a secret. It's not that it's deliberately been withheld as part of some elitist Vedantic plot to keep the masses ignorant!

This knowledge has always been available. The problem is, most people have little value for it. The average human being is far too busy seeking happiness in worldly objects and the pursuit of money, power, sex, consumer goods and the never-ending distractions of mundane life. Our culture values and promotes such pursuits, but hardly anyone recognises moksha as the legitimate means of attaining lasting happiness.

Until you know what moksha is and have the appropriate value for it, you'll naturally expend your attention, effort and life energy elsewhere. You'll keep trying to squeeze whatever drops of happiness you can get out of worldly objects, while continuing to suffer the self-perpetuating frustrations and sorrow of samsara.

If you were to offer a young child the choice between a bar of chocolate and a bar of gold, the child will almost certainly take the chocolate. While a bar of gold might indeed buy a lifetime supply of chocolate, if the child doesn't understand the value of the gold, they simply won't have a desire for it.

The same holds true with Vedanta. Most people would rather pursue the tantalising objects of the world because they fail to see the value of Self-Knowledge. So although the teaching of Vedanta is freely given, unless a person recognises its value, they won't be inclined to pursue it.

That's why this royal knowledge remains the greatest of secrets. Only a precious few understand its value. Even for those who are seeking enlightenment, Vedanta requires a qualified mind and will not yield fruit without one. The first two steps are therefore to recognise the value of the teaching and then make sure that your mind is suitably prepared to receive it.

The Beggar Who Was Prince

Ordinarily, the amount of effort it takes to attain an object is proportional to the object. In other words, the greater the object of your desire, the harder you usually have to work to get it.

That's why enlightenment might seem an impossibly daunting task. Chasing finite objects takes enough effort as it is—so you might therefore assume that an infinite accomplishment will require an infinite amount of effort.

The good news, however, is that enlightenment doesn't require some superhuman effort. To attain the Self, you simply realise that you are Self. This isn't even an 'attainment' as such, but an already accomplished fact. All that's required is knowledge. This knowledge takes the form of a particular *vritti*; a thought in the mind that removes your self-ignorance.

There's an old story that perfectly illustrates how knowledge can change your entire life in an instant. Once upon a time, an ancient kingdom was invaded by barbarian forces and the king was slaughtered in battle as he defended his land. To spare the king's newborn son, a servant snuck the child out of the palace and gave him to a peasant family living in a far-off village. The family agreed to raise the boy as their own and to conceal the child's royal identity for his own safety.

By the time the king's forces had overthrown the usurpers and regained the throne a number of years passed. The boy's adoptive family had since died and he was now a teenager living on the streets. When the king's men eventually found him begging for food, they told him that he was actually a prince and that it was time for him to come and reclaim his throne.

The boy was understandably astonished. In a split second, he'd gone from being a beggar to being a prince! This remarkable transformation had required no effort on his part. When ignorance is the problem, knowledge is the only solution. All the boy needed was the knowledge of his true status—that he was actually a prince and heir to the throne. The only thing he then needed to do was let go of the notion that he was a pauper.

Swami Dayananda points out:

> As far as happiness and fulfilment are concerned, we all think that we are paupers. We always beg for happiness at the altar of life, waiting for the hands of chance to shape a moment of joy. We keep on praying or manipulating so that some situation will become so conducive that we are happy for a moment.

This never works for long, however, because finite objects can only ever deliver finite results. What's more, the problem isn't that we were ever lacking to begin with. We only assume that we're lacking due to our ignorance of our true nature. We think that we're paupers when we're actually kings.

The solution isn't trying to add anything to ourselves or trying to 'become' a better and more successful person. The solution is Self-knowledge.

Vedanta provides that knowledge. The scriptures make it clear that you are the Self; the totality of all that is. You are already free, because freedom is your very nature. Your sense of bondage is nothing but an erroneous thought of self-limitation conditioned by ignorance.

It takes little effort on your part to listen to this knowledge. All that you have to do is prepare your mind to receive the knowledge and then have faith in the knowledge until you can verify its truth for yourself.

The beggar needed to have faith in what the king's men were telling him. If he lacked faith in their words and assumed it to be some kind of cruel joke on their part he may never have travelled to the palace to learn the truth for himself. Instead he'd likely have spent the rest of his life on the streets begging for scraps of food, never knowing the truth of his royal birthright.

Similarly, as an inquirer, you require faith in the initial stages of the teaching. If you reject it out of hand, the only who who loses out is you—and the loss an infinite one, because the Self is infinite. The 'gaining' of the Self is an infinite gain, and its 'loss' (through ignorance) is an infinite loss.

The All-Pervading Self

The core of this chapter sees Krishna again expounding the nature of the Self and the origin and nature of the world of form. This royal knowledge is not unique to the Bhagavad Gita, but is in fact the distilled essence of the Upanishads, the revealed knowledge of the ancient *rishis* (seers), which we call Vedanta.

According to Vedanta, the Self is the very ground of existence; that which supports and sustains the entire creation.

We tend to think of existence as a property belonging to objects. We might say that this pen, or tree, or person *exists* and that at some point they will lose their existence. Our understanding of existence is, therefore, in relation to the idea of non-existence.

Vedanta, however, turns this understanding on its head. Existence is not a variable attribute belonging to discrete objects. Existence is the non-variable constant; the eternal substratum of all things.

We've already established that all objects are mithya, meaning they're not independently real, because they don't possess an existence of their own. Like any effect, they borrow their existence from the underlying cause—which is satya, the Self, or pure consciousness.

Let's consider the analogy of a gold chain. When you call it a 'gold chain', you're assuming that the chain is the substantive and 'gold' is merely an adjective; an attribute or quality belonging to the chain. But in actuality, the chain doesn't exist separately from the gold. The 'chain' is simply the gold in a certain configuration; the gold with a particular name and form. Therefore, the 'chain' is only an apparent creation. The gold was there before the chain came into apparent existence, and the gold will remain there after the chain is broken. That's why, in this instance, the chain is mithya, and the gold is satya.

Mithya, the apparent creation, is only a configuration of satya—satya plus a certain name and form. The Self is the only substantive factor in existence. It is the very essence of existence, and all the objects of the manifest universe only temporarily 'borrow' their existence from the Self.

That's why Krishna says that although the Self is beyond objectification and is not available for sensory perception, it pervades all that exists. It pervades and sustains everything because it is everything, just as gold pervades the chain and is the chain. Nothing exists apart from the Self.

Shankara explains:

> Underlying our changing, successive experiences, and unaffected by them, is our true Self which experiences them as they arise. This Self is the sustaining ground of all our experiences, in the absence of which the latter cannot stand and operate.

While our experiences are manifold, the Self is one, eternal, and unaffected by anything in the world of form.

Krishna makes an important point in this chapter. The Self isn't located *in* the creation. To be in a thing, one must first be separate from it. That would be like me that saying that 'part of me' was in my dream last night. In actual fact, I wasn't in my dream. My dream was in me.

Thus, the Self isn't located in the creation. The creation is located in the Self. Indeed, the creation is nothing but the Self. There is no world other than the Self, just as there is no dream outside of consciousness. Consciousness is that which contains, enables and sustains the dream, and the Self is that which contains, enables and sustains the entire creation. Only ignorance makes the two appear to be separate.

The Dance of Creation

Explaining the nature of the creation, Krishna says:

> All beings have their existence in Me, yet I am free from all form. The world of the manifest appears to exist in Me. By my nature I bring forth and sustain all beings, yet I am not confined by them.

In the last chapter, we saw how, by the power of maya, Ishvara 'breathes' the universe in and out of being.

At the beginning of a cycle of time, all the worlds and jivas arise from the causal body; the unmanifest seed state of prakriti. The light of the Self pervades the creation, setting the worlds and beings into motion in a ceaseless dance of movement, growth and decay. Then, at the end of a cycle, the creation and all the beings in it again resolve into the causal body, much as consciousness folds into deep sleep at night.

Krishna says, "[These beings] move in Me as the wind moves through space."

Although the Self seems intimately associated with the creation, like space, it is actionless, taintless and unaffected by anything that happens.

Space is often used as a metaphor to help us understand the nature of the Self, and so is light. The light in a room enables all kinds of activity to take place, yet the light cannot be said to be 'doing' this activity. Actions take place by virtue of the light, but these karmas do not belong to the light, which is actionless and unchanging.

Another good metaphor is that of electricity. The presence of electricity allows countless appliances to function; from our lights and computer, to our television and kettle. But although it is the same electricity bringing each appliance to life, the appliance will function according to its own particular nature. A kettle will function as a kettle, and a radio as a radio. The electricity granting both life is impersonal and doesn't impose its will on the appliance.

In the same way, the Self grants life to all beings, yet it does so impersonally, without imposing a will of its own. The jiva's mind and body, enlivened by the reflected light of pure consciousness, function according to their nature, as determined by the gunas and the jiva's particular karma.

Therefore, like space, light and electricity, the Self is That which enables the creation to exist, while remaining unaffected by it.

An Apparent Creation

You might wonder how can the Self remain free and untouched by the creation. The answer to this can be found in Krishna's words, "The world of the manifest appears to exist in Me." The words "appears to exist" are an important qualifier, implying that this isn't an actual creation, but an apparent creation.

Swami Chinmayananda writes:

> In pure awareness, there never was, never is, and never can be any world of pluralistic embodiment, just as for the waker, the pleasures of the dreamworld are never available. For the Self there is no cognition of the pluralistic world, which is born out of forgetfulness of the infinite.

In other words, the creation appears to exist only from the relative standpoint of mithya. From the standpoint of the Self, there is no separate creation, for there is only the Self.

If the Self is by nature limitless, how can any form of limitation apply to it? Limitation only appears by virtue of the upadhi (the conditioning adjunct) of maya, which makes the infinite appear as a finite world of form.

But like a dream, this is only an appearance. Maya has no independent reality. As Swami Dayananda clarifies:

> It really does not exist. From one standpoint there is maya, from the other, there is no maya; only Brahman. Just like your shirt has no existence apart from its fabric, similarly, maya is not a substance separate from Brahman. [...] Like the capacity to burn is not independent of fire, the power of maya is not independent of Brahman.

Again, the analogy of dreaming is helpful. The dream is only real from the standpoint of the dreamer. From the perspective of the waker, the dream wasn't real at all—it was simply an appearance in consciousness. The dream pertained only to a lower order of reality.

Similarly, the empirical creation exists only from the standpoint of maya. From the perspective of the Self, there is nothing other than the Self, because it is limitless and formless.

Just as you exist with or without a dream yet the dream cannot exist without you, the Self exists with or without maya, but maya cannot exist without the Self.

The Curse of the Deluded

Once again, the basis of samsara is ignorance. By taking appearance to be real, you fall under the spell of the enchantress and deceiver that is maya. As Krishna says:

> The deluded fail to recognise My presence. Devoid of wisdom, of vain hopes and fruitless action, their lives are fraught with calamity and suffering.

The hopes of the worldly, even when attained, are always in vain. The samsari is tragically seeking permanent satisfaction and fulfilment in an impermanent world in which all things are ephemeral and subject to change and decay.

Samsara is, therefore, a case of false expectation. Those who spend their lives expecting to find security, happiness and permanent in an ever-shifting world of impermanence must endure continual frustration and suffering.

As we've seen, the true purpose behind any pursuit is the attainment of freedom. What all people seek, no matter how they seek it, is freedom from a sense of lack.

The Self is already and eternally free. Lack cannot exist for that which is infinite.

Not knowing this, the deluded continue seeking freedom in the world of objects—an endeavour doomed to perpetual failure.

Samsara is a slippery slope. Owing to lack of Self-knowledge, discrimination becomes impossible. Without discrimination, a person's thinking will be conditioned by ignorance. Ignorance creates delusion. Deluded souls, deep under the spell of maya and prone to adharmic behaviour, may then become what we call *rakshashas* or *asuras*.

The rakshasha is someone who, with a predominance of rajas, is driven by ambition, greed, and selfish desire. Rakshashas put their own interests ahead of everything else, and in order to get what they want, are more than willing to destroy anyone in their path. This rakshashic mindset is all too common in the business world, where corporations are willing to destroy competitors, rivals, and even the very planet in order to achieve their profit-driven objectives.

The asura is an equally undesirable soul with a predominance of tamas. Like the rakshasha, asuras are completely wrapped up in their own interests, desires and greed, with no regard for the well-being of others. Lustful and self-obsessed, if they get a desire, they'll act upon it irrespective of the harm it causes to others or themselves.

Lazy, yet wilful, they cut corners and disregard rules and laws as a matter of course. Sadly, if the business world attracts the rakshasha, the political world often attracts the asuric. Either way, both inflict untold misery on others and themselves. Such people remain bound to samsara, forging ever greater chains for themselves with each new adharmic act.

The Solution

It doesn't have to be that way, of course. Krishna says that even the lowliest of people, those whose actions have been highly adharmic, can attain freedom by purifying their mind and turning within to seek the Self.

Whatever your karma, the past doesn't have to be your future. At any moment, you have the potential to turn things around and create a different, better destiny for yourself; a destiny of freedom.

There's actually no such thing as a bad person anyway, only an ignorant person. And the solution to ignorance? Knowledge.

As we've established, knowledge can only take root in a fertile mind; a mind sufficiently purified by karma yoga and an unwavering commitment to dharma. With each and every action, you condition your mind. That's why you alone are responsible for whether your mind becomes your greatest asset or your greatest liability.

Our sadhana, spiritual practice, isn't an end in itself. It's a means to an end, and that end is a pure and sattvic mind. That's how one is in time "gifted with a spiritual disposition", as Krishna puts it.

The mind and senses are naturally extroverted, and hence completely under the spell of maya. As a result, the jiva remains deeply entrenched in worldly pursuits and, taking itself to be the doer and enjoyer of action, is subject to continual rebirth.

Shankara makes it clear in *Vivekachudamani* that the highest blessing in life is to be born as a human being with a spiritual disposition and the desire for liberation. Such a soul is rare. It requires significant merit to be born into conducive circumstances with access to the teaching and a teacher, as well as to have a qualified mind, proper values, and a discriminating mind. Such fortune should never be squandered.

This grace isn't a mere quirk of fate. It is earned, as the result of good karma. Cultivating a pure and qualified mind creates *punyam* (positive karma), which in turn makes the mind a sufficient receptacle for Self-knowledge. As Krishna promises, "Those whose minds are fit for inquiry come to realise themselves as non-separate from Me."

The Three Levels of Understanding God

This section of the Gita explores the topic of bhakti, or devotion, in great detail. While Krishna makes it clear that the highest form of devotion is to realise our essential non-separation from Brahman, the expression of our devotion can take many forms and is determined by our level of understanding. This naturally varies from person to person. In recognition of this, Vedanta presents a three-fold definition of God encompassing each level.

That explains why, in spite of teaching that the Self is the formless and limitless, we also have the notion of personal deities, such as Krishna, Shiva, Kali, and the countless other faces of divinity. According to a person's level of understanding, there is a place for both non-dual and dualistic understandings of the divine.

The threefold categories for understanding God are as follows:

1. The Absolute, Formless Self (Nirguna Brahman)

The highest understanding of God is as Nirguna Brahman: the formless, indivisible, eternal and deathless Self that is the essence of all things.

Brahman, which is another name for the Self, is the very substratum of existence; self-shining, self-existent and self-luminous. This formless essence is *sat*, or satya; that which alone is independently existent, relying on nothing else for its creation or sustenance. The essential nature of this all-pervading Self is pure awareness/consciousness.

The problem is that most people find it hard to understand and relate to such an abstract understanding of God. After all, Brahman is not available for objectification. It cannot be known as an object, because it is the eternal subject.

A very mature and refined mind is required to be able to appreciate the Self as the propertyless totality of existence, much less to be able to claim this as one's own self—to realise the non-difference between the jiva and Brahman. The highest form of worship is said to be the application of Self-Knowledge to mind, because this shatters all illusion of separation and otherness. You 'become' the Self by knowing there is nothing other than the Self.

Again, this requires a highly qualified mind. Until one cultivates a sufficiently pure and subtle mind, it's extremely difficult to contemplate the absolute order of reality. For this reason, and to explain the existence of the world and the individual, Vedanta provides another definition.

2. The Cause and Substance of the Universe (*Saguna Brahman*)

The intermediate understanding of God relates to what we commonly associate with the term Ishvara: the intelligence that creates the material universe, as well as the substance of which it is made.

Arising within limitless awareness, the power of maya allows for the apparent creation of an entire universe of differentiation. Thus, Nirguna Brahman, the Self without form, appears as Saguna Brahman, the Self with form.

The Self, awareness, plus the power of maya equals Ishvara: the universal intelligence that shapes and governs the laws of creation. Ishvara is a universal God, appearing as every conceivable form and experience. That's why Krishna says:

> I am the One from whom this phenomenal universe is born, and into Me it again resolves. There is no source other than Me and nothing separate from Me. All universes are woven in Me like pearls in a necklace.

When the light of the Self shines upon the inert matter of prakriti, the entire universe comes to life. Ishvara, as governor of maya, is not only the creative intelligence but also the very form and substance of the universe.

When you understand the universal nature of Ishvara, you realise you don't need to go to churches or on pilgrimages in order to find God, because God is already everything everywhere! Because Ishvara creates out of its own essence just as a spider creates its web out of itself, there is nothing and nowhere that God is not.

3. A Personal God (*Ishta Devata*)

Some people find it difficult not only grasping God as the unmanifest absolute, but also as the totality of the manifest universe. That's why God can also be envisaged as a personal deity.

For the purposes of worship (upasana yoga), it's obviously easier to establish a relationship with a deity that has a name and form, and India alone has literally thousands to choose from. Krishna himself is one of the most popular, being an incarnation of Vishnu, who, along with Brahma and Shiva is said to oversee the creation, maintenance and dissolution of the cosmos. There are countless other deities available for worship, both male and female, and the mythological Puranas relate the legends and exploits of these various gods.

To the uninitiated, Hinduism might appear to be a polytheistic chaos. However, the Vedas are clear that, in essence, there is only one, all-pervading God, and it is none other than Brahman, the Self; the innermost essence of all beings. The various gods and goddesses are symbols of this one Self, much as a single ray of light passing through a prism (maya) appears as the different colours of the rainbow.

Problems may arise when immature seekers, unaware that all form is mithya, and that the object of his or her worship is in fact a symbol for a deeper truth, become dogmatic and sectarian. The notion of 'my God versus your God' has been a problem since time immemorial. Tragic though it is, the most devout can become asuras, lost in the illusion of maya.

In Krishna's words: "Unable to perceive beyond the world of changing appearance, people fail to see Me as the changeless essence."

A personal God provides an object of focus for the devotee. As the inquirer deepens their understanding, they should expand their meditation to encompass not just a personal deity, but also an understanding of Ishvara as the universal cause and substance of the creation—and finally, knowledge of the eternal Self as the one, formless totality of all existence.

This automatically leads the devotee from dualistic devotion to non-dual devotion, which is synonymous with Self-knowledge; the key to liberation.

Such a mature mind is fit for Vedantic inquiry, and the object of their bhakti, devotion, then becomes Self-knowledge. Prior to this, one's bhakti was aimed at purifying and integrating the mind. Now, the highest bhakti is the knowledge *Aham Brahmasmi:* I am the Self.

Vedanta is unique in that it allows for dualistic devotion and a subject/object relationship between the devotee and God, even as it unfolds a vision of non-duality in which all separation between the individual and the divine is negated.

The Two Types of Devotion

As we saw in chapter seven, Vedanta categorises two basic types of devotion: sakama bhakti, which means devotion motivated by the attainment of personal or worldly desires, and nishkama bhakti, motivated by the desire for liberation alone.

1. Desire for Worldly Gain

Sakama bhakti literally means devotion with desire. This type of bhakti is motivated by the desire for worldly benefits and is by far the most prevalent form of devotion.

Whether they admit it or not, such devotees always have an ulterior motive for their worship. They may appear very devout; always making a point of going to the temple to perform devotional offerings, or attending church every Sunday and saying their prayers each night before bed.

Their devotion, however, isn't for merely the sake of devotion. It's not an end in itself, but rather a means to an end. Perhaps they want more money, a new job, a relationship, for their child to get married, or their health to improve. In the modern spiritual world, these are the people who tend to be into the law of attraction in a big way, always keen to find new ways of manifesting their dreams and desires.

The Vedas do acknowledge sakama bhakti as a legitimate pursuit, and, in fact, prescribe various means for the attainment of such desires, whether they relate to artha (wealth), kama (pleasure) or dharma (virtue).

There's nothing wrong with such pursuits in themselves. The problem, as we've established, is the expectation that material objects will provide lasting fulfilment, happiness and security. This is impossible, not least because everything in maya is in constant flux and every pleasure contains within it the seeds of future pain.

In every endeavour and undertaking, what you're actually seeking is the happiness, peace and security of your own limitless nature. It's your own Self that you're seeking. That's why Krishna says, "Those who worship other gods with faith are also worshipping Me, although they know it not." By 'other gods,' he means whatever you happen to elevate to the status of godhood, whether it's fame, fortune, sense pleasure, food, relationships or any number of worldly objects.

Speaking as the Self, Krishna makes it clear that, "I am the object of all rituals and all seeking," and that, "those who fail to Realise my nature again succumb to samsara." The worldly, prone to seeking in all the wrong places—and desperately trying to find the lasting in the fleeting and the real in the unreal—remain bound to samsara.

2. Desire for Moksha Alone

There is hope, however. Worn down by samsara's relentless grind of desire and frustration, in time, by Ishvara's grace, you finally come to realise that permanence can never be found in the world of the impermanent. That's why not getting what you want can be the greatest of blessings in disguise.

Your entire focus then changes. Instead of chasing worldly objects in a desperate bid to squeeze whatever drops of happiness you can get from them, you see the futility of settling for the finite, and you instead set your sight on the Infinite. You decide that you're not going to be the child who chooses a bar of chocolate instead of a bar of gold. Why settle for something of limited value when you can have that which has limitless value?

When you decide to pursue liberation directly, sakama bhakti becomes nishkama bhakti, which means devotion without desire. In actuality, that's not strictly true, because nishkama bhakti is, in fact, motivated by one, very powerful desire: the desire for moksha.

It's paramount that you always have clear understanding with regard to your goal. As the Brihadaranyaka Upanishad states, improper understanding leads to improper desire, which then leads to improper actions, and this inevitably brings improper results.

The nishkama devotee is no longer motivated by worldly concerns. As a nishkama bhakta, you remain clear that your true goal is moksha.

Why a Devotional Attitude is Important

For the ardent seeker of liberation, the path to liberation is clearly laid out. You don't have to stumble around in the dark and hope that you happen to find your way by yourself. The way is clearly signposted.

The key to liberation is Self-knowledge, as provided by the scriptures and unfolded by a qualified teacher. In chapter seven, Krishna calls this yoga of Self-knowledge the highest form of devotion. The greatest bhakti, therefore, is knowing and abiding as your true Self.

There's actually no effort involved in being what you already are. You don't have to add anything to yourself in order to be yourself, just as you don't have to add any water to the ocean in order to make it the ocean. The Self is already attained. You are, therefore, already free.

This freedom cannot be apprehended or enjoyed, however, until the intellect's bubble of ignorance has been burst, and the volatile, restless mind, agitated by its entrenched likes and dislikes, has been brought to bear.

Vedanta itself is very easy. You sit and listen as the teacher explains the nature of the Self and reality. The tricky part is acquiring the qualifications necessary for the mind to recognise and reorient to this basic truth of who you are.

That's why karma yoga is an essential first step for purifying the mind. In addition, you should also have a firm understanding of and commitment to dharma, and clarity with regard to your values, which must always determine your actions and choices. It's also essential to integrate and steady the mind, and for this, Vedanta prescribes meditation, as we learned in the sixth chapter.

A mindset of devotion is the final key to purifying the mind. Bhakti can take many forms, depending upon your level of understanding and your conception of Ishvara. Whatever form your bhakti takes, the key is to convert your emotional attachments to a devotional attachment. Attachment to the finite can only ever bring suffering, whereas attachment to the infinite is the only secure attachment there is.

Swami Dayananda says, "If you are intellectually convinced about the pursuit of moksha but your heart is distributed into a hundred different things, it does not work."

Emotion is the engine driving our actions. We naturally focus on what we love, and this love determines our actions and pursuits. Until you develop an overwhelming love for Truth, for God or the Self, your heart will inevitably remain in conflict.

If you have even the slightest uncertainty about your intended destination—if you still secretly crave worldly pleasures and glory—your priorities will remain muddled. You won't devote the necessary time and energy to seeking the Self by purifying the mind, studying Vedanta and practicing self-inquiry.

Whatever you worship, you eventually attain. If your worship is of finite things, you will attain finite things. Unfortunately (or fortunately!), no one can ever be satisfied with the finite. That's why you should always keep the Infinite as your goal. Krishna says, "Those who worship Me will reach Me."

Your entire life must be oriented to Self-inquiry. By seeing the divine Self in all things, by worshipping Ishvara with your every thought, word, and deed, you invoke Ishvara's grace by purifying your mind. A pure mind is like a tranquil lake in which the clear light of the Self shines in all its glory, and liberation through Self-realisation is attained with ease.

Krishna's Promise

Krishna says, "Fix your mind and heart on Me, offer your actions to Me, and surrender all results to Me." In order to attain a goal, you must never lose sight of it. That's why a devotional mindset becomes essential. Only when you are truly devoted to your goal will you have the necessary drive and determination to pursue and attain it.

Earlier in the chapter, Krishna makes a promise: "For those who remember and meditate on Me constantly, I will provide for all their needs."

The Self is the sustenance and support of all beings; what the Tao Te Ching calls the 'Great Mother' of the universe. While our physical forms have certain material needs, these should never be the entire focus of our life's endeavour.

By seeking the Ultimate through the assimilation of Self-knowledge, we find, often to our astonishment, that all else is taken care of. For that is Krishna's promise: "By knowing in your heart that Self-realisation is the ultimate goal, and pursuing it with all your heart, you will be united with Me."

CHAPTER TEN

The Divine Glories

1-3 "Listen further, Arjuna, as I reveal to you My divine splendour. Neither the gods nor sages can fathom My full glory, for I am That out of which the gods and sages are created. The one who knows Me as the unborn, beginningless, and limitless Lord of Creation is released from delusion and cleansed of impurity.

4-5 "Truly the greatest of all qualities in man—knowledge, understanding, discrimination, truthfulness, self-mastery, peace of mind, the transcendence of pleasure and pain, birth and death, fear and fearlessness; as well as nonviolence, equanimity, contentment, spirituality, charity and honour—all these are from Me alone.

6-8 "The ancient seers and the ancestors whose minds were resolved in Me were born of My mind. From them came all the beings in this world. Whoever sees this glory of Mine as it shines through the worlds of form, is gifted with clear vision. The wise know Me as the source from which all creation comes and because of Whom all life is sustained.

9-11 "Those whose minds are fixed on Me, whose lives are devoted to Me, who teach one another and speak of Me always, are ever satisfied and happy. To reward their steadfast devotion, I grant such souls spiritual vision and understanding. For them, out of compassion, I illuminate their minds, destroying the darkness of ignorance with the shining lamp of Self-knowledge."

12-16 Arjuna said, "Oh Krishna, you are indeed the limitless Brahman; the light of all lights and purifier of misdeeds. You are That of which the sages and seers speak: the Eternal Being, creator of all the gods; unborn and infinite. All this you have now told me, and I believe it to be true. Neither the gods nor the demons know what you are, Oh Lord. Indeed, you alone are capable of knowing the glories by which you pervade all these worlds.

17-18 "What is the best way to meditate upon you, O greatest of yogis? How can I know you? In what forms are you to be meditated upon? Please share with me your wonder and glory, leaving nothing unspoken. I listen with delight to your words, but I am left wanting more."

19 Krishna said, "As you ask, Arjuna, I will tell you of My divine glories, revealing only the most prominent, for there is no end to My splendour.

20-22 "I am the eternal Self shining in the hearts of all beings. I am the cause of their creation, sustenance and dissolution. Among the gods, I am the Sustainer; among the luminaries, I am the sun lighting the world, and I am the moon illumining the night. Of the scriptures, I am the pure wisdom of the Vedas; of the gods I am Indra; of elements, I am fire; of the senses, I am the mind; and at the heart of living beings, I dwell as consciousness.

23-25 "Among the demons, I am the destroyer; among the priests, I am the purest; among the armies, I am the commander-in-chief; among all bodies of water, I am the ocean. Among sages, I am the wisest; among words, I am the sacred syllable Om; among rituals, I am the repetition of the holy name; and among mountains, I am the Himalayas.

26-28 "Among the trees, I am the tallest and oldest; among the celestials, I am the most revered; among the horses and elephants, I am those belonging to the gods, for I am the king of all men. Among weapons, I am the thunderbolt; among cows, I am the wish-fulfilling cow; among lovers, I am the power behind love, union and procreation.

29-31 "I am the cosmic serpent, the god of water, the king of all ancestors and Yama, the god of Death. I am scourge of the demons; I am time itself; among wild animals I am the lion; among birds I am the eagle. Of the purifying elements, I am the wind; of warriors, I am the brave Rama; of fish, I am the shark, and of rivers, I am the Ganges.

32-33 "Indeed, Arjuna, I am the beginning, the middle and the end of all creation. Of knowledge, I am the knowledge of the Self. Of those who speak, I am the words pointing to truth. Among all letters, I am 'a', and of speech, I am the sweetest. Of time, I am infinity. I am the giver of all actions and My essence pervades all.

34-38 "As Prosperity, I bestow all things, and, as Death, I take all things away. I am wisdom, prosperity, constancy, speech, memory, intelligence, fortitude and equanimity. I am the sweetest of mantras, the first of months and of seasons I am the flowering Spring. I am the game of dice and that which plays it, and I am the radiance in all that shines. I am the victory of the triumphant, the clarity of the wise and the goodness of the virtuous. Among the noble lineages, I am Krishna; among the Pandavas, I am Arjuna; among the seers, I am Vyasa and among the sages, I am Usana. I am the discipline of those who enforce order; I am the justice of those who lead; I am the silence of the unknown; and I am the intelligence of the wise.

39 "Arjuna, I am the cause of all things. I am the root of existence. Without Me, no form could exist, either sentient or insentient.

40 "There is no end to my divine splendour, Arjuna. I have spoken only briefly of the most prominent of my glories.

41-42 "Whatever is blessed with any grace or splendour, power or strength, springs from Me and reflects but a fraction of My glory. But of what use are such details to you, Arjuna? It is enough for you to know that I alone Am, and that, with a small fraction of My being, I give rise to the entire cosmos."

COMMENTARY

The title of this chapter is *Vibhuti Yoga*, which means the 'topic of the glories of the Lord'. At Arjuna's request, Krishna, speaking as Ishvara, recounts His many glories as manifest in the world of form. A number of the examples he cites would undoubtedly prove baffling to those unfamiliar with the intricacies of Indian mythology. For that reason, I simplified a number of those references in this translation to make them more universal while retaining the essence of Krishna's words.

The Relationship Between Jiva and Ishvara

Before we get to the heart of this chapter's message, it may be helpful to consider the relationship between the jiva and Ishvara. In essence, both are the same—the formless Self; pure consciousness—but according to one's standpoint, they appear to be different.

Swami Paramarthananda explains:

> Jiva is an expression of pure consciousness obtaining in the microcosmic gross, subtle, and causal bodies, while Ishvara is an expression of that same consciousness obtaining in the macrocosmic gross, subtle, and causal bodies. Although the expression differs according to the composition of the reflecting medium, it is the same consciousness that animates and pervades both.

At the empirical level of reality (vyavaharika satyam), the relationship between jiva and Ishvara, the individual and the total, is analogous to waves and the ocean. The waves are seemingly separate formations, yet they don't exist independently of the ocean. From the standpoint of each wave, there is a clear difference between itself and the ocean. A wave can claim to be part of the ocean, but it cannot claim to be the ocean. It exists at a certain point in space and time, and there will come a time when it ceases to exist.

In the same way, from the standpoint of each jiva, there is a clear difference between itself and Ishvara. The jiva is a finite body and mind, subject to limitation and decay, while Ishvara is the totality of all bodies and minds; and the intelligence that created them. That's why you, as a jiva, cannot claim to be Ishvara—because quite clearly, you as a person are not responsible for the creation and maintenance of the universe.

From the perspective of Ishvara, there is no separation between itself and the jivas. The jivas are a part of it, just as each wave is a part of the ocean. Waves have no independent existence of their own. If you subtract the name and form, all that you find is water. In the same way, jivas appear in Ishvara, out of Ishvara, as temporary waves; time-bound configurations of name and form.

From the standpoint of the Self, or the absolute order of reality (paramartika satyam), there is no distinction between Ishvara and the jiva at all. In fact, they are as good as nonexistent; for all that ultimately exists is pure, undifferentiated, formless consciousness. To go back to the wave and ocean analogy, you might say that at the absolute level, there is no wave or ocean at all; there is simply water.

In summary, Ishvara and jiva are united in that they are both, in essence, the Self; pure consciousness. This consciousness expresses in differing ways according to the upadhi with which it is associated. That's why, at the empirical order of reality, both appear to be different. At the empirical level, the jiva cannot claim to be Ishvara, even though it is part of Ishvara. But it can claim its identity as the Self, which is also the essential identity of Ishvara.

Avoiding Enlightenment Sickness

One of the reasons that Vedanta is intended only for sufficiently qualified, pure minds, is the danger of the ego co-opting the knowledge. Self-knowledge, when properly integrated, ought to humble the ego into submission by realising that it is, in fact, only mithya; an epiphenomenon with no independent existence of its own.

However, left unchecked, the ego will try to create a new identity for itself out of this knowledge: a super-identity. This is called superimposing satya on mithya.

The ego is sly and extremely tricky. Its entire purpose is to cement itself and to create a better, firmer, more solid sense of identity. When an immature, unqualified, rajasic mind is exposed to Vedanta, the potential for disaster is great. Indeed, Vedanta is a veritable heaven for the narcissistic mind. The scriptures affirm that, far from being limited and lacking, you are actually the limitless, eternal, boundless Self. But this teaching is not designed to aggrandise the ego. Vedanta's only intent is to neutralise the ego by revealing that it, and the instruments of body and mind, are but mithya; appearances in consciousness and entirely dependent upon consciousness.

However, by knowing that the Self is everything and that I am the Self, the ego can potentially inflate itself to absurd proportions. This accounts for what Vedanta calls 'enlightenment sickness', where the ego surreptitiously co-opts Self-knowledge for its own ignoble ends.

The 'spiritual ego' can be far more dangerous than a regular ego. Such an ego is still under the sway of samsara, and still seeking wholeness in the mithya world, but it now does so under the guise of being 'enlightened' and whatever superiority it believes this confers. Spiritual teachers who abuse their followers and compulsively violate dharma are usually victim to enlightenment sickness—which is, in fact, a distortion of true Self-knowledge, and therefore not enlightenment at all.

If the student has a good teacher, has properly followed the dharma of the teaching, and undertaken the necessary purification of mind, this is less likely to happen. Sadly, however, in a materialistic, often adharmic society in which 'anything goes' spiritually, it's not uncommon for the ego to misinterpret and distort spiritual teaching for its own ends, thus creating the dreaded 'spiritual ego'.

God is Not Dead

This chapter of the Gita is, therefore, an important one. You might think of it as the ego-busting chapter. It compels you to acknowledge the role of Ishvara as both the intelligent and efficient cause of the creation.

Krishna declares that whatever beauty, wonder and majesty you perceive in the world is but a manifestation of His (Ishvara's) glory. He further states that the highest qualities of humankind, such as intelligence, beauty, bravery, compassion, and wisdom—all of which the ego is quick to claim ownership—actually belong to Him. Whatever greatness you think you possess, and whatever gifts or talents you might have, are there only by the grace of Ishvara.

Swami Dayananda says:

> If you recognise all glories as Ishvara's glories, your pride, your ahamkara (ego), diminishes. That paves the way for understanding what Ishvara is. What stands between you and Ishvara, after all, is your ego.

Very often modern teachers and seekers shy away from acknowledgment of Ishvara. For them, Ishvara sounds too much like an outmoded concept of God. Indeed, after centuries of misuse at the hands of various self-seeking religions, many proclaim that 'God is dead'. This is based on a very limited understanding of what God is.

Accordingly, Vedanta presents a three levelled understanding of Ishvara. At the first level, Ishvara is viewed as the creator of the world; as the intelligent cause that fashions the creation much as a carpenter crafts furniture.

As the seeker matures and becomes more discriminating, certain questions naturally arise: such as, where is this God? If He stands outside of the creation, doesn't that mean there's another creation of some kind? And where did He get the materials to build the universe?

To answer this, Vedanta explains that Ishvara isn't separate from the creation. Ishvara creates the universe out of itself. This entire creation is a manifestation of Ishvara, just as heat is a manifestation of fire. Therefore, Ishvara is not only the intelligence that shapes the universe, but also its very shape and substance.

Where, therefore, do you need to go to worship such a God? You don't need to go to any temple or church. You can find God everywhere. The entire cosmos is the body of Ishvara. This chapter of the Gita highlights that the glory of all creation belongs to Ishvara, for Ishvara pervades the entire creation as both the unmanifest cause and the material effect.

This, in time, leads to the final level of understanding. The idea that God is both the source and the substance of the creation leads to an inevitable problem. If God has become this world of multiplicity, does that mean that God is no more? After all, when you churn milk it becomes butter and the milk is forever lost.

That isn't the case here, however. Vedanta explains that Ishvara doesn't become the universe, because to become something necessitates change. Rather, Ishvara appears as the creation. The creation itself is not an actual creation; it is an apparent creation—an appearance.

Shankara summed this up with the words: *Brahma satyam, jagat mithya, jivo brahmaiva naparah.* This means that Brahman, the Self, is real (or satya; the independent cause) and the world is unreal (mithya; the dependent effect). Furthermore, the jiva is non-different to Brahman, because Brahman alone exists.

The knowledge that the Self is at once the creator and the creation (Ishvara and jiva) while remaining formless and undifferentiated is the highest level of understanding and requires a significant degree of intellectual maturity. This chapter and the next explore the intermediate level of understanding, which presents Ishvara manifest as the world.

Nothing Here Belongs To You

When you realise that the entire creation is born of—and is—Ishvara, there's absolutely no room for vanity. Nothing actually belongs to you—not even 'your' body. The entire universe is created for us, along with everything in it, including our bodies and minds. In actuality, we ourselves do and own nothing. Everything is given to us on loan by Ishvara.

As noted, modern spiritual teachings, such as Neo-Advaita, generally bypass Ishvara. They may talk about the jiva and the Self, but have no recognition of Ishvara's role as That which creates and sustains the universe. They perhaps see it an irrelevancy, when, in fact, acknowledgement of Ishvara is crucial.

By acknowledging that you (whether you are talking as a jiva or as the Self), aren't the one running this show, you become objective. At the level of the empirical world, Ishvara is not only the one running the show—Ishvara is the show. Everything is bestowed by Ishvara's grace alone.

Recognising this, you develop the mindset of a devotee. This is not something that can be manufactured or forced. A sense of devotion arises naturally the more you study the teaching and come to understand and appreciate the role of Ishvara in the creation. A devotional mind is a pure mind; a mind fit for inquiry and the assimilation of Self-knowledge.

Everything Belongs to Ishvara

Theists and atheists vehemently argue about whether or not there is a God, but Vedanta asserts there is nothing but God. This isn't a remote, far-off God, or a 'spark' of divinity within things. Just as all ornaments made of gold are nothing but gold plus name and form, everything in the creation is nothing but Ishvara plus name and form.

Ishvara's glory is, therefore, everywhere. It's in every sight, sound, and taste; every sunset, every flower, every act of kindness. It's in the sky and the rivers, in the sun and the rain, and in whatever is deemed sacred, wondrous, powerful or auspicious.

Krishna recounts His glory using multiple examples. Even these, he later states, are but a small fraction of His limitless wonder.

The implication is that you should always keep the ego in check. As a jiva, there's nothing in the world that you can legitimately claim as your own. Everything here belongs to Ishvara. If Ishvara is not only the intelligence behind the creation, but the actual creation itself, then how can it not belong to Ishvara?

Whatever you find praiseworthy in yourself has its source in Ishvara. Whatever you happen to achieve is not a source for pride either, because it is only by the grace of Ishvara that you achieve anything. Indeed, Ishvara is the giver of the results of all actions. All accomplishments belong to Ishvara—and, so too, do your perceived faults and failures.

We've seen how tricky the ego can be. It wants to survive and propagate itself at all costs. It's always looking for ways to cement itself and strengthen its identification with what it deems positive and desirable. The knowledge that everything belongs Ishvara ought to break the ego into submission.

Swami Paramarthananda says that, "Seeing everything as God creates the utmost humility."

Such knowledge minimises the binding likes and dislikes that obstruct self-knowledge. By realising that all success and all beauty and positive attributes belong to—and are blessings bestowed by—Ishvara, you eliminate pride, vanity, and conceit in yourself.

You no longer claim any glory as your own, but recognise it as Ishvara's glory. Similarly, it's impossible to be jealous or resentful of others when you know that other people's success, beauty or talent belongs not to them, but to Ishvara. You can then celebrate their merits without a trace of jealousy or resentment, in worshipful appreciation of the divine beneficence.

A Worshipful Mind

When you see Ishvara as everything, your resistance to the flow of life naturally diminishes. A mind caught in the grip of binding likes and dislikes is a mind subject to constant tension. Such a soul will feverously pursue certain experiences and outcomes while rejecting others.

But when you see God everywhere, your relationship with reality changes. You find yourself at peace with the present moment, even if it doesn't take the form you might have chosen.

Non-resistance means taking all of life as prasada; as a divine gift. Because you can't change the past, or even the present, you gracefully accept what Ishvara has brought, while taking advantage of your capacity to change the future.

Knowing that Ishvara is present everywhere, the entire world becomes your temple; the altar of your worship. Simply to appreciate the sky, the glory of a sunrise or sunset, the beauty of a tree, a flower, or a dewdrop on a blade of grass, is to appreciate the divinity of all life.

The poet William Blake was speaking of this when he wrote the immortal lines:

> To see a world in a grain of sand
> and heaven in a wild flower.
> Hold infinity in the palm of your hand
> and eternity in an hour.

To know and see everything as a blessing rather than an entitlement naturally fills you with wonder and gratitude. Such gratitude is one of the greatest secrets to a happy life. To live with gratitude and to appreciate even the simplest of things, such as a sip of tea, or the fragrance of a rose, is to be truly fulfilled—filled with with divinity of all things.

Swami Paramarthananda says:

> There may be failures in life, but as long as God-vision is there, you never look upon your life as a failure. Appreciating God everywhere, there is fulfilment.

By recognising that all things belong to Ishvara, you pierce the blight of the seemingly mundane and develop divine vision.

Every moment then becomes sacred and every second filled with beauty.

CHAPTER ELEVEN

The Cosmic Vision

1-4 Arjuna said, "Your great words have dispelled my ignorance, Krishna. I now know the greatest of secrets: the supreme power of the Self. You have explained to me the origin and the dissolution of all creatures, and the wonder and glory of your infinite Being. But words alone are insufficient to convey your divine magnificence. I now long to see it with my own eyes. O Lord Krishna, if you think me capable of seeing it, please reveal to me your eternal cosmic form."

5-8 Krishna replied, "It is not possible for you to see with your own eyes alone. So I now give you the divine eye. With this spiritual vision, observe my wondrous power! Behold and see hundreds and thousands of my forms—of infinite shapes, colours and variety. Look and see the entire universe in my body!"

9-13 Having spoken these words, Krishna revealed to Arjuna his wondrous cosmic form. Arjuna beheld an all-pervading form of countless eyes, mouths and arms reaching in every direction. An infinitude of jewels and celestial ornaments danced around it like stars in orbit, and it was strewn with garlands, robes, and anointed with sweet fragrances. Brilliant and effulgent, it was endless; the source of all wonder; spanning an entire universe in every direction. If a thousand suns were to illumine the heavens all at once, this would barely match the blinding radiance of this supreme Lord.

14 There, within the body of this universal form, Arjuna beheld the world, and countless others, each seemingly separate and yet all connected. Overwhelmed with ecstasy and awe, his hair standing on end and his body trembling, Arjuna fell before the Lord, his hands joined together and head lowered.

15-16 Struggling to relate his vision in words, Arjuna said, "O Krishna, in your body I see all the gods and every living creature in existence. In your magnificence, you have infinite eyes, arms, mouths and stomachs and you are embodied in every form. I can see no beginning, no middle and no end to you, O Lord of creation. The cosmos itself is your body.

17 "With a crown, a mace and a discus, your form is a dazzling mass of light. It is hard to see you for the light. Its radiance is blinding as it shines infinitely in every direction. Unlike any other form, you cannot be known as a limited object.

18-19 "I can see you as imperishable and limitless, the changeless Reality, the One that is be known. The source of creation, you are impervious to change and modification and protector of the eternal laws of the universe. You are eternity and infinity—shining as the innermost being of all things. With unyielding power, countless faces and endless arms, the moon and the sun shine as your eyes and your mouth is fire, from which you animate the cosmos with your own light.

20-22 "Your divine presence pervades all things and indeed the space between all things. If they were to see this wondrous yet frightening form of yours, those of the three worlds would tremble before you. I see a multitude of good people seeking your grace. Some pray with folded hands, crying out to you from the depths of their suffering; others seek you through the bliss of meditation. Great saints and seers sing your name with wonder, praying "Let all be well!" Those of the various worlds, turning their eyes to you, are awestruck by what they see.

23 "O mighty Krishna, at the sight of your immeasurable form of billions of eyes and mouths, arms and legs, feet and stomachs and of sharp, fearful teeth, the people tremble in terror, and so do I.

24-25 "Your form stretches across the heavens, radiant and multi-faceted, open-mouthed with glowing, all-seeing eyes. Courage and composure have deserted me, O Lord! Seeing your fanged-mouths, burning like the fires of time, I reel in fear and disorientation. Please, Lord, be merciful!

26-29 "I see the armies of the battlefield—the sons of Dhritarashtra; the kings, and Bhisma, Drona, and Karna; and our great warriors—and they are falling into your terrible jaws, only to be crushed by your ferocious teeth; their heads sticking between your mighty molars. Just as flood-swollen rivers rush to the ocean, all creatures pass into your fiery mouth like moths darting to a flame, full speed toward their own oblivious destruction.

30 "Devouring these beings with your flaming jaws, you swallow entire worlds and universes, while licking your lips, ready to consume yet more. Set alight with your terrifying brilliance, the whole of creation ignites in flames.

31 "Tell me, O Lord, who you are! I ask for your grace and mercy. Tell me why you take this most terrible form? I do not understand your actions."

32 Krishna said, "I am Time, destroyer of worlds. I not only give birth to all beings, but I cause them to age and die. Even without any action on your part, all the warriors gathered at Kurukshetra will die. To the living, death is inevitable. To the unborn, death exists not.

33-34 "Therefore arise, Arjuna! Conquer your enemies and free your kingdom. As unconquerable Time, I have already slain all these warriors. You will merely be My instrument, Arjuna. Do not hesitate to act as you must. Fight in this battle and the Pandavas will be victorious."

35-38 Hearing these words of Krishna, Arjuna's limbs trembled in fear. Again he saluted this glorious and terrifying form, and he spoke in a faltering voice: "It is right that the world rejoices and sings your praises, O Krishna. While all evil flees from you, the saints and sages bow before you, exalting your glory. How could they not worship you? You who is creator of all the gods; who is both cause and effect; who is limitless and will never cease to be. You are the timeless and all-pervading first among the gods. You are the ultimate and all-pervading abode of creation; the knower and that which is to be known. You are the home of all beings, and the seat of creation and dissolution. There is nothing not pervaded by you, O Lord, whose forms are endless!

39-40 "You are the Lord of air, the Lord of death, the Lord of fire, the Lord of water. You are the moon and the ultimate progenitor of all beings. A thousand salutations to you. I bow before you and again and again salute your supreme perfection. The one of infinite strength and immeasurable glory, you pervade everything and therefore you are everything.

41-42 "Before I knew of your true nature, I thought of you as only my friend—as only a man. Please forgive me for any times I spoke causally, rashly or in jest to you. Such comments I made before I knew the truth of your nature.

43-44 "Your glories are truly without parallel. You are the father and mother of this universe; of the sentient and insentient. You are the object of all worship and the first and greatest of all teachers. You are without equal and none is more powerful than you. That is why I prostrate myself to you, O Lord. I ask you to forgive my ignorance and my misdeeds as a father would forgive a son, as a friend would forgive another friend, or as a lover would forgive his beloved.

45-46 "I rejoice that I have now seen what was previously unseen. But I am afraid of this fearful form! Please, O Lord, I beg you return to your original form. Though you are the embodiment of the entire cosmos, Lord of a thousand arms, may you again become that form with which I am familiar."

47-49 Krishna said, "The cosmic form I have revealed to you, a form of limitless brilliance—radiant and without beginning or end—is a form never before seen by mortal eyes. Even the most learned scholars, devout devotees or committed ascetics could not have perceived this form of My infinitude, Arjuna, bravest of the Kurus. May you have no more fear or confusion at seeing this frightening form of Mine. I again resume the form of the friend you have always known."

50 As these words left his mouth, Krishna again resumed his familiar human form, much to Arjuna's relief.

51 With a smile, Arjuna said, "I'm pleased to again see my beloved friend stand before me."

52-54 To that, Krishna said, "The vision you were given is most difficult to attain. Even the gods are unable to see Me in such a way. Neither study of the Vedas, nor austerity, charity, or worship can bring about such a vision. But through my grace and your unfailing devotion, Arjuna, you have attained the vision of My true nature. It is with this one-pointed devotion that I can be known and united with.

55 "He or she who performs all actions for My sake, for whom I am the supreme goal, who are devoted to Me and free of both attachment and enmity toward all beings, comes to realise Me, Arjuna."

COMMENTARY

The previous chapter detailed the divine glories of Ishvara at great length. As we learned, Ishvara isn't separate from the creation. Rather, the creation itself is Ishvara. That's why Krishna says that in whatever is brilliant, beautiful and wondrous, the glory belongs to Ishvara alone.

This creates something of a problem, however. If life, joy and beauty are a reflection of Ishvara's glory, then what of death, sorrow and ugliness? If Ishvara is truly everything, by definition that must also include the less pleasant aspects of life. Chapter eleven deals with this predicament.

Seeing With New Eyes

Spiritual seekers are generally experience hungry, and Arjuna is no exception. That's why, although affirming that he's understood everything Krishna has told him, he asks to see this all-pervading cosmic Self with his own eyes.

In actuality, he already is. The entire universe is the embodiment of Ishvara. Because the universe is always present and available to the senses, every experience that we have is, therefore, an experience of God.

But even though the cosmic form is around us at all times, only a certain mind is capable of apprehending the inherent divinity of all creation. A mundane mind will see only mundane objects, and have no appreciation for their inherent divinity.

Swami Paramarthananda uses the example of an old guitar sitting in a secondhand shop. This guitar might be damaged, have strings missing, and may even be incapable of playing music. Objectively it appears to have little value. But what if it was discovered that this guitar had belonged to one of the Beatles in the 1960's? Suddenly, this worthless old instrument has immense value. The object itself hasn't changed, but the way we look at it will definitely change—as will its price tag!

Similarly, although the cosmic vision is available for anyone with the eyes to see it, this treasure is hidden in plain sight. To gain the vision of Ishvara, all that needs to change is the way that we see things. To see and apprehend God, we must develop new vision; the ability to not only see the objects in front of us, but to recognise their value.

Although grandly dramatised in this chapter of the Gita, the cosmic vision isn't some earth-shattering event. It's simply a change of perspective—the ability to see what was always there in a new light.

That said, Krishna stresses how difficult it is to attain this vision. It requires what he calls 'spiritual vision'; the eye of wisdom, or what might some call the 'third eye'. This simply means a pure mind, refined by dharmic living and made steady by the practice of karma yoga, meditation and self-inquiry. With this eye of wisdom, we come to see the true nature of reality. We realise that both the manifest and unmanifest are nothing but Brahman; the limitless, eternal Self.

What we see isn't as important as the way that we see it, and this is determined by our level of understanding.

To the materialist, the universe is nothing but an accident; random bundles of matter combining to form objects and, supposedly, by some inexplicable quirk of fate, consciousness. Those with spiritual vision, however, see the entire creation as arising from universal consciousness; the divine creative essence. All the worlds, objects and beings are simply Ishvara assuming different names and forms, just as every bracelet and bangle is a different form of the same gold.

Wherever the wise look, and in whatever they see, they see God.

This chapter uses a dramatic device to convey the simple truth that everything is Ishvara. On account of this vision of infinity, Arjuna is overcome by wonder. He sees Krishna's eyes, mouths and feet everywhere! He beholds Krishna, or Ishvara, as not only the source of all creation, but as the very form of that creation—all-pervading, as brilliant as a thousand suns, and blinding in radiance and power.

Ishvara is Both Life and Death

What started as a vision of wonder, however, becomes a nightmare when Arjuna sees the fearsome jaws of Ishvara hungrily devouring both friends and foes alike.

Ishvara, he realises, isn't just life and creation—but is also destruction and death. After all, creation cannot exist without destruction any more than birth can exist without death. Without exception or concession, all mortal beings get consumed by the merciless jaws of time; chewed up and eventually swallowed. What is born must eventually die, from the tiniest cell to the largest galaxy; for that is the law of Ishvara.

Swami Dayananda explains:

> When he asked for this vision, Arjuna expected to see something wonderful, and he did. But he was not prepared for the other side of it. Ishvara is not only the one who sustains everything, but the destroyer, too. What Arjuna is seeing here is the destruction that is constantly taking place in the creation. It is a necessary part of creation, so has to be included in the vision of the cosmos. The continuous process of destruction, creation, and sustenance is Ishvara. But the destructive aspect is not easy to look at.

It takes a mature mind to appreciate Ishvara as both the creative and destructive principle of life. One cannot exist without the other. The entire phenomenal reality is a play of opposites; of birth and death, day and night, growth and decay, health and sickness, strength and weakness, union and separation, joy and sorrow.

The mind naturally clings to the good and resists the bad, but both must be accepted as part of this worldly existence. Arjuna found it easy to accept God as the creative force of the universe; as that which is all beauty and benevolence. What he sees now—Ishvara devouring all beings without a hint of remorse—confuses and disturbs him. How can he reconcile such a cruel and ferocious God?

In his Gita commentary, Swami Chinmayananda writes:

> No creation of a thing is possible without the corresponding destruction of its previous condition. The world is created by a continuous process of destruction. Today has arisen from the graves of yesterday. Childhood dies before youth appears. And when youth passes away, old age takes birth.

The Order of Creation

The laws of the universe are exacting and inviolable. It is through these laws that Ishvara maintains the order of creation, allowing meaningful action to take place.

We have no option but to submit to these laws, for there is no changing them. We can't expect Ishvara to bend or rewrite these laws simply to appease our particular desires and whims. For example, gravity cannot be suspended because one person happens to be falling. Even a momentary suspension of the law of gravity would have repercussions for everyone else.

With exacting precision, Ishvara maintains the laws of creation and delivers the results of all karma. All beings depend upon these laws for their existence. The Earth rotates around the sun at exactly the right distance, tilt and speed in order for it to sustain life. If the variables of its orbit were to change even minutely, our planet would become an uninhabitable ball of ice or fiery rock.

There is no question of compassion or cruelty when it comes to Ishvara. These qualities are superimposed by man. As the giver of the results of our karma, Ishvara will seem to be cruel or loving depending upon our likes and dislikes. When we get what we want, it's easy to praise Ishvara and glorify God's grace. But when we fail to get what we want—or, indeed, when we get what we don't want—we must also accept this as divine grace.

Being at friction with reality only causes suffering. In any transaction with the material world, we must accept that in all likelihood the results of our actions will not conform to our likes and dislikes. Instead of seeing unpleasing results as evidence of cruelty on Ishvara's part, we should accept what comes and use it as an opportunity to purify the mind by practicing karma yoga. That's how a simple shift of attitude can transform misfortune into spiritual gain.

Surrender is the Only Option

While Arjuna's reaction to this cosmic vision began as wonder and then turned to fear, it eventually becomes one of acceptance and surrender.

Ishvara ordains the physical and moral laws of the creation; and to these laws all beings must submit. That's why surrender to the cosmic order is the only sane response to life.

By seeing with the eye of wisdom and knowing the entire universe to be Ishvara, you naturally develop a reverential attitude for all of life. Knowing that no part of your life is separate from God, you not only become more accepting of the opposites of duality, but you naturally live with greater reverence and devotion.

You find your attitude shifts from small-minded egocentrism to an all-encompassing sense of gratitude and awe. Instead of complaining when life fails to deliver the results you want, you learn to take the rough with the smooth, knowing everything to be part of a divine tapestry of perfection.

Your actions are no longer motivated solely for the gratification of your mind and senses, but are performed out of respectful devotion to Ishvara. What you do naturally conforms to dharma, for you know that dharma is Ishvara.

Krishna ends the chapter by again summarising karma yoga—which is, in fact, bhakti, or devotion, in action. It is with an unfailing attitude of devotion, he tells us, that one comes to realise the Self. This devotion to Brahman is life's only secure attachment because the Self is always present and, unlike material forms, is subject to neither change or decline. When this Truth becomes the object of your greatest devotion, the false, the ego, is negated and freedom is attained.

Devotion

¹ Arjuna said, "There are those who worship you as a personal god and those who seek you impersonally as the everlasting Reality beyond objectification. Which of these devotees knows you best?"

²⁻⁴ Krishna answered, "Those whose minds are fixed upon Me with unflinching devotion and who meditate upon Me consistently are most exalted. However, there are those who seek Me as That which is not subject to decline and which is beyond form and the reach of mind; ever-abiding, unmoving and eternal. Having complete mastery of their senses, a tranquil mind, and taking joy in the welfare of all beings, they are non-separate from Me.

⁵⁻⁸ "Yet this can be a difficult path for those whose identification with body and mind is strong. However, those who worship Me and to whom I am the supreme goal—who have relinquished all actions to Me and fixed their minds on Me with a devotion that knows no otherness—I will liberate from the ocean of samsara. Keeping your mind and thoughts on Me, there is no doubt you will abide in Me alone.

⁹⁻¹¹ "Should you find yourself unable to keep your mind continually absorbed in Me, then it is through the practice of upasana meditation and contemplation that you will reach Me. If you find yourself unable to do this also, then you must commit to karma yoga, performing all actions for My sake. If you are not able to do even this, then with a disciplined mind, you must simply renounce the results of all your actions to Me.

¹² "Knowledge surpasses the mere practice of yoga. The full realisation of that knowledge through meditation on the Self surpasses mere knowledge. But surrendering attachment to the results of one's actions brings immediate peace of mind.

13-14 "Beloved to Me is the one who harbours no malice, who is friendly to all, compassionate, free from covetousness, unburdened by the notion of doership, equally disposed to the duality of the opposites, accommodative, contented, self-controlled, resolute, and whose heart and mind are resolved in Me. Such a soul is completely satisfied, has mastery over the mind, firm ascertainment, and a mind and intellect that are resolved in me.

15 "Beloved to Me is the one who neither disturbs the world nor is disturbed by it; who is beyond the sway of elation, intolerance, fear and anxiety.

16 "Beloved to Me is the one who remains free of dependence on external things; who is pure, stable, free from fear and disinclined to initiate ego-driven undertakings.

17 "Beloved to Me is the one who relinquishes hostility, grief and desire; who lets go of notions of 'good' and 'bad'; and who allows things to come and go with a spirit of devotion.

18-19 "Beloved to Me is the one who looks upon friend and foe with equal regard, as well as honour and disgrace; and who retains equanimity with regard to heat and cold, pleasure and pain, praise and blame. Unattached to objects, he or she is of firm knowledge, disciplined in speech, satisfied with what life brings and sees all places as home.

20 "Those who live this life according to dharma, who are filled with faith and see Self-realisation as the supreme goal are exceedingly beloved to Me."

THE DIVINE SONG   259

COMMENTARY

The Gita has established Ishvara as not only the intelligence shaping the creation, but also its essence and substance. The previous chapter demonstrated this in visceral terms by revealing the entire cosmos to be the body of the Lord.

Arjuna's initial reaction to this cosmic vision is one of awe-struck wonder. His amazement turns to fear, however, upon realising that, as the sum total of all things, Ishvara isn't only all that is beautiful and wondrous, but is also time, decay and death. It's only when Arjuna manages to reconcile this eternal dance of creation and destruction that his fear becomes not only acceptance, but worshipful wonder.

Accordingly, this middle section of the Gita now closes with a short but potent chapter on the topic of bhakti, or devotion. As Swami Paramarthananda points out, all discussion of Ishvara should naturally lead to devotion for Ishvara.

Reverence For Ishvara

Whether we take ourselves to be a jiva or the Self, it's clear that we ourselves have no direct control over the order of the cosmos. The universal laws of the creation belong to Ishvara alone. As long as we remain associated with a mortal form, we have no option but to play by those rules or else suffer accordingly.

This arrangement generally works well for us. After all, we don't have to worry about keeping the Earth spinning or the stars and galaxies in motion. That's not our job. Everything that we need has been supplied to us by Ishvara. We've been given the gift of a body and mind and everything necessary for them to survive and hopefully thrive. That's why an attitude of respect, gratitude and reverence for Ishvara is the only appropriate response for the enlightened and unenlightened alike.

The wise see everything as belonging to Ishvara. All that we have is on loan; a temporary loan that must eventually be repaid. As trustees, it behooves us to act with graciousness and respect for the cosmic force that has created and sustains our lives and the universe of which we are a part.

Devotion Requires Knowledge

In order to have devotion for Ishvara, you first require knowledge of Ishvara. If you think about it, it's impossible to either love or hate someone of whom you have no knowledge. Until you know a person, your feelings toward them will be neutral. It's only when you get to know them that you develop feelings for them, either good or bad. These feelings are shaped by two factors: firstly, by your knowledge of this person and secondly, by your likes and dislikes, which, as we've seen, filter our entire experience of reality.

In our materialistic age, many people refuse to even acknowledge Ishvara's existence. Or perhaps they have a negative attitude toward God based upon the distorted dogma pedalled by religion and the adharmic actions of some fanatical believers.

However, both those who refuse to acknowledge the existence of Ishvara and those who use their concept of God as a means of justifying adharmic behaviour are under the spell of ignorance. The former are incapable of bhakti because they believe Ishvara to be nonexistent, and the latter have misplaced bhakti owing to ignorance about the nature of Ishvara.

It's our knowledge, therefore, that determines our attitude toward Ishvara. One of the most important implications of the Gita's teaching is that Ishvara expresses as dharma; the innate order of the cosmos. Any concept of God which promotes or justifies adharma is not divine. It is demonic.

Fighting For Dharma

A sticking point for some people when it comes to the Gita is that Krishna repeatedly implores Arjuna to enter battle and kill his enemies.

Again, this highlights the importance of discrimination. The battle of the Gita is a battle between dharma and adharma. A grave injustice has been committed and an entire kingdom thrown into darkness. Arjuna's duty as a warrior, a prince, and a follower of dharma, is to overcome this adharma and restore order and peace. The Gita is not about war, nor should Krishna's words ever be taken as a glorification of violence. The Gita is both a *dharma shastra* and a *moksha shastra*; a teaching about dharma and a teaching about enlightenment.

Just as Ishvara sustains the universe, maintaining the eternal cycle of birth, life and death—so too are all jivas, as microcosmic aspects of Ishvara, responsible for contributing to the creation by fulfilling their dharma.

All beings are born with a specific and preordained personal dharma. By honouring our nature and following this dharma, we each serve Ishvara and play our part in the creation. Those who live according to this dharma, which Swami Dayananda defines as "dedicated action to Ishvara", are called bhaktas, or devotees.

The Bhakti Confusion

A great deal of confusion surrounds the topic of bhakti. At the root of this confusion is the notion that bhakti is a specific path and an end in itself; an idea that can be traced to the works of Swami Vivekananda. Around the turn of the 20th century, Vivekananda became one of the first teachers to export Vedanta to the West. He obviously did the world a tremendous service in doing so. The way he presented some aspects of the teaching, however, was not always in line with the Vedanta *sampradaya* (teaching tradition).

In particular, Vivekananda spoke of four distinct paths to enlightenment which, he believed, could be adopted according to one's personal temperament. He presented jnana yoga, the pursuit of Self-knowledge, as the appropriate path for intellectuals. For extroverted, action-oriented people, he recommended karma yoga. For the more 'feeling', emotion-oriented types he recommended bhakti yoga. Finally, for those who were more physically focused, he suggested hatha yoga.

This notion of a four-fold path, however, is not to be found in the Vedas, the Gita, nor any other Vedantic scripture. In fact, the Gita makes it clear that there are only two 'paths' to moksha: the path of knowledge (jnana yoga) for those with a contemplative lifestyle and temperament, and the path of action (karma yoga) for those with worldly ties and obligations. Karma yoga doesn't lead to enlightenment itself, but it does prepare the mind for jnana yoga, the application of Self-knowledge, which alone liberates the mind.

This makes Vivekananda's pronouncement problematic. Vedanta doesn't view bhakti as a separate yoga or a path in itself.

The main branches of Hinduism, such as Shaivism and Vaishnavism are based on *agama* traditions, and place great emphasis on bhakti and the worship of a personal deity. Devotees pray, chant and perform all kinds of pujas (devotional offerings). These, however, are all actions (karma), and actions fall into the category of karma yoga.

Bhakti means love for the divine. Love is not something that you do; it is not an action or a series of actions. Bhakti is what motivates and informs your actions—a spirit of love and devotion for the Lord, in whichever form you conceive Him or Her. Such devotion is not limited to a single path or a specific action, but encompasses every stage of the spiritual path.

For the karma yogi, who accepts Ishvara as the very law of dharma, every single action is performed as an act of devotion, consecrated to the divine.

That's why, as Swami Dayananda clarifies:

> We can never say that the karma yogi is without bhakti. And neither is the sannyasi without bhakti, because sannyasa is only to know Ishvara. There is no bhakti yogi. Lord Krishna has said, in this world there are two committed lifestyles for moksha: that of a sannyasi and that of a karma yogi.

While one person may be emotional in nature and another more intellectually-oriented, all of us have emotions, all of us have an intellect, all of us have a tendency to be extroverted, and all of us have a body. That's why assigning a single yoga according to the superficial predilections of the personality doesn't work. Integration must be achieved on all levels.

Only Self-knowledge leads to moksha. According to Vedanta, the other yogas are tools for preparing the mind for knowledge—each a rung in the ladder to liberation. As such, they are all necessary, but only the top rungs will take you where you ultimately need to go. Bhakti is not a specific yoga, but a blanket term for all of the stages of the path to liberation.

Arjuna's Question

Chapter twelve begins with a question from Arjuna. He wants to know which is the best form of devotion: worship of Nirguna Brahman (the Self as the formless, all-pervading totality) or worship of Saguna Brahman (the Self in the form of Ishvara, whether conceptualised as a personal deity or the cosmic form he's just witnessed).

This question echoes Arjuna's earlier doubts about whether he should choose the path of renunciation or the path of worldly duty and karma yoga. The sannyasi worships the Self through deep contemplation leading to assimilated Self-knowledge, while the worldly devotee directs his or her devotion to the Self symbolised as a personal deity.

Krishna has already made it clear that the highest form of worship is to realise one's non-difference to Him. But while it might be the highest form of bhakti, and indeed the key to moksha, Krishna admits that this knowledge does not come easily unless one has a sufficiently qualified, sattvic mind. Fortunately, there are forms of bhakti appropriate to every temperament and stage of development.

A Map of the Entire Spiritual Path

In this chapter, Krishna reveals the different stages of bhakti appropriate to each person's level of understanding. What follows is a five-step map of the entire spiritual path. Each step is a different form of bhakti.

1. Karma Yoga With Personal Desire (*Sakama Bhakti*)

The average human being, almost completely driven by their likes and dislikes in the form of binding vasanas, will find it impossible to fix the mind in steady contemplation of the Self. Such a mind, subject to the endless sorrows and agitations of samsara, is unlikely to gain the necessary qualifications for moksha overnight.

However, Vedanta doesn't leave such a person high and dry. According to Krishna, at the beginning stages of the spiritual path, you are free to follow your desires and take action in the world, so long as this doesn't contravene dharma.

This first stage of karma yoga doesn't require all your actions to be done for Ishvara alone, and you are still permitted to indulge your likes and dislikes as you pursue various personal goals. The only stipulation is that you recognise that all results are given by Ishvara and should, therefore, be accepted as prasada (Ishvara's will).

Understanding that the results of your karma are dispensed by Ishvara should bring immediate peace of mind.

According to Swami Dayananda, our likes and dislikes lie at the root of every emotional pain we experience. The only way to neutralise them is to graciously accept the results of our actions, whether good or bad, as prasada. Though our likes and dislikes still remain, in time they become non-binding and incapable of creating the same emotional upheavals.

2. Karma Yoga Without Personal Desire (*Nishkama Bhakti*)

After practicing the first stage of karma yoga for some time, you'll find your mind naturally becoming more refined and pure. It's then you may begin to wonder if there isn't more to life than simply pursuing desires for your own personal gratification. You realise that life will be more fulfilling if you were to help others or the society in some way, perhaps by offering your time, energy, wealth or knowledge. It now occurs to you that success is proportional to how much you give rather than how much you can take.

By recognising the limitations of desire-based happiness, you progress to the second stage of karma yoga. You are no longer devoted solely to your own desires, but to something greater. All your actions are now performed for Ishvara and for the purification of your mind. Recognising the importance of dharma, and accepting that the results of your actions are always determined by Ishvara, your every action becomes an act of worship.

By no longer acting solely for yourself and the fulfilment of selfish desires, you lessen the ego's tenacious grip and begin to neutralise the mind's entrenched likes and dislikes. By relinquishing your attachment to outcomes, the stress inherent in action diminishes. As your vision becomes increasingly clear, you become firmly committed to the pursuit of moksha as life's highest goal.

3. Meditation on Ishvara as a Personal Deity (*Ishta Devata Upasana*)

The third and fourth rungs on the bhakti ladder are both forms of *upasana yoga*. *Upasana* is a term that can have different meanings, but in this context, Krishna defines upasana as meditation or contemplation upon Ishvara.

Having attained a certain peace and evenness of mind through the practise of karma yoga, you are now able to turn your attention inward and focus the mind in contemplation of Ishvara. As Krishna states: "Those whose minds are fixed upon Me with unflinching devotion and who meditate upon Me consistently are most exalted."

Because it takes a pure and highly refined mind to be able to contemplate Nirguna Brahman, the formless, all-pervading Self, for beginner and intermediate seekers, it's much easier to worship Saguna Brahman; the Self in the form of Ishvara.

Most people find it helpful to have a symbol for Ishvara. That's why the first stage of upasana yoga is to visualise Ishvara as a particular form or deity, thus giving the mind a clear focus and outlet for devotional practice. That's why Hindus place pictures or statues of Krishna, Shiva, Ganesha, Kali, or any number of other deities upon their altar. Such a devotee will perform daily puja to their personal deity by offering prayers, chants, flowers, food and incense. Such rituals are beneficial for purifying the mind and cultivating a calm, even-minded and devotional disposition.

Whatever symbol of divinity you choose, whether it is Krishna, Allah, Jesus or an Archangel, it should be seen as a representation of the eternal, all-pervading Self. By offering all your actions to and affirming your devotion to this divine symbol, you generate a tremendous amount of love.

Instead of deriving your emotional support from external relationships, objects and circumstances, bhakti converts your emotional attachments to a devotional attachment. Attachment to Ishvara is the only secure attachment you can ever have because, unlike the ever-changing objects of the world, Ishvara is changeless and eternal, and will therefore always be there for you.

The cultivation of this bhakti, divine love, helps qualify the mind for moksha by reducing your attachment to worldly objects. The mind naturally gravitates to what it loves and the key to liberation, as Krishna says here, is to keep your mind fixed upon the Self with "a devotion that knows no otherness". The reward, he promises, is liberation from samsara.

4. Meditation on Ishvara as the Universal Form (*Vishvarupa Upasana*)

The second stage of upasana yoga is a natural progression from the first. You keep your mind and thoughts fixed on Ishvara, but rather than confining your worship to a particular deity or symbol, you now expand your understanding of Ishvara to include the entire creation.

By expanding your conception of Ishvara in this way, you realise that wherever you go and whatever you encounter, you are meeting God. Your love is no longer confined to a particular form but flows outward to embrace the entirety of creation.

You appreciate the divinity in each moment, in every sight and sound and experience. Depending on your nature, your bhakti may find expression in love of nature's boundless beauty; in the twinkling of the stars in the night sky; the sound of birdsong, and the colour and fragrance of a flower. Every person and animal that you meet can be a recipient of your bhakti, because every being is an expression of Ishvara.

This expanded vision helps us to see things from a more elevated perspective. Our entrenched likes and dislikes are further neutralised, and we find it easier to accept others and to embrace the flow of life, taking the good with the bad and seeing all things as divine. This qualifies the mind for the final and highest stage of bhakti.

5. Pursuit and Actualisation of Self-Knowledge (Jnana Yoga)
A lover always seeks to be close to his or her beloved. For the bhakta, the ultimate devotion is the realisation that we are nonseparate from the true object of all our love, devotion and worship—the one, eternal Self. The highest devotion is therefore the realisation of our innermost Self as the limitless, formless, non-dual essence of Existence.

As the Kaivalya Upanishad states:

> Experiencing one's own Self in all beings and all beings in the Self, one attains [the realisation of] limitless awareness and not by any other means.

All the stages prior to this have been necessary to prepare the mind for Self-knowledge. This final stage of bhakti takes the form of Vedanta's threefold teaching methodology: listening to the teaching (shravana), systematically resolving any doubts or confusion (manana) and applying this knowledge to the mind to make it a living reality (nididhyasana).

Thus, the highest devotion is to know that you *are* God—the one, independent, all-pervading Reality that is Brahman, the Self. The assimilation of this knowledge strips away lifetimes of ignorance-induced suffering as you come to realise the fullness and freedom of your own nature.

An Erroneous Question

As it turns out, Arjuna's opening question was an erroneous one. Whether one worships the formless Self or a personal deity will depend upon the stage they are at in their path and their corresponding level of understanding. Both forms of bhakti work together; the former preparing the mind for the latter.

The five stages of bhakti take the seeker from basic karma yoga to upasana yoga, and eventually culminate in jnana yoga, or the teaching of Vedanta. Because self-ignorance is the cause of samsara, only Self-knowledge can remedy it. The problem, as Krishna states, is that few people are qualified to jump straight to jnana yoga. That's why, for most people, it's necessary to start at the beginning and systematically progress through each of these five steps.

The Self-Realised Mind

The closing verses of chapter twelve beautifully explore the fruits of Self-realisation and the characteristics of the jnani.

Until you realise the fullness of your nature and the richness of your inner world, you will naturally look to the outer world for fulfilment. Your entire view of reality thus remains subjective. Being emotionally dependent upon objects for your happiness, and seeing everything through the lens of your likes and dislikes, you divide the world into 'good' and 'bad'. You love those objects which you believe bring happiness and hate those which seem to obstruct it.

To live in such a way is to be at perpetual war with reality. For the samsaric mind, driven by a crippling sense of lack, whether physical, emotional or intellectual, every action is an act of struggle—the struggle to force reality to conform to your likes and dislikes. Swami Paramarthananda defines struggle as 'any action motivated by a sense of incompleteness'—which, for the samsari, is pretty much every action!

The jnani, however, knowing his or her true nature to be whole and complete, never acts from a place of struggle. The enlightened have nothing to gain in this world, because they've already found wholeness within themselves. In the words of Swami Chinmayananda: "A real devotee is completely independent of the world and he draws his inspiration, equanimity and joyous ecstasy from a source deep within himself."

For the jnani, all activities become *lila*; a divine play. Life is no longer a desperate struggle to make yourself whole by grasping at ephemeral objects. As a jnani, no longer dependent upon external factors for your happiness, life can be enjoyed free of expectation and demand.

The removal of self-ignorance cuts away the knots of the heart. As the closing lines illustrate, the jnani harbours no hatred or malice for anyone. Knowing yourself to be the essence of fullness and love, this naturally expresses in all your interactions with the world, and you regard all with compassion, equanimity and kindness.

As well as having an open heart, you also have a thick skin and rarely get perturbed by the ups and downs of maya or the ignorant behaviour of others. Whereas the worldly are only happy when they get they own way, the jnani's happiness is far more durable, for it is a happiness independent of external factors.

Swami Dayananda says:

> [The jnani] does not take issue with himself, the world and God on any account and is happy with himself. He is free from any sense of imperfection in spite of the fact that the body, senses and mind are imperfect, because the self does not have any of these features. They belong to anatma (not-self), which is mithya and thus do not in any way condition the Self, which is the satya from which they draw their very existence.

When you know who you are, you are at home wherever you find yourself. You are naturally impartial, unattached to objects and have negated the ego's sense of doership and ownership. You automatically live according to dharma and are satisfied with whatever blessings Ishvara brings your way. Such is a life of freedom; the life of a true devotee who has realised the unity of all life.

CHAPTER THIRTEEN

The Field and the Knower of the Field

Arjuna said, "I wish to know more about existence, Krishna. Tell me about prakriti and pursusha; about the world of appearance and the one who knows this world; about the means of knowledge and that which is to be known."

¹Krishna said, "The body is matter, Arjuna, and all material existence is called the 'field'. The one who knows this is called 'the knower of the field'.

²"As the Self, I am the knower of the field in everyone. True knowledge is having knowledge of both the field, the manifest universe, and the knower of that field, the Self.

³"Listen and I will explain the nature of the field, the modifications that take place within it, and the nature of the knower.

⁴"These truths have been sung by the great rishis (seers) of the Vedas in a variety of ways. They have revealed the nature of Brahman with great reasoning and precision.

⁵⁻⁶"The field is comprised of the subtle elements, the unmanifest cause (maya), the sense organs and their respective sense objects, and the components of mind: cognition, intellect and ego. Modifications that take place in the field are the qualities of desire, aversion, pleasure and pain, the physical body, intelligence and will.

⁷⁻¹¹"Those who know this are free of conceit and pretence. They commit non-injury, are generous, straightforward, devoted to their teacher, inwardly and outwardly pure, steadfast with mastery of the mind, and dispassionate toward the objects of the senses. Free of pride, they realise the limitations and suffering of birth, old age, disease and death. With no sense of ownership, they do not get compulsively entangled in the affairs of

family and home and retain evenness of mind regarding gain and loss. Their unswerving devotion to Me is accompanied by a keenness for solitude and indifference to social life. Firm in Self-knowledge, they know that seeking the Self is the ultimate goal of life and all else is ignorance.

12 "That which is to be known is the Self; knowing which one attains immortality. The Self has no beginning, is limitless, and is neither existent as an object nor non-existent.

13-14 "Pervading everything, it dwells in all beings. Everywhere are its hands and feet; everywhere are its eyes and faces. Though free of the senses, it shines through the functioning of all senses. The sustainer of all, it is beyond the three gunas yet it enjoys their play.

15 "That which is both within and without all beings, it is immovable, yet is the cause of motion. Both near and far, its nature is so subtle that most beings fail to perceive it.

16 "Though indivisible, it appears divided into separate beings and objects. It is the support of all beings and elements—their creator, sustainer and destroyer.

17 "The light of all lights, it is beyond darkness and ignorance. Present in the minds of all, its nature is knowledge; that which is to be known and that by which it is known.

18 "I have briefly explained the field, the knower of the field, and what is to be known. Those who are devoted to Me, with this knowledge, attain liberation through Self-realisation.

19-20 "Know that both prakriti (the material world) and purusha (the Self) are without beginning. It is prakriti that gives birth to the gunas and all the modifications of the field. The physical body and its senses are born of the field.

21-22 "It is purusha, the Knower, that appears to experience pleasure and pain. Obtaining in the field, the Knower enjoys the attributes born of prakriti. Through ignorance of one's nature, attachment forms to the objects of sense and experience, and this causes subsequent births, both good and bad. The one experiencing the body, the field and all its modifications is ultimately the Self; the limitless creator, witness, sustainer and enjoyer.

²³ "The one who gains knowledge of the nature of prakriti and purusha, the field and the knower, and the interplay of the gunas, is freed from the cycle of rebirth.

²⁴⁻²⁵ "Some, by virtue of a pure mind, realise the Self through contemplation. Others attain the Self through inquiry and direct knowledge. Others must reach the Self by first practicing karma yoga. Some, being unfamiliar with these approaches, can attain liberation by applying the teachings of an illumined teacher.

²⁶ "Any existent form, whether animate or inanimate, is born of union between the field and the knower of the field.

²⁷⁻²⁸ "The one who sees the Self shining in the heart of all beings, and who knows it to be That which survives the death of form, sees truly. In seeing the Lord as one and the same in all beings, one is no longer impelled to harm others, or oneself, and will attain the supreme goal of Self-realisation.

²⁹ "The one who sees that all actions are generated and performed by the field, and that the Self is not the doer of action, sees truly.

³⁰ "Liberation comes to he who sees unity in diversity; who understands the manifold forms of the world are all expressions of the one Self.

³¹ "This limitless Self is eternal, imperishable and indivisible. Even though it dwells as the inmost essence of body and form, it performs no action, nor is it affected by the results of actions.

³²⁻³³ "Just as space pervades the cosmos and remains unaffected by whatever takes place within it, so too, is the Self unaffected by whatever happens within it. Just as the sun illumines the entire world, so too, does the Self illumine the entire field.

³⁴ "Those who understand the distinction between the field and the knower of the field achieve freedom from the bondage of material existence and attain the ultimate goal."

COMMENTARY

This thirteenth chapter is considered one of the Gita's most important, and with good reason. It not only distills the essence of the Upanishads into a mere thirty-four verses, but also marks the beginning of the final section of the Gita.

It's believed that Arjuna's question at the start of the chapter was added to the Gita at a later date. This was perhaps to ease us into the subject matter instead of diving headfirst into a weighty philosophical discourse about the nature of reality.

Arjuna asks Krishna to elaborate on prakriti and purusha; two terms that were introduced back in chapter seven. Prakriti and purusha might be equated to matter and spirit; the world of material existence and the consciousness pervading and illumining it. It's from this marriage of matter and spirit that the world of form arises.

Krishna here introduces two new terms: 'the field' and 'the knower of the field'. The field is another term for praktriti. The knower of the field means purusha, or the pure awareness/consciousness that is the Self. The field, then, is the inert realm of matter, and the knower of the field is the sentience that illumines and enlivens it.

This pivotal chapter therefore unfolds three main topics: the nature of the field, the nature of the knower of the field, and how discrimination between the two is the key to liberation.

The Field

Krishna provides a succinct definition of the field: "The body is matter, and all material existence is called the field."

He begins by stating that the body belongs to the field because the body is, for most people, their primary point of identification.

However, it's important to note that the mind also belongs to the field. Whereas the physical body is made of gross matter and is readily observable as an object, the mind is made of subtle matter and, although not perceptible to the eyes, is also known to us as an object of perception. If you think about it, we are aware of our thoughts, our emotions and feelings as objects in consciousness. Anything objectifiable, whether gross or subtle, belongs to the field of prakriti.

Krishna then says: "The one who knows this is called the knower of the field." As we shall see, one of Vedanta's key teaching methodologies is to distinguish between these two orders of reality: the seen and the seer.

The field is basically whatever you can experience with your mind and senses. The world around you—all the stars, planets and galaxies—and the private world of your own thoughts, dreams and imagination all belong to the field. Swami Paramarthananda notes that even the heavens are part of this field, because they themselves are subtle objects of experience.

The field is material in nature, whether gross or subtle; visible or invisible. Physics tells us that although matter can change form, it can neither be created or destroyed. Prakriti is, therefore, an eternal principle, which can exist in both a manifest (visible) or unmanifest (invisible) state. The three gunas, which we shall explore in the next chapter, are the primordial qualities comprising this field.

All material objects are subject to change and modification, decay and disintegration. This is a fundamental characteristic of matter. The very cells of our bodies undergo a continuous cycle of decay, death and rebirth. Material forms are subject to both internal damage, such as disease and ageing, as well as external damage from accident, injury or environmental factors.

Finally, it's essential to understand that matter itself is inert. The field of prakriti has no life or sentience of its own. In order for the field to come alive, another factor is required. Just as the moon has no light of its own, the field has no life without the enlivening presence of consciousness.

The Knower

Most people spend their lives completely fixated by the field of objects—by their body and mind, the bodies and minds of others, and the world around them. Enmeshed in the spell of maya, they rarely, if ever, consider the second principle of which Krishna speaks: the knower of the field.

Every experienced object automatically presupposes an agent of experience: a subject. After all, without a subject, no experience would be possible.

This knower is pure awareness; the Self. This chapter again uses the term purusha. Like electricity, purusha is that which illumines and animates the field of matter.

Swami Chinmayananda describes the relationship of prakriti and purusha in terms of matter and spirit:

> Spirit itself has no expression except when it plays through matter. When purusha weds prakriti, the world of plurality appears, and the experiences of good and bad, in legion, are born. Electricity in itself can't manifest as light. But when it weds the bulb, it is manifested as light.

Certain forms within prakriti (specifically, the body-mind-sense complex) are capable of serving as a reflecting medium for awareness/consciousness. Thus, by the light of purusha (the Self), the instruments of body and mind are granted a certain borrowed sentience. This enables consciousness to know and transact with the world.

As the instruments of body and mind are finite, their borrowed sentience lasts only as long as they are capable of functioning in their reflecting capacity. When consciousness departs a form, we consider it 'dead'. This 'death' only relates to the outer form, however. As the Self is limitless and without beginning or end, the original consciousness ever abides, whether the reflecting medium is available or not. Consciousness, then, will always outlast the form through which it expresses.

Observing the world around us, we might assume that because there are many bodies and minds, there must also be many consciousnesses. There is only one consciousness, however. Just as the same electricity can power any number of bulbs, and the same sun shines on all the reflective surfaces in all the world, only one consciousness pervades, illumines and enlivens all bodies and minds.

The Eternal Subject

The difficulty we have understanding the Self, the eternal subject, is that it cannot be experienced as an object. It's the one thing that's unavailable for objectification. If it were, it would be part of the field and thus subject to the field's limitations.

If you think about it, a camera can take photographs of anything within its range, but the one thing it can never photograph is itself. The mere existence of the photograph, however, presupposes the existence of the camera. Similarly, the very existence of objects and experiences presupposes a subject/experiencer.

The heart of this chapter is a meditation upon the nature of the Self. Krishna says: "As the Self, I am the knower of the field in everyone."

This Self is without beginning or end. It is limitless, pervades all things, and dwells within all beings—or, to put it more accurately, all beings dwell within it. It is the support of all creation; "the sustainer of all." It enables the world of creation to exist, yet remains untouched and untainted by the creation.

This Self is not a part or product of the body. As we have established, the field of matter is inert and insentient. Sentience cannot arise from the insentient. It can only be lent by that which is of the nature of sentience. Just as the sun lends its light to the moon, making the moon appear to shine by itself, the Self lends the body consciousness for an allotted time.

The materialist assumes consciousness to be a product of the brain, even though science cannot substantiate this claim. How can sentience arise from the insentient? To assume that the brain creates consciousness is like an ignorant man turning on a radio and somehow believing the radio set itself to be the source of the broadcasts. The radio set is only a medium through which radio signals can be received and played. In a similar way, the apparatus of mind and body is a medium through which consciousness expresses.

As a light bulb shines in the presence of electricity, consciousness enlivens and animates the otherwise inert body and mind. When the bulb is damaged, however, it loses its ability to function. The electricity is still there, but that particular bulb is no longer a medium for its expression.

When the brain dies, like a fused bulb, it can no longer serve as a reflecting medium for consciousness. Consciousness, however, continues existing even when the body has disintegrated. Mortality is a feature of the body and not the Self.

Like the sun, shining upon good and bad alike without any hint of favouritism or reservation, the light of the Self illumines all things equally. Whether the body is in health or sickness, and whether the mind is peaceful or agitated, the light of consciousness cannot be contaminated in any way. Regardless of the presence or absence of the body and mind, the Self is ever present, ever free and ever actionless awareness.

A Process of False Superimposition

Our inability to distinguish between the field (the world of objects), and the knower (the eternal subject) accounts for mankind's existential sorrow.

Recall that maya is the creative principle by which the entire universe of multiplicity appears within the one, formless Self. This awareness/consciousness is the essence of what we are—the very ground of existence; the substratum upon which all things appear and upon which they depend for their being.

Ignorance, however, causes us to mistake the objects appearing in awareness (specifically the body/ mind/ego) for who we are. In a process of false superimposition, we take these objects to be our self. In other words, under the spell of ignorance, we superimpose selfhood upon these objects, investing them with a sense of 'me' and 'my-ness', while mutually superimposing their attributes onto the Self.

Believing ourselves to be a limited form subject to the ravages of time, we adopt a false identity and an erroneous sense of doership and ownership. Overcome by limitation, this falsely invested sense of 'I' compels us to act according to the mind's

likes and dislikes and its countless desires and fears, attachments and compulsions.

In itself, the world is neutral. Like a coloured gel placed over
a white light, the presence of our likes and dislikes colours our
entire experience of life. We then come to inhabit our own subjective world of good and bad, desirable and undesirable. The
moment we label a thing either good or bad, it has the capacity to cause us pleasure or pain and so we find ourselves swept
away by samsara's endless cycle of frustration, desire, action
and reaction.

Discriminating the Knower From the Known

The heart of the problem is a fundamental misapprehension
about the nature of our existence.

We know that the world exists because we experience it
with our senses. We also know that we exist, because our sense
of beingness, of "I am", is the most fundamental aspect of our
everyday experience. Our existence is not something that's
open for debate. Nor is it something that somebody had to tell
us one day. That we exist is a self-evident fact.

The problem occurs when we misplace our sense of "I am".
Instead of understanding ourselves to be the knower of the
field, we identify with the body and mind, which, as material components, belong to the field. Because our sorrow arises
from a case of false superimposition—mistaking mithya for
satya—the problem is lack of discrimination, and the only solution is discrimination.

Enlightenment is nothing but the shifting of our identity
from the body/mind/ego to the awareness in which they appear. As we have already established, this awareness, which is
the nature of the Self, is free from lack and limitation and is
eternal and all-pervading like space.

That's why the ability to discriminate the objects from the
subject, the transient from the eternal, is the key to freedom.
This is a core part of Vedantic teaching and practice. The term
for it is atma-anatma viveka, which means discriminating the
Self from that which is not the Self. By knowing ourselves to

be pure awareness, we are no longer bound by the shackles of mortality and the pain inherent in believing ourselves to be a limited, incomplete entity helplessly at the mercy of a cruel external world.

You Escape the Snake by Realising There is No Snake

The tricky part in claiming the knowledge of ourselves as the all-pervading Self is that, as jivas, we experience constant limitation. Owing to maya, the infinite is perceived as finite, and the formless, limitless Self appears bound by form and limitation.

The oft-cited example in Vedanta is the analogy of the snake and the rope. As you may recall, late at night, a weary traveller freezes in fear upon catching sight of a snake at the edge of the well, apparently poised to strike. It's not until another man arrives with a lantern that he realises that the 'snake' is, in fact, a piece of coiled rope.

The snake, which seemed so real to the man that his heart seized and his body trembled in terror, was merely the product of ignorance. Only the light of knowledge can dispel such ignorance. To know the truth of reality, the traveler needed to discriminate between the apparent and the actual; the appearance of the snake and the actuality of the rope.

Although as the Self we are immortal and unbound, the mind takes what it perceives to be real. Thus, through ignorance, we assume the limitations and sorrows of a mortal form and, in our delirious attempts to free ourselves, become chained to the wheel of samsara.

In this, we're no different from the traveller mistaking the rope for a snake. In actuality, the snake is nothing but a projection, a trick of the mind, but the resultant fear and panic is most certainly real. It's only by careful discrimination that we remove this projection and realise that our suffering was based on nothing more than delusion.

An Inquiry Into Existence

For any superimposition to occur, there must first be a ground onto which the mind projects its delusion. The form of the snake is projected onto the rope, thus the rope 'lends' its existence to the non-existent snake.

This notion of borrowed existence is an important one. Back in chapter two, we defined the Self as satya and all objects as mithya. Satya, you may recall, means that which is self-existent; the independent cause out of which the dependent effect (mithya) arises. Satya means 'real', and mithya 'unreal'. Mithya is unreal because, like the snake in our example, it has no inherent existence of its own.

Another metaphor Vedanta often uses is of gold and jewellery. Let's imagine that I show you a piece of jewellery. You might say, "what a nice gold bangle." Notice that the word 'gold' is used as an adjective to describe the bangle. Our natural assumption is that the bangle has an inherent existence of its own, of which 'gold' is simply an attribute.

In actuality, it's the other way around. Gold isn't a property of the bangle—rather, the bangle is a property of the gold! The bangle has no existence outside of the gold. 'Bangle' is simply a name given to the gold in a particular form. So it would be more accurate to call it 'bangly gold' than 'gold bangle'. If I were to melt it down, the bangle would disappear and the gold alone would remain. The gold, therefore, is satya, the essence, and the bangle is mithya, an incidental attribute. The only existence the bangle had was entirely borrowed from the gold.

So it is with the field and the knower. An effect cannot exist independently of, or in isolation to, its cause. Every phenomenon, every object in the field, must necessarily be the result of a cause. The world of objects, therefore, has no independent existence of its own. As mithya (a dependent effect), it is entirely dependent upon satya (the independent cause) for its existence, just as the snake depends on the rope for its existence and the bangle the gold.

When you look around a room and see various objects: such as a clock, a light, a window, a door, the natural assumption is that each of these objects has an existence of its own. The clock exists, you might say. However, if you were to analyse the clock, you'll find it is simply an assemblage of various parts. Where is the actual 'clock'? 'Clock' is just a name given to a certain configuration of metal, glass and plastic.

Existence is not an attribute of objects themselves. Existence doesn't come from objects. Objects come from existence. Existence is the noumenon from which phenomena arise; the substratum from which the world of name and form derives its existence.

Because our senses are hooked to the world of objects—and the subject, awareness, is not an object of perception—the average person is completely unaware of the formless substratum that is the Self. Ignorance obscures our perception and the ego superimposes "I-ness" onto the inert objects of the field, namely the body and mind, while oblivious to the one independent principle that brings it all to life—the Self; which is Existence itself.

The Field Appears in the Knower

In all that exists, its existence belongs to the Self alone, as both the essence and the substance of creation.

Thus, in ultimate analysis, the field and the knower are revealed to be non-separate. If the Self is truly limitless and non-dual, then nothing can exist outside of it. Therefore, the field can't be a separate principle, but must exist as part of the knower.

Krishna says: "Liberation comes to he who sees unity in diversity; who understands the manifold forms of the world are all expressions of the one Self."

The world of form appears within awareness like a dream arising in the mind. Just as the dream has no existence apart from the dreamer, the field has no existence apart from the Self.

Returning to our clock analogy, an inquisitive person might take the clock to bits to try to find which part of it makes it a 'clock'. But the clock has no existence outside of its component parts. You could use the most powerful microscope available and you'll find that no object has any inherent substance of its own. Every object in the field is ultimately reduced to nothing but space. And where does this space appear? In awareness. Awareness is the one thing you can never get rid of; the one thing that you can never objectify, modify or eliminate in any way.

Action and Actionlessness Revisited

Toward the end of the chapter, Krishna again makes it clear that the Self is neither the doer of action, nor is it affected by the results of actions. The Self can no more act than space can act. Indeed, as Krishna tells Arjuna:

> Just as space pervades the cosmos and remains unaffected by whatever takes place within it, so too, is the Self unaffected by whatever happens within it. Just as the sun illumines the entire world, so too, does the Self illumine the entire field.

Action is generated by the field of prakriti when enlivened by the animating consciousness of purusha. Like the sun illumining the Earth, the Self is that by which all action happens, while itself remaining ever actionless.

Swami Dayananda elaborates:

> It is the nature of prakriti to engage itself in action. When a person says "I do," it is due to ignorance—for atma is akarta (actionless). For the ignorant, the actions of the sense organs, mind, and organs of action are superimposed upon atma and they believe they perform action and are affected by the results.

The ignorant assume themselves to be the doer of all actions, even though the ego (the sense of doership) is only one among many factors responsible for action. After all, isn't it true that the eyes automatically see, the ears automatically hear, and the tongue automatically tastes? Yet, the self-ignorant person will say, "I see," "I hear," and "I taste." In actual fact, the "I" is being superimposed onto these bodily functions.

In reality, the ego's sense of doership and ownership is an erroneous projection; a superimposition of satya upon mithya. By knowing that all action belongs to mithya, and that, as the Self, you are free of mithya, you attain liberation.

Fix Your Mind on the Self Alone

Krishna states that with a sufficiently pure mind, one can attain liberation by meditating upon His words. Most people, however, will need to take the longer route by first practicing karma yoga and upasana meditation in order to tame and refine the mind.

When you have cultivated a mature and contemplative mind, you then are ready for the three-fold teaching methodology of Vedanta. To recap, you first hear the teaching, work through any doubts or confusion and then apply this knowledge to the mind in a rigorous and consistent manner.

This final stage is a process that cannot be skipped. After all, once you eat a meal, the food must be fully digested. It can take only a few hours to hear the teaching of Vedanta, but it may take years to fully assimilate the knowledge. It's this assimilation of Self-Knowledge that liberates the mind. Until the knowledge is actualised, it will have little impact on the ignorance-induced sufferings caused by the samsaric mind. To use a modern analogy, you can download new software for your computer, but it won't do anything at all until you properly install it.

Being hard-wired as it is, ignorance will manifest in a seemingly endless number of ways. That's why sustained effort is required to keep the mind qualified and to shift its point of identification from the ephemeral to the eternal.

One way of doing this is the practice of subject-object discrimination, the core teaching of this chapter. By discriminating the field from the knower of the field, you re-train your mind to identify as the Self, rather than the body, mind and ego.

All thoughts conditioned by ignorance—particularly any thoughts of self-limitation, lack and inadequacy—must be subject to the rigorous application of self-inquiry.

Unfortunately, old habits die hard. Left unchecked, the mind will simply keep replicating its existing thought patterns, reactions and habits. Your job is to initiate the process of change by questioning every self-ignorant thought and replacing it with the opposite thought. Tending to the garden of your mind, you must patiently weed out thoughts of ignorance and replace them with thoughts of truth.

It's not by chance that Krishna refers to the mind and body as 'the field'. A field is a piece of land used for planting seeds and growing crops. In the same way, the mind and body are fields in which we sow the seeds of our future karma—in the form of our thoughts, values, actions and habits—which will in turn determine our future lives. It is through the body and mind that we reap this future karma.

As well as taking proper care of the field, we must tackle the root problem of superimposing "I-ness" onto the field—of believing the rope to be a snake—which is the direct cause of samsara. The treatment is found not by trying to remove the symptoms, but by tackling the underlying cause. That's why, if ignorance is to be resolved, only knowledge will do the job.

In the closing verse, Krishna makes a promise: "Those who understand the distinction between the field and the knower of the field achieve freedom from the bondage of material existence and attain the ultimate goal." So ends one of the Gita's most challenging yet important chapters.

CHAPTER FOURTEEN

The Gunas

1-2 Krishna said, "I shall again share with you the highest knowledge, by which one attains liberation. It is by Self-knowledge alone that one reclaims their unity with Me and is freed from birth and death. Those who have realised their oneness with Me are not reborn into the creation, nor do they perish at the time of its dissolution.

3-4 "My maya is the primordial cause out of which all things are created and sustained. Everything born comes from the womb of prakriti, and the seed of all creation is from Me. I am, therefore, the father of all manifestation.

5 "Arjuna, it is the three gunas of prakriti—sattva, rajas, and tamas—that bind the changeless indweller to the body.

6-8 "Sattva, which is pure, luminous and free from affliction, binds by attachment to happiness, beauty and knowledge. Rajas colours the mind with passion, craving and attachment. It binds the indweller of the body by a compulsive need for action. Tamas is born of ignorance and covers the mind with delusion and confusion. It binds one by doubt, indifference and sloth.

9 "Sattva causes bondage to pleasure, rajas causes bondage to action, and tamas causes bondage to apathy by distorting the mind and senses."

10 "When sattva predominates, rajas and tamas recede. When rajas dominates, sattva and tamas recede. When tamas predominates, sattva and rajas recede.

11-13 "With sattva, the mind and senses are clear, allowing for knowledge and illumination. When rajas predominates, a person is overcome by greed, restlessness and compulsive action. Dullness, laziness and indifference result when tamas is predominant.

14-15 "When the body dies, if one has a sattvic disposition, he or she enters the pure worlds of the wise. Those whose minds are rajasic when they die will be reborn with a strong compulsion toward action. Those with a predominance of tamas will be reborn into the wombs of those lacking discrimination and wisdom.

16-18 "The fruit of sattvic actions is virtuous and results in pure knowledge. Rajasic actions yield suffering and greed. Tamasic actions result in ignorance and delusion. Those abiding in sattva evolve upward, those who abide in rajas remain where they are, and those belonging to tamas degenerate.

19-20 "The wise understand that all action is the result of the gunas. Knowing him or herself to be beyond the gunas, he or she understands My nature and attains liberation. By transcending the gunas, which are the cause of the body, one is released from birth, death, old age and sorrow, and gains immortality."

21 Arjuna said, "Oh Lord, what are the characteristics of someone who has transcended these three gunas? How do they act, and how have they managed to transcend these three qualities?"

22 Krishna said, "Such people are not averse to any state of mind. They are unmoved by the harmony of sattva, the compulsiveness of rajas or the delusion of tamas. Nor do they crave particular states of mind.

23-25 "They remain impartial and unperturbed by the interplay of the gunas. Knowing the gunas alone to be the agent of action, they abide in their own nature as actionless and changeless awareness. Thus established within themselves, they see all things with equal vision: pleasure and pain, positive and negative situations, praise and criticism, friends and enemies. A clod of earth, a stone, or a lump of gold are no different to them. Such a person, having relinquished all self-directed undertakings and dedicated themselves to worshipping and seeking Me with unswerving devotion, has transcended the gunas and is qualified for liberation.

26 "Indeed, I am the abode of the limitless Self which is immortal and unchanging, the eternal dharma, the support of all

things and source of the ever-lasting joy that is not subject to sorrow."

COMMENTARY

Krishna begins chapter fourteen by summarising the previous chapter's topic: the nature of prakriti and purusha. He states that, born of the power of His maya, it's the union of these principles—matter and consciousness—that gives birth to the universe of form. Like the sperm and egg, these two factors unite to produce the phenomenal reality.

Having already explored the nature of consciousness in depth, this chapter turns its attention to the material aspect of prakriti.

Prakriti is comprised of what we call the gunas—the three qualities, or 'threads', woven by Ishvara to create the tapestry of the phenomenal universe. As the building blocks of the creation, these gunas constitute, shape and determine the nature of all phenomena, including our bodies and minds.

While ultimately everything is the Self alone—pure consciousness/existence—at the empirical level of maya, all beings and all forms are subject to the gunas. That's why it's essential for the spiritual inquirer to have a clear understanding of how these forces work and how they can be mastered and eventually transcended.

Maya in Hard Form

If Ishvara could be likened to the great artist of the cosmos, the gunas are the three colours with which He/She paints the universe. All material forms, whether gross or subtle, are the product of these gunas.

The word guna has no direct equivalent in English. Translations include 'thread', 'cord', 'rope', or 'quality'. Some people may find it easier to think of them as the three basic 'energies' of creation.

Much as cotton threads combine to form a shirt, the 'threads' of these gunas constitute the field of material existence. And, like a rope, the gunas seemingly bind us to matter. Swami Chinmayananda, in his book The Holy Gita, explains:

The gunas are born of matter. Produced by the 'field', they generate a feeling of attachment and successfully delude the indwelling Self and chain it, as it were, to the cycle of birth and death in a stream of constant change and pain. Like cords, they seemingly bind the Spirit to matter and create, in the Infinite Spirit, the painful sense of limitation and sorrow.

"This delusion," Swamiji adds, "is maintained in each of us by the play of these three gunas."

The gunas, then, as maya in hard form, are responsible for avidya. Avidya is the deep rooted self-ignorance that keeps us misidentified as a limited body and mind rather than the boundless awareness in which they appear.

As long as you inhabit this world, you necessarily possess a gross and subtle body, and these instruments are composed of—and are constantly shaped and conditioned by—the interplay of the gunas. Every aspect of prakriti is determined by their play, from the atoms of your body to the birth and death of stars, planets, and galaxies.

Because there's no escaping the effect of the gunas, even for the enlightened, the secret is therefore learning to understand and manage these qualities, wielding them to your advantage rather than being an unwitting victim to them.

The Three Gunas

Present in all things in varying degrees and combinations, the three gunas are called *sattva, rajas* and *tamas*.

Sattva is the highest and most refined of the three qualities. Because energy in its purest form is light, sattva is often depicted as being a luminous white light.

If sattva is energy at rest, then rajas is energy in dynamic motion; responsible for movement, change and activity. Finally, as the densest of the three qualities, tamas enables energy to be condensed into mass or matter. Therefore, each of the gunas plays an important role in the creation and sustenance of the world.

Sattva is characterised by balance, clarity, and the capacity for clear knowledge. When sattva predominates in the mind, you experience a sense of peace, brightness, happiness, creativity, friendliness and the desire to know and understand.

Rajas is the mode of activity and passion. Whereas sattva, owing to its reflective capacity, opens the mind to learning and knowledge, rajas orients the mind to action. This dynamic quality expresses itself in both positive and negative ways. Rajas can be positive in that it provides us with the desire, motivation and energy to undertake action. This passion, however, can also manifest as self-centred desire, ambition, greed, attachment and anger.

Tamas is associated with dullness, inertia, sloth, indifference and negativity. When tamas predominates, you feel tired and sleepy. All you'll want to do is laze around, and watch television, scoff junk food and oversleep. Whereas rajas extroverts the mind, tamas obscures it. It becomes difficult to see things with clarity, much less to discriminate and make decisions. As with the other two qualities, tamas has its place and function. Tamas is essential for us to rest and enjoy a good night's sleep.

The Capacity to Bind

Each of these qualities has the potential to bind the jiva. Even sattva, as pleasing as it is, can cause bondage through attachment to knowledge, learning and purity. The predominantly sattvic person values peace, harmony and quietude above all else. They find it very difficult when their much-cherished serenity is shattered. If you've ever seen someone in a library get outrageously agitated and angry when somebody makes a noise, you'll understand attachment to sattva.

A rajasic mind is prone to almost unquenchable desire and longing. The tormented rajasic soul is never satisfied. No matter what they possess, there's always something better out there and they are filled with the unrelenting determination to get it. However, almost the moment they attain it, their mind immediately locks onto something else—something different, better, and more exciting. This driving passion and desire can lead the rajasic person to compromise and violate dharma in all kinds of ways. This always results in pain and suffering.

Tamas binds through ignorance and inertia. When tamas predominates, both knowledge and action become exceedingly difficult. Unable to think clearly, the tamasic person will have little energy or drive and virtually everything in life becomes a struggle. Whereas excess rajas can lead to conditions such as anxiety, high blood pressure and insomnia, excess tamas leads to apathy and depression.

Three Buckets
A good analogy for understanding the gunas and the way they affect the mind and body is to think of three buckets of water sitting in the sun.

1. Sattva
Let's imagine the first bucket of water is clean, clear and completely still. Free of impurity or agitation, this water is the perfect medium for the light to shine. That's why sattva has a revealing quality. A sattvic mind is capable of seeing things as they actually are. It's only then that true knowledge is possible.

2. Rajas
The second bucket has been shaken and moved about, making the water choppy and unsettled. Although you can see sunlight reflected on the water surface, you might mistakenly conclude that the light is in motion because the water itself is moving. Therefore, a mind under the influence of rajas, the projecting guna, has partial knowledge but it isn't accurate due to the agitated quality of the reflecting medium.

3. Tamas
The third bucket is thick with mud. Even though the sun is shining, it's impossible to see any reflection in the water because it's too muddy, cloudy and murky. Because tamas obscures the light, it's extremely difficult to gain knowledge. The mind, filled with impurity, is incapable of perceive anything with clarity.

How to Tell Which Guna is Predominant

Each guna can be known by its effects in the body and mind. However, while people may be predisposed to a particular guna, these qualities are constantly changing and cycling throughout the course of the day.

As the gunas exert their particular influence, our mood, energy levels and our thoughts and feelings are affected accordingly. For instance, tamas sends us to sleep at night and rajas wakes us up in the morning. During the day, sattva helps us to know what is to be done and rajas gives us the motivation and energy to do it.

While a balance between the three is necessary, the cultivation of a sattvic mind is essential for all spiritual seekers, and anyone who wants to live a healthy, balanced and happy life. Krishna says that when sattva predominates, the mind and senses are clear, reflective and fit for the attainment of knowledge.

Because knowledge is the key to liberation, all spiritual practice is geared toward cultivating a pure and sattvic mind. Such a mind is open, relaxed and naturally inclined to dharma and spiritual advancement.

A mind under the sway of rajas is easy to recognise. The rajasic mind is active, restless, and prone to dissatisfaction. Driven by insatiable longing and desire, the rajasic person is always hooked onto some goal or another, and is subject to continual agitation, anger and frustration. A highly rajasic person can't even sit still for a moment without fidgeting. The rajasic mind knows little peace—only a steady stream of avarice, desire and anxiety. The fruits of excess rajas are greed and pain, and the inability to progress spiritually.

Tamas can be recognised as dullness, laziness, inertia and indifference towards performing action of any kind. Excess tamas clouds the mind in a narcotic haze. This makes it exceptionally difficult to see things clearly, and so the tamasic person is prone to delusion and erroneous conclusions. This creates indecision and difficulty with regards to initiating any endeavour. Even the simplest action becomes a struggle. The consequence of tamas, then, is ignorance and inaction. Whereas sattva enables spiritual growth and rajas blocks such advancement, tamas leads to spiritual deterioration.

An Objective Inventory

The proportion of the gunas not only determines the quality of your experience in this life but, according to the Gita, your next life as well.

In terms of basic cause and effect, the condition of your mind today is a product of your thoughts, actions and behaviour yesterday, and the days, months and years preceeding that.

The subtle body is a malleable instrument. Indulging rajasic and tamasic patterns for any length of time imprints the subtle body and naturally generates more of the same. That's why your next birth will be determined by the quality of your subtle body now. It is, after all, the same subtle body that transmigrates to a new gross body.

As a seeker of liberation, it's essential to take an objective inventory of how the gunas are conditioning your body, mind and intellect. If you find yourself prone to rajasic or tamasic tendencies, it's important to learn to manage and minimise these gunas and cultivate a greater proportion of sattva.

Guna Management

The previous chapter stated that all action is a product of the field and this chapter clarifies that the field is comprised of the the gunas. As Swami Dayananda explains:

> Action is done by the body-mind-sense complex, which is born of maya, consisting of the three gunas. Being awake to the nature of the Self, which performs no action, one sees that there is no agent [of action] other than the gunas.

All action is, therefore, driven and determined by the gunas, which, furthering our discussion of action and doership from chapter four's commentary, you might think of as Ishvara in motion.

This should not engender an attitude of resignation or fatalism, however. You don't have to be a victim to the gunas. Rather, you can learn to actively manage them. That, as it happens, is the entire purpose of spiritual practice.

Our experience is shaped by what we do. Every aspect of our lives, from our lifestyle to our diet, choice of work, home environment, media exposure and circle of friends has a profound effect on the way we think and feel.

A rajasic lifestyle conditions the mind to excess rajas, and we must endure the resultant anxiety, dissatisfaction, craving and greed. Similarly, tamasic life choices inevitably leave us feeling lethargic, demotivated and depressed.

Moksha necessitates a predominantly sattvic mind. Only a sattvic mind is capable of properly receiving and assimilating Self-knowledge. That's why it's necessary to examine all aspects of your life and commit to cultivating sattva in every way that you can.

The good news is that sattva isn't actually something that you need to 'add' to yourself. The mind is by its very nature sattvic. If it wasn't, it wouldn't be able to reflect the light of consciousness. Swami Dayananda notes that, "Every human being has enough sattva to make him self-conscious, and enough rajas and tamas to cause confusion."

All that you need to do is to learn to manage and minimise excess rajas and tamas. This is done using the spiritual practices unfolded in the Gita: following dharma, and practising karma yoga and upasana yoga, or meditation upon Ishvara as the cause and substance of the cosmos. Actively managing and transcending the gunas is called *triguna vibhava yoga*. The concluding chapters explore this yoga of the three gunas in greater detail.

A Line of Progression

Swami Paramarthananda says that the entire spiritual path is "a gradual journey from tamas to rajas to sattva." Indeed, the gunas work in a line of progression. When you find yourself overcome by tamas, it's almost impossible to jump straight into a purely sattvic state. You must first cultivate some rajas to burn off the excess tamas.

As you may recall from chapter twelve's commentary, the spiritual path consists of five sequential stages. It begins with karma yoga motivated by personal desire. Because tamas leads to apathy and demotivation, the initial stage actually endorses the pursuit of personal desire. A deliberate injection of desire, which is rajasic in nature, helps offset the deadening effect of tamas and stirs the aspirant into action.

The next stage of spiritual practice is to convert desire-prompted karma yoga to nishkama karma yoga, which means action unmotivated by personal desire. By now, you've recognised that moksha alone leads to liberation, so your actions are now consecrated to Ishvara and done not as a means of achieving desires, but as a way of purifying the mind by neutralising its binding likes and dislikes.

The following stage is to practice upasana yoga, or meditation upon Ishvara/the Self, which helps to master and refine the rajasic tendencies of the mind. The aim is now to convert this rajas to sattva.

When the mind is sufficiently sattvic, the final stage is jnana yoga, the yoga of self-knowledge. The inquirer must now follow the three stages of Vedantic practice: listening to the teaching (shravana), reflecting and removing doubts (manana) and then applying and internalising the knowledge "I am awareness" (nididhyasana).

How to Transcend the Gunas

At the level of maya, there's no escaping the gunas. The jiva, the body-mind-sense complex invested with a sense of "I", is forever subject to their effects. Even a highly sattvic person remains subject to the influence of rajas and tamas.

But it is possible to transcend them, and that's what Krishna addresses in the final section of this chapter. You transcend the gunas by knowing that, as the Self, you are already beyond them.

As Vedanta makes explicitly clear, you are not the jiva. The jiva's body and mind are instruments used by you, awareness, for transacting with the world of form. Just as a boat will carry you across a lake, the body and mind are nothing more than vehicles for navigating the world.

The application of Self-knowledge means affirming that you are neither the body or mind. These are objects known to you. They belong to the field of prakriti—of which you, awareness, being of a higher order of reality, are independent.

As long as you identify with the body and mind, you claim their attributes as your own, and its problems become your problems. Rather than seeing the body as fat, you think, "I am fat". Rather than seeing illness as a predicament of the body, you believe, "I am ill." This is the mutual superimposition at the heart of samsara: projecting the subject (awareness) onto the object and superimposing the attributes of the objects onto the subject.

Owing to this false superimposition, the ignorant readily identify with the gunas and their effects. They believe that the restless agitation of rajas and the lethargic daze of tamas some-how belongs to them.

However, Krishna makes it clear that by knowing yourself to be beyond the gunas, you come to realise your nature as aware-ness and will thus attain liberation. The Self is that by which the gunas function. But, like space, which pervades all things, it remains ever-unaffected by them.

Swami Chinmayananda writes that the sorrows of matter, such as birth, growth, disease and pain "belong to matter and not the consciousness illumining it. One who has realised him-self to be awareness transcends all these sorrows."

That's why transcendence is the key. You don't have to get rid of the gunas because, in fact, at the level of maya, you can't. But, as the Self, you are already free of them.

Knowing this, your attitude towards them changes. The en-lightened accept that the body and mind function according to their nature. The mind naturally fluctuates and disturbances inevitably happen. What changes is your reaction to these fluctuations.

Most of our suffering comes not from the mind's natural re-action to events, situations or the influence of the gunas, but from our reaction to our reaction. We feel bad about feeling bad! We resist the state of our mind and berate ourselves for having reacted. This only leads to frustration, anger, grief, depression and endless self-recrimination.

It is the nature of all things, including the body and mind, to be as they are. Problems only arise when we fail to accept this; when we find ourselves at friction with reality.

With clear Self-knowledge, we remain rooted in our nature as awareness. We no longer resist the fluctuating states of the mind or the various favourable and unfavourable conditions of life. Our vision moves from the subjective to the objective and we enjoy *samatvam*, or evenness and imperturbability of mind.

It's not that we *become* free of the gunas. Rather, we recognise that, as awareness, we are already free. We see the gunas for what they are— impersonal forces by which the world turns and by which all action happens—and know that, as the Self, we are always free, taintless, and untouched by anything in this world.

CHAPTER FIFTEEN

The Supreme Being

¹Krishna said, "The sages liken maya to the imperishable *ashvat-tha* tree, with its roots above in awareness, and its limbs stretching below into the world of man. On its branches, the Vedas grow as leaves. The one who knows this is a knower of Truth.

² "Nourished by the gunas, its foliage spreads upwards and downwards, with the sense objects growing as buds. Secondary roots, the karmas, reach down into the world of mortals, binding them to the wheel of death and rebirth.

³⁻⁴ "The true form of this tree is imperceptible to those on earth. It has no beginning, no end, and no visible source. You must cut its well-entrenched roots with the sharpened axe of detachment! Then approach the path from which no return is necessary—the path of Self-inquiry. Seek and surrender to That from which this entire creation has come.

⁵ "Relinquishing the need for respect, surrendering attachment and binding desires, and being even-minded with regard to the duality of pleasure and suffering, fix your mind on the Self and you will attain that eternal goal.

⁶ "Neither the sun, nor the moon, nor fire can add further illumination to the light of My limitless abode. Those who enter it do not return to separate existence.

⁷⁻⁹ "In the world of form, a part of Me exists as the jiva, the indweller of the body, and it is eternal. When the indweller leaves the body, it gathers the mind and the five senses and enters a new body, taking these with it just as the wind carries the fragrance of a flower far from its source. With the use of the ears, eyes, the senses of touch, taste, smell, and the mind, this eternal jiva experiences the sense objects anew.

¹⁰ "The deluded fail to see the one who, acting via the gunas, experiences through the body and then departs when the body ceases. Only those with the eye of Knowledge see the truth.

¹¹ "Those who resolutely purify their mind through yoga are able to see the Self shining through the minds of all. Those whose minds are immature and who lack discrimination, may seek but will ultimately fail to recognise this innermost Self.

¹²⁻¹⁴ "May you know that the brilliance of the sun that illumines the entire world, the radiance of the moon, and the heat of fire all come from Me. I am in the earth, sustaining all beings with my strength; I nourish all vegetation and dwell within all beings as the essence and life-giving breath. I am also the fire in the stomach which digests all food and sustains life.

¹⁵ "I am in the hearts of all. I give the power to remember, to know and to forget. I am the object of all knowledge in the scriptures. I am the author of the Vedanta. I am the knower, the known and the knowing.

¹⁶⁻¹⁷ "Two orders of reality pertain to this world: the perishable and the imperishable. All separate forms and elements are called perishable, and the changeless unmanifest is imperishable. Beyond these is the limitless Self, the changeless Lord animating and bringing life to the three worlds.

¹⁸ "I am the supreme Self, renowned by the scriptures as beyond both the changing and the changeless.

¹⁹ "Those beyond delusion, with the wisdom to know Me as the totality; gain Me as the Self of all.

²⁰ "I have shared this most profound teaching with you, Arjuna. By assimilating this knowledge, you attain enlightenment and accomplish all that is to be accomplished in this life."

COMMENTARY

The Gita's fifteenth chapter succinctly condenses the essence of Vedanta into a mere twenty verses. Krishna provides insight into the nature of samsara, the means of escaping it, and again explores the nature of the jiva, the field and the all-pervading Self.

These are topics that have been dealt with previously, of course. It's important to note that repetition is an essential part of the teaching process. Subtle truths must often be repeated a number of times, and in different ways, in order for the mind to fully grasp and assimilate what is being taught.

The Tree of Samsara

Krishna likens samsara to the ashvattha tree, a type of fig tree known for its dense foliage and secondary aerial roots. This 'tree of samsara', he says, has its roots above, while its trunk, branches and leaves plunge down into the material world beneath. This is a metaphor borrowed from the Katha Upanishad:

> The ancient tree of life has its roots above
> And its branches below on earth.
> Its pure root is the Immortal Brahman,
> From whom all the worlds draw their life,
> And whom none can transcend.
> The entire cosmos issues from Brahman
> And by his power alone it reverberates,
> Like thunder crashing in the sky.

This tree's roots are not in the earth, but above, in the Self; the universal consciousness from which all life has its being.

The pervading scientific paradigm of our modern age still hinges on the assumptions of the Newtonian materialist. It purports that the universe was somehow created from the bottom up; from the gross to the subtle. According to Vedanta, however, such a reductionistic analysis gets things literally upside down! As can even be inferred from the Big Bang, the cosmos evolves from the top down; from the subtle to the gross. The cosmos began as energy, and this energy then condensed to create the atoms, form and structure of the physical universe.

The subtlest of the subtle, and beyond all objectification, is the Self; the invisible yet all-pervading essence of existence. The Self, courtesy of its power of maya, is at the root of creation. While the roots of a tree aren't visible, we can infer their existence by the very fact the tree exists. After all, were there no roots, there would be no tree. Similarly, while the roots of the tree of samsara aren't visible, the world of form must necessarily have a cause, and that cause is the Self.

The branches of this tree grow far and wide and the buds take the form of the various sense objects that capture our attention. Krishna likens its foliage to the Vedas, the ancient scriptures relating to karma, dharma and ritual action. Just as leaves are essential for the life and growth of the tree, so are our actions necessary to the cycle of creation.

Our preset actions, themselves a product of our past action, in turn become the seeds of our future karma. Every action that we take is influenced by and further strengthens the vasanas. This cycle of action and reaction which keeps us bound to the material world is likened to a set of secondary roots, which in the case of the ashvattha tree can grow almost as thick as the trunk.

As our actions strengthen these roots, the fruits of our karma grow upon the branches of this tree. Some of these fruits are sweet, and others bitter. In a world of duality, it's impossible to have one without the other, so the jiva is subject to both happiness and sorrow.

The Upanishads liken the jiva to a bird perched upon a tree branch, hungrily pecking at the fruits of samsara. Like a bird, we have the ability to move up or down the branches of this tree. Moving down the tree of samsara brings us closer to the material world, where we risk falling deeper under the spell of maya; ever-more driven by our desires and aversions, and enmeshed in the delusion of separation.

Ascending the tree, on the other hand, brings progress in our spiritual path, as we come closer to the realisation of our true nature as pure awareness.

The Axe of Detachment

Fortunately, like any tree, the tree of samsara is vulnerable to the blade. Krishna exhorts Arjuna to cut it at the roots with "the sharpened axe of detachment!"

Detachment in this case means ceasing to falsely invest the world of objects with a sense of 'me' and 'my-ness'. It means discriminating between the subject and the objects; between satya and mithya. Swami Dayananda explains it as follows:

> By distinguishing between the subject and object, the erroneous identification of oneself with the physical body, senses and mind is withdrawn. The axe of detachment is the enquiry into the nature of the Self and not-self. With this, the tree of samsara is felled.

This ability to exercise discrimination is crucial to Self-knowledge. Because samsara is a tree of self-ignorance, it can only be destroyed by knowledge—specifically, Self-knowledge.

When you know who you are, you must then divest all sense of identification with the world of form and objects, including the body and mind, and place it where it belongs: the pure awareness/consciousness of the Self. Only this will destroy samsara at its root.

Like any great tree, you're unlikely to fell it with a single strike. In fact, it may take repeated swings of the axe. You must do this by applying self-inquiry to the mind with rigorous consistency.

Like the 'snake' in the rope, samsara has no inherent existence. It's a superimposition born of ignorance of the nature of Reality. Such a superimposition has no beginning or end. You can't say that the 'snake' has a beginning, because it was never there to begin with. Because it was never there to begin with, it can't logically have an end, either. All that was ever there was a delusion in the mind, and all it takes to remove that delusion is knowledge.

Mental Preparation is Everything

In order to know the Self, we must learn to see with the eyes of objectivity. In our ignorance, we 'lose' ourselves in the mithya world by associating 'I', the subject, with the world of objects appearing in us. Not only that, but we superimpose false values and attributes upon those objects, believing that they're somehow capable of bringing us lasting happiness and wholeness.

Objectivity means stripping the world of our subjective superimpositions. Only then can we see with clear vision.

As we've established, such 'divine vision' requires a mature and contemplative mind. In this chapter, Krishna again enumerates some of the qualifications vital to the cultivation of such a mind, starting with dispassion and freedom from slavery to the opinions and approval of others.

The seeker of liberation must weed out such insecurities by mastering the mind and converting binding desires and attachments into non-binding preferences. A mind gripped by binding likes and dislikes is a veritable battleground, with little capacity for sustained contemplation.

Only a tranquil mind unperturbed by samsara's duality of pleasure and pain can rest in steady contemplation of the Self. Such a mind, tamed by the practise of karma yoga and upasana meditation, is then ready for Vedanta's threefold discipline of listening, reasoning and integrating the teaching.

The Heart of All Beings

The deluded, Krishna says, are those whose minds are incapable of seeing Reality as it truly is. The gunas, specifically the merry dance of rajas and tamas, keep such souls bound to a strictly surface-level understanding of reality. Such materialists, seeing only what is visibly real, remain ignorant of what makes it all possible: the underlying substratum of existence that is the imperishable and all-pervading Self.

The phenomenal world has no independent existence of its own any more than the pot exists separately from the clay. An effect cannot exist independently of its cause. Therefore, this entire universe is inseparable from its cause—the Self, which is the foundation and basis of all that exists.

The heart of this chapter is a meditation upon the nature of this Self, echoing the poetic words of the Mundaka Upanishad:

> The Lord of Love [Brahman] is above name and form.
> He is present in all and transcends all.
> Unborn, without body and mind,
> From him, comes every body and mind. [...]
> Bright but hidden, the Self dwells in the heart.
> Everything that moves, breathes, opens and closes
> Lives in the Self.

From the perspective of the jiva, it's true to say that the Self dwells in the hearts of all beings as the innermost spark of life and sentience. It grants life, light and knowledge to the inert field of matter.

From the vantage point of the Self, however, it's more accurate to say that all beings exist in the Self. After all, the Self is the only factor in reality; the all-pervading 'one without a second'. Therefore, all beings exist within this universal consciousness. How could anything exist outside of that which is all-pervading?

By the power of maya, this indivisible, formless consciousness appears as a divisible universe of form—and, thus, out of non-duality, we experience a realm of apparent duality.

The Light of All Lights

Vedanta often uses the analogy of light to describe the Self. In this context, light is that by which things are perceived and known. As the light of all lights, consciousness is that by which physical objects are known, and also that which illumines our thoughts and dreams. The radiance of the sun comes and goes, but the light of consciousness is eternal, ever shining, self-luminous and self sustaining.

As another great verse from the Mundaka Upanishad states:

> Know [the Self] as the radiant light of lights.
> There shines not the sun, nor moon, nor star,
> Nor flash of lightning, nor fire lit on earth.
> The Lord is the light reflected by all.
> He shining, everything shines after him.

Krishna goes on to examine the nature of the jiva.

By themselves, the body and mind are, like all things in the field of matter, inert, insentient and perishable. When illumined by the consciousness of the Self, these instruments are granted life, courtesy of this reflected consciousness.

When this body-mind apparatus is no longer capable of functioning in its reflecting capacity, it appears to us as though the light is withdrawn and the physical form perishes. However, the consciousness enlivening the subtle body, like a caterpillar moving from one blade of grass to another, simply moves to another body.

Therefore, you might say that the gross and subtle bodies act as a mirror; a reflecting medium for the light of consciousness. A mirror, when blessed by the light of the sun, is capable of illuminating a dark room. Although it's the sun providing the illumination, the sun doesn't illumine the room directly. A reflecting medium, in this case the mirror, is needed to shine the light. This mirror represents the jiva's body and mind, which, by the light of consciousness, are granted sentience, enabling the world of maya to be experienced.

The Proof of Existence

By itself, awareness or consciousness is incapable of transacting with the world, for it is indivisible and formless. On the other hand, because matter is by itself inert, it is incapable of independent transaction. The union of the two, however, allows consciousness to function in the world through the reflecting mediums of the body and mind.

Krishna again makes reference to prakriti, which he divides into two categories: the perishable and the imperishable, or the manifest and the unmanifest.

The manifest is the ever-changing world of objects as perceptible to the senses. This world of gross and subtle matter has its basis in the causal body, or the unmanifest seed state. You might marvel at the beauty of a garden and all its wonderful colours and fragrances. It's the unseen factors beneath the soil, however, that enable the flowers and trees to exist. In the same way, the visible world has its root in the unmanifest; the invisible causal body from which all forms arise.

Beyond both the visible and the invisible, the Self is the universal consciousness 'lending' existence to the world of matter. Eternally luminous, awareness needs no other light to reveal it. Without beginning and end, it exists as the innermost 'is-ness' of all things.

The proof of its existence is existence itself. Whatever you see and experience in the world, and whatever thoughts and dreams you experience in your mind, is all made possible only by the presence and light of the Self.

To doubt the Self is to doubt your own existence. You needn't search for this Self, for it is already and always present everywhere. As That which enables you to experience everything, it exists as your innermost sense of 'I am'.

The ignorant, failing to realise this, and forever seeking the wholeness of the Self in the world of objects, are therefore subject to the endless frustrations and sorrows of samsara. The wise, however, knowing this Self to be supreme, seek it through Self-knowledge; the attainment of which liberates the mind. Such a soul, Krishna says, attains all that is to be attained in life.

CHAPTER SIXTEEN

The Two Dispositions

1 "Arjuna," Krishna said, "in this world, two basic dispositions prevail. One is born of sattva and the other of rajas and tamas. Cultivate a sattvic mind by being fearless, pure-minded, steadfast, generous and self-controlled. Realise the truth of the scriptures, perform rituals to purify the mind, be disciplined, unattached to objects, and keep your every thought, word and deed in alignment with truth.

2 "The sattvic person harms no one, for he has compassion for all living beings; is resolved of anger, gentle, kind, truthful, modest, tranquil and free of anger, craving and agitation.

3 "Intelligent, composed, courageous, clean and devoid of all thoughts of malice and exaggerated self-opinion, such a soul has cultivated the very qualities of the gods.

4 "On the other hand, some people are rife with demonic qualities. They act with hypocrisy with regard to dharma, displaying pride, arrogance, anger, and cruelty. They need and demand respect from others, and exhibit a fundamental lack of discrimination.

5 "The divine qualities lead to freedom and the demonic lead to bondage. Do not grieve, Arjuna, for you have attained much in the way of spiritual wealth.

6 "In this world, there are two types of people: those with divine, dharmic tendencies, and those inclined to demonic or adharmic actions. The divine I have spoken about at length. Listen to me now as I describe the adharmic.

7 "The ignorant and self-indulgent lack clear vision. They cannot distinguish between what they should do and what they should avoid doing. Their minds are impure, their conduct unbecoming, and their words untruthful.

⁸ "Staunchly materialist, they view the world as being without truth or moral order; as godless and purposeless. They see themselves as nothing more than the body and believe the cause and basis of life is sexual union.

⁹ "Such people are driven by passion and self-interest alone. Because their minds are limited, their thinking distorted and their actions cruel, they are enemies of the world.

¹⁰ "Overcome by desire, pretension, pride, and the need for respect, their actions, coloured by delusion, are destructive to themselves, others and the world around them.

¹¹⁻¹² "Driven by fear of death and diminishment, and an insatiable craving for objects of enjoyment, they believe that the only purpose in life is the gratification of their desires. They live on hope as they strive to accumulate and hoard wealth in order to satisfy their cravings.

¹³ "Ever intent on gaining this or that, they depend on what they have for their self-esteem. Wilful and competitive, they don't care who or what they have to destroy in their quest for wealth and self-gratification.

¹⁴⁻¹⁵ "I am the ruler of my life," they think. "I am successful, powerful and happy. I am from a good family and people think well of me. I perform acts of charity to show the world how good I am."

¹⁶⁻¹⁷ "But such people, ensnared by delusion and greed, and totally driven by attachment to objects and sense pleasure, inevitably suffer. Those who are self-important, vain, and prideful because of their seeming wealth and power, do good deeds only out of pretentiousness.

¹⁸ "Egotistical, aggressive, and arrogant, they are poisoned by their own lust and anger. Such people have no value for My divine virtues in themselves or in others.

¹⁹⁻²⁰ "These lowest of men, hateful and cruel, are repeatedly despatched by Me back into the wombs of those with similarly negative tendencies. Paying the price for their lack of discrimination, they fail to realise Me and continue to suffer.

²¹⁻²² "This doorway to self-destruction is three-fold and is created by desire, anger, and greed. Therefore, one should re-

nounce all three. Those who bypass these three gates to suffering and seek what is best will attain life's highest end.

23 "But the ones who, driven by binding desire, disregard the teachings of the scriptures, never attain maturity or happiness, much less enlightenment.

24 "Therefore, Arjuna, the teaching of the shastra (Vedanta) is the means of knowledge for understanding what is to be done and what is not to be done in order to attain liberation. Allow the teachings to guide you and act in accordance with them."

COMMENTARY

Chapters sixteen and seventeen are something of a departure in that they don't deal directly with the Gita's central theme of Self-knowledge. But as we have established, the fruits of this knowledge can only ripen in a suitably qualified mind. These chapters demonstrate the necessity of cultivating such a mind.

Krishna here describes two basic human temperaments—the 'divine' and the 'demonic'. The divine refers to those with a mature, dharmic and spiritually oriented disposition, while the demonic are those driven by materialistic, egoistic and adharmic tendencies.

This analysis should in no way be construed as judgemental or fatalistic. Today neuroscientists talk about the neuroplasticity of the brain. Indeed, much like a potter at the wheel, we shape and mould our mind with our every thought, word and deed.

Although the fruits of past action determine the current condition of our mind, we have a choice as to how we act in the present. It's always up to us whether we choose to adopt higher values or whether we fall prey to our lower nature and feed the ego and all of its gratuitous desires, attachments and adharmic impulses. One choice leads to liberation, and the other to ever greater suffering.

This chapter invites us to take a fearless moral inventory. By honestly assessing our predominant values, how we use our mind, how we relate to others and deal with our vasanas, desires and compulsions, we can ensure that we're living a lifestyle conducive to self-inquiry and moksha.

The Path to Maturity

At the material level, all beings are born the same. We're each given a body and mind, and we all have the same basic requirements for food, shelter and safety. Human beings and animals are no different in that regard, for we share the first two goals of life—the need for security (artha) and, to a lesser extent, the desire for pleasure (kama).

We grow up compelled to seek security and, when that is attained, our focus becomes indulging our desires for pleasure and enjoyment. Many people never progress beyond this. They live in a subjective world, driven by their likes and dislikes. Materialistic to the core, such people concern themselves only with worldly goals and ends. While they might be intelligent and educated in worldly terms, because they are ignorant of life's higher goals, they are spiritually illiterate.

As a person matures, they begin to seek more than mere sense gratification. No longer mindlessly pushed and pulled by their likes and dislikes, they commit to following dharma and cultivating spiritual values or what the Gita calls 'inner wealth.' In short, they're less focused on what they can get out of life and more interested in bettering themselves and giving something back to the world.

In time, these mature souls come to realise that, owing to its impermanence and perishability, nothing in maya can deliver lasting happiness and fulfilment. That being the case, freedom based on attachment to external variables is no freedom at all. No longer robotically driven by the desire for security and pleasure, the wise understand the importance of dharma and, when exposed to the teaching of Vedanta, they recognise its value and commit to the attainment of moksha as life's highest goal.

The Divine Disposition

Krishna begins the chapter by first exploring the values and qualities of those whose minds and hearts are committed to the 'divine path' of inner wealth. This provides a template for anyone seeking moksha and desirous of cultivating a pure, refined and inquiry-fit mind.

The first quality Krishna mentions is fearlessness. Fear has its basis in duality, which is born of avidya (self-ignorance). As the words of the Taittiriya Upanishad state:

> When one realises the Self, in whom
> All life is changeless, nameless and formless,
> Then one fears no more.

Until we realise the Unity of life,
We live in fear.

Krishna next mentions purity of mind, which comes from clear discrimination and a healthy value system. Steadfastness refers to sustained contemplation upon the teaching. This steadfastness is only possible when you understand the true value of the teaching as your means of liberation.

As Swami Dayananda notes:

A human being is here to accomplish the particular end of moksha. Whether or not one discerns this, it is what everybody wants. Nothing less will satisfy the human heart. Since the basic problem is one of self non-acceptance, acceptance is possible only when a person discovers the self to be free from any lack; in other words, complete. And the Self happens to be complete. Discovering this fact releases the individual from his erroneous sense of imperfections.

Without unrelenting devotion to the teaching, this Self-knowledge will never be assimilated. The mind will simply default to existing patterns and you'll find yourself pulled back into samsara.

Krishna also lists charity or the spirit of generosity as another key value. On this topic, Swami Chinmayanda says, "Charity must come from one's sense of abundance. Charity only springs from a sense of oneness in us—oneness between the giver and the recipient."

Self-control means mastering your sense organs rather than being a slave to them. Instead of unquestioningly feeding the senses, the seeker of liberation should exercise moderation and judicious restraint. Continually indulging the senses only strengthens the corresponding vasanas, creating further desire for sense gratification.

Krishna next prescribes upasana yoga, which may take the form of devotional rituals and offerings (pujas), prayers, chanting, meditation, and so on. This includes the study of the Vedantic texts, which Krishna has said is the highest devotion; the offering of knowledge. In addition, the practice of tapas, asceticism, is the ability to relinquish certain comforts or pleasures in order to develop fortitude and strength of mind.

Alignment of thought, word and deed is another key value. This value relates to integrity: to only saying what you know is true and to always doing as you say. In other words, you learn to integrate your ethical and moral values with your words and actions. It's not enough to talk the talk, you must also walk the walk!

Non-injury is another essential quality to cultivate, as is truthfulness. Krishna uses the word *akrodha*, which means 'lack of anger'. Shankara clarifies this as meaning the ability to resolve anger. After all, to be human is to have feelings, and denying or repressing those feelings only leads to psychological dysfunction. The secret is learning to sublimate rather than suppress our emotions and, through mastery of the mind, to deal with anger and other difficult emotions as they arise.

Other divine qualities include the ability to renounce attachment to the results of action, peacefulness and quietude of spirit, refraining from finding fault in others, compassion toward all living beings, and non-covetousness, which Swami Dayananda defines as "an absence of longing in the presence of desirable sense objects."

Those who cultivate this inner wealth will be kind, modest and free of self-aggrandisement. Naturally gentle and peaceful, they have calm and abiding minds, free from the defects of restlessness, fickleness and agitation. Always composed, they shine with an inner radiance and demonstrate fortitude in the face of pain or discomfort.

Krishna makes reference to cleanliness, which relates to both physical purity and inner mental purity. Physical purity can be cultivated through healthful living, a good diet, getting adequate exercise and rest and adopting a predominantly sattvic or yogic lifestyle.

A person's mental and emotional health are just as important as their physical health. Today's epidemic of mental health disorders are a reflection of our society's adharmic values and the increasing stress and turbulence affecting us all. That's why it's essential that we learn to manage stress, deal with difficult emotions, and cultivate a calm and tranquil mind. The tools for this include a commitment to following dharma, practicing karma yoga, meditation, upasana yoga and applying knowledge of the three gunas to every aspect of our lives.

Finally, forgiveness and unpretentiousness are also important qualities, along with courageousness and humility.

These, Krishna says, are the qualities of the gods. Some people, owing to a good birth, a cultured upbringing and meritorious karma, find these traits in natural abundance. But anyone can, with a clear intent and steadfast resolve, adopt and nurture these qualities in themselves.

The Demonic Disposition

If the divine temperament is the gateway to liberation, the opposite disposition is what Krishna calls the 'doorway to self-destruction', meaning continued bondage and suffering. Krishna spends the better part of the chapter examining this 'demonic' disposition in vivid detail.

Those with a preponderance of negative qualities are called asuras, a word often translated as 'demon'. India's Puranic stories are full of such demons; the dark forces who oppose the gods and perpetrate adharma, causing untold chaos and misery for all. In this context, the word asura should not be taken to mean some otherworldly, supernatural force. When Krishna uses the term asura, he is referring to the lower aspect of human nature: our gross, materialistic tendencies and the destructive impulses of greed, lust, attachment and egoism.

Swami Dayananda explains:

> The altercations between the devas (gods) and the asuras (demons) represent our internal conflicts. Everybody enjoys the qualities of a deva to some extent. Absence of

hurting, compassion, love, and so on, are all very natural. And the qualities of an asura are also often there. These two are always at loggerheads. Even if there is a person who seems to embody the qualities of an asura, it is not because he is bad, but because his thinking is wrong. All conflicts first happen within, and then express themselves in the external world. Every war is first waged in the mind. If it cannot be resolved there, it expresses itself externally.

The literal translation of the word asura is 'sunless'. It refers to those whose mind, personality and psychology are shrouded in darkness (ignorance), thus obscuring the reflecting light of Truth. As Swami Dayananda said, this is not because such people are innately bad. A mirror covered in grime isn't a bad mirror; it just has an obstruction preventing it from reflecting the light.

The asura is of the same divine consciousness as the greatest saint, or any other being for that matter. However, their capacity to reflect this consciousness has been compromised by an impaired reflecting medium (ie., a distorted mind). Self-ignorance is responsible for this impairment, not to mention the subsequent false values and erroneous thought patterns that prompt adharmic behaviour.

The Asura

Although the terms are often used interchangeably, a person might be categorised as either an asura or a rakshasha. Both have negative and adharmic tendencies, but to differing degrees depending upon their predominant guna.

Asuras are generally tamasic and driven by their binding likes, desires and attachments. Their lives are characterised by lust—lust for money, power, fame, pleasure and all kinds of sense gratification. Staunchly materialistic, they are extroverted in nature; hooked to the world of objects with little capacity to turn inward and absolutely no value for spiritual matters.

An asura is motivated by relentless self-interest and greed. Owing to their tamasic disposition, they are unable to exercise clear discrimination and are, therefore, inclined to adharmic behaviour. If an asura wants something and it feels good, they'll do it, with little regard to the harm they might cause others or even themselves in the long run. They live only to indulge the whims of their lower nature.

Wilful materialists, they believe that only what is visibly real exists and they see life as without purpose or moral order. Because they fail to recognise Ishvara as the cause of the creation, they have no understanding of karma and therefore believe they have nothing to account for.

Because their own desires and self-interest are the epicentre of their existence, they see the world as one big dispensing machine. Overcome by lust and greed, they try to snap up as much as they can, irrespective of the consequences to others or the environment.

When a person believes that the end justifies the means, they become willing to lie and cheat in order to get their way. This mindset is only possible when one has no comprehension of dharma, karma and Ishvara. All their actions are calculated as they seek to satiate their desires and acquire and accumulate whatever takes their fancy.

The problem isn't only the immediate results of these adharmic actions and the negative karma they generate. Every action you take strengthens the vasanas that prompted it. The vasanas are, you may recall, the hardwired tendencies to repeat certain thoughts and actions. They create an 'itch' that may be slight at first, but which, with repeated scratching, becomes an irresistible and maddening compulsion. The vasanas determine a person's entire psychological makeup and necessitate continued rebirth in order to express and, hopefully, at some point, resolve those itches. Alas, like a ravenous fire, the more the vasanas are fed, the stronger and more destructive they become.

Clearly, such people are best avoided. Although they generally don't set out to harm others, asuric people are out for themselves and place their own desires and gratification above dharma. In other words, you can count on them to do what they want rather than what is right.

The Rakshasha

If the asura should be avoided, the rakshasha is someone you actively have to protect yourself from.

The term rakshasha means 'man eater', and as the name implies, these are harmful, destructive people. They have all the traits of the asura, but owing to a rajasic temperament and a general focus on their dislikes rather than their likes, they are always at war with everyone around them. They want to get ahead and to win at any cost—and they don't care what they have to do in order to win.

The rakshashic mindset, which ranges from sociopathic to psychopathic, is all too prevalent in the worlds of business and politics. Rakshashic people aren't just out for themselves and their own self-interest; they will actively destroy anything or anyone standing in their way.

Aggressive and cynical, they habitually cause suffering, either intentionally or unintentionally, with their words and deeds. With blatant disregard for dharma, they don't hesitate to lie, cheat and inflict pain and misery on others.

Unfortunately, owing to their devious nature and willingness to scheme, deceive and resort to violence, these rakshashas often end up in positions of leadership and governance. Once they secure power, the rakshashic leader has no regard for the people they ought to be serving. These cruel dictators will do anything, including go to war and cause untold suffering and death, just to maintain their own power and dominance.

Those who perpetrate adharma are like a cancer to the world. Adharma is the great sickness of society and, just as a body can't survive certain diseases, a profoundly adharmic society has little hope of long term survival. Adharmic actions sow the seeds of the society's disintegration and eventual destruction. Such people cannot be allowed to continue their adharmic ways, which is why the Gita hinges on Krishna's insistence that

Arjuna's duty, as a warrior, is to fight and defeat the adharmic Duryodhana.

Abusing the Gift of Life

Fortunately, most people don't fall into the extreme category of the asura or rakshasha. However, given the fiercely materialistic orientation of our society, just about all of us will, if we are honest, find some of the qualities of the 'demonic disposition' in our own temperament.

From a young age, our culture indoctrinates us to believe that material objects alone bring lasting happiness and security. As children we have no ability to discriminate and question the values that are instilled into us. It's therefore only natural that we grow up believing the lies of the social order. That's why we end up believing ourselves to be inherently lacking beings who must rearrange and manipulate the circumstances of our lives in order to be whole and complete.

This false notion lies at the root of samsara. Our basic sense of self-lack compels us to seek and attach to certain objects, and this object-dependence becomes the source of our bondage. Because all objects in maya are subject to change and impermanence, our dependence on them inevitably brings as much sorrow as it does happiness. Once the psychological attachment has been formed, it can be very difficult to break.

A human life is a wonderful gift, yet it must be used wisely. If you are given a plot of land in which to create a garden, the soil must be cultivated and the seeds planted, nourished and cared for. Only then will the flowers bloom to make the garden a place of beauty, colour, and sweet fragrance. All of us have the capacity to cultivate such a life for ourselves. However, it's just as possible to let our garden go to waste or ruin. By our own misdirected thoughts and actions, we may let the garden become overrun with weeds, or kill it with neglect, overwatering, or the use of toxic chemicals. The responsibility is ours alone.

Those whose lives are devoted entirely to the fulfilment of their own desires and compulsions, and who pay little regard to dharma, remain ignorant of life's highest goal: moksha. Living only to feed the senses, they squander the precious gift of life. There's no spiritual progression for such a person and, until drastic changes are made, no hope of liberation from samsara.

The Doorway to Self-Destruction

Krishna closes the chapter by making reference to the three-fold 'doorway to self-destruction'. This gateway is comprised of three negative qualities: desire, anger, and greed.

Swami Dayananda warns: "A human being is caught and destroyed by these three things. He is destroyed in the sense that his mind is so disturbed that he is no longer fit for any purusartha (life goal), let alone moksha."

Binding desire, when left unchecked, escalates to greed; the cause of so much adharma in the world. When we fail to get what we want, as is often the case in life, the mind reacts with anger. This anger consumes the mind, creating delusion by robbing us of our ability to discriminate. Our thoughts, words and actions are then contaminated by this anger and delusion, leading to endless worlds of pain and suffering.

The Only Solution

Krishna implores us to "renounce all three" and to "seek what is best and attain life's highest end." Recalling the garden metaphor, our mind and temperament are ours alone to plant and tend. There may well be weeds caused by past ignorance and false values, such as our dependence on external objects for security and happiness. However, it's up to us to take charge and master the garden of our mind.

This necessitates a careful examination of our values, beliefs and priorities by holding them up to the light of truth. The application of discriminative self-inquiry must extend to every aspect of our psychology and lives. Only then can we progress from the self-destructive tendencies of the demonic disposition and begin to adopt the dharmic qualities of the divine disposition.

This whole chapter is an exploration of the qualifications necessary for attaining moksha. Even without moksha, to live according to these higher values will unquestionably lead one to a happier, more peaceful and fulfilling life.

CHAPTER SEVENTEEN

The Three Types of Faith

¹ "Krishna," Arjuna said, "what is it that motivates those who perform religious rituals with faith but without truly understanding the words of the scripture? Do they act from sattva, rajas, or tamas?"

²⁻³ Krishna answered, "People's understanding and faith is born of the quality of their mind, whether that is sattvic, rajasic, or tamasic. Whatever one's faith, it is reflective of their nature, and to that all people conform. Listen, and I will elaborate further.

⁴ "Those with sattvic minds worship God for knowledge and the purification of their mind. Rajasic people do so to attain worldly treasures. Tamasic people observe superstitions and worship out of fear or ignorance.

⁵⁻⁶ "Those with demonic dispositions, riddled with pretension and egotism and motivated by desire and longing, subject themselves to physically harmful penances not endorsed by the scriptures, injuring not only their bodies, but Me, who dwells within the body.

⁷ "The way one eats, performs rituals, disciplines oneself and gives to charity reflects the predominance of a particular guna. I will now describe these different ways.

⁸ "Foods that are fresh, nourishing, fortifying and pleasing to taste, which increase longevity and promote mental clarity, strength and health, are favoured by sattvic people.

⁹ "Foods that are bitter, sour, salty, excessively hot, astringent, and which cause inflammation, discomfort and ill health, are highly desired by rajasic people.

¹⁰ "Food which is stale or inadequately cooked, leftover, putrid, and from which the nutritional value has gone, is preferred by tamasic people.

11 "In terms of ritual, the sattvic perform offerings enjoined by the scriptures with no expectation of results, other than the purification of their mind.

12 "On the other hand, rituals that are performed to attain worldly results or for the sake of show, are motivated by rajas.

13 "The tamasic, with dubious intentions and improper understanding, fail to perform the ritual in the proper way or with the proper spirit.

14 "Worshipping the divine, honouring wise teachers, and maintaining purity, honesty, self-discipline and non-injury, is true discipline of the body.

15 "Speech which does not cause distress, which is true, pleasing and beneficial, and which conveys the wisdom of the scriptures, is true discipline of speech.

16 "Inner calm, cheerfulness, absence of compulsion to talk aimlessly, mastery over the mind, and pure intent, is true mental discipline.

17 "This three-fold self-discipline, when practiced with faith and without attachment to results, is sattvic in nature.

18 "When such self-discipline is practiced ostentatiously for the sake of seeking honour, respect, or admiration, and is inconsistent and short-lived, it is rajasic in nature.

19 "When this self-discipline is done for the sake of harming another, or the deluded notion that to torture the body is spiritual, it is tamasic in nature.

20 "When charity is dutifully given at the appropriate time and place, and to a worthy recipient, without expectation of return, it is considered sattvic.

21 "Charity that is painful to give and motivated by the desire for getting something in return, is rajasic.

22 "Charity given improperly and contemptuously at inappropriate times and places, and to unworthy recipients, is tamasic.

23 *Om Tat Sat:* These three words, uttered at the beginning, are an expression of Brahman, from which the Vedas (scriptures), the rituals, and the path to Self-realisation were born.

24 "Therefore, those who know the Vedas always repeat the word 'Om' before all rituals, charities, and religious disciplines.

[25] "Those who seek liberation, yet remain unattached to the result, speak the word Tat when performing the rituals, charities, and disciplines.

[26-28] "The word Sat is used to signify a pure and righteous life and to sanctify one's karma. To be steadfast with reference to a ritual, a discipline, and giving, is called sat, and all actions done for the sake of the Self are also called sat. However, rituals, disciplines, and offerings given without faith are called asat, and yield no fruit, either in this life or the next."

COMMENTARY

At the end of the previous chapter, Krishna advised Arjuna to let the Vedantic scriptures guide his life. The lives of those who have neither faith in the scriptures nor interest in moksha are governed by an altogether different authority: that of their own personality and disposition.

Allowing yourself to be driven by temperament alone is a perilous path to go down. The modern exhortation to "be yourself" might seem like sound advice until you stop to question which 'self' is being referred to. Is it the ego self, a mental abstraction based on conditioned desires and aversions, or is it your actual Self? Until you truly know who you are, the advice "be yourself" is best treated with caution.

In chapter sixteen, Krishna spoke at length about the two basic dispositions of humankind. One leads upward in terms of spiritual evolution, and the other leads to spiritual destruction. Anyone desiring happiness and freedom is advised to cultivate a sattvic mind and to minimise the influence of rajas and tamas, both of which lead to suffering and spiritual disintegration.

A Fertile Mind

As we've seen many times, the purpose of the teaching is not only to gain the Self-knowledge necessary for moksha, but just as importantly, to prepare the mind in order to receive this knowledge.

Gaining the knowledge is actually the easy part. You simply find a qualified teacher and, setting all preconceptions aside, expose your mind to the teaching. Arjuna did this back in the second chapter. He got down on his knees and beseeched Krishna to teach him the secret of liberation. This Krishna did, with words of great power, beauty and succinctness. It wasn't enough, however, to resolve Arjuna's doubts and set him free. If it had been, there would have been no need for the subsequent sixteen chapters.

The hard part is ensuring that your mind is qualified to not only understand, but to internalise and assimilate the teaching.

That's why the seeker's mind, values and lifestyle must be judiciously refined and purified. Ideally, this should be done prior to being taught, just as you would prepare the soil before planting a seed. However, it's never too late to go back and make the necessary adjustments to your mind and lifestyle. If you have heard and understood the teaching but have yet to enjoy the fruits of this knowledge, it's a sure sign that you need to go back and work on re-qualifying the mind.

That's the predominant topic of chapters sixteen and seventeen. It might seem strange that, having covered a range of weighty philosophical, psychological and cosmological topics, Krishna now turns his attention to such mundane matters as diet and lifestyle. The theme of these chapters, however, is ensuring that the mind is fit for the actualisation of Self-knowledge.

If the first six chapters of the Gita were about understanding the jiva, and the middle six about Ishvara, these final chapters provide the tools and understanding necessary for integrating and aligning our mind, lifestyle and actions with the highest Truth: *Tat Tvam Asi*—That I Am. The assimilation of this knowledge is the gateway to freedom.

Faith Determines Everything

The title of this chapter is 'the yoga of the three types of *shraddha*'. In this context, yoga means topic. The word *shraddha* is a little harder to define. The closest translation is 'faith', but it's a term with a deeper and more nuanced meaning. Shraddha refers to the innermost axis of your heart and psyche; to your deepest and most fervently held convictions and beliefs. Swami Dayananda clarifies that shradhha isn't something external, but rather, "it is in your thinking, your understanding, your value structure, and your priorities."

We are each nothing but an expression of our shraddha. When we have faith in something, we naturally develop a value for it. The opposite is true as well: to lack faith in something automatically renders it valueless to us. Therefore, our faith determines our values, and our values, in turn, determine our priorities.

Our actions and life choices are always a reflection of our priorities and values. I know a guy who is unhappy with his weight and general health. He often tells me that he wants to get fit, lose some weight and shape up. The problem is that his value for McDonalds and cake, which he associates with pleasure, is greater than his value for losing weight and improving his health. As long as that remains the case, nothing is going to change, no matter how much he protests.

That's why it's crucial to examine your priorities and the values underpinning them before you can hope to affect any kind of lasting change in your life. You'll find at the heart of it all is your shraddha; that in which you have unwavering belief.

Your Life is Your Worship

One of the themes of this chapter is worship and the way a person undertakes that worship. The term 'worship' has a broader meaning than simply going to a temple and saying prayers or chanting a mantra. In a sense, every action that you perform is a form of worship, for it is an expression of your shraddha; that in which you have faith, whether it be spiritual or secular.

Swami Chinmayananda writes:

> Every man in life brings his entire devotion and offers it at one altar or another, and seeks fulfilment from the benefits that accrue from the invocations. In scriptural terms, this is called 'worship'. The term worship here embraces a wider implication. Every one of us is a worshipper at some altar chosen by him. Even atheists are worshippers—perhaps they devote themselves to the altar of sense objects, of wealth, or power.

By this definition, everyone is devotional at heart. We each worship at the altar of our own particular choice. Some place their faith in God, in enlightenment, or in materialism, sense pleasure and the pursuit of money, fame or virtue. It's our faith in a thing—and the results and benefits we believe it will bring us—that motivates us to pursue it. In the absence of this faith, what would compel us to take action?

Action and the Influence of the Gunas

When it comes to action, three primary factors come into play: our motivation behind the action, the way that we perform the action, and our attitude with regards to the fruit of that action. Each of these is coloured by the predominance of a particular guna.

The entire aim of spiritual practice is to reduce the impurities of rajas and tamas and to cultivate a predominantly sattvic mind.

For the sattvic person, whose mind is clear, tranquil and reflective, spiritual values naturally supersede materialistic ones. Such souls have an impeccable commitment to dharma and see life as a gift rather than an entitlement. Instead of continuously trying to manipulate objects in order to obtain certain ego-driven results, sattvic people follow dharma as best they can with an attitude of humility and gratitude.

The karma yogi performs all actions, however great or small, as an offering to Ishvara and a way of serving the world, the society, and one's fellow man. By understanding that Ishvara dispenses the results of all actions according to the greater good of the total, the karma yogi no longer stresses over outcomes and accepts everything as a gift from the Lord.

Such a mindset is utterly foreign to those with rajasic and tamasic temperaments. The motivation behind rajasic action is always personal gain, whether in the form of wealth, power, prestige or sensual pleasure. Relentlessly passionate and driven, the rajasic are inclined to cut corners and violate dharma in order to get their own way. They generally worship at the altar of materialism and are very much attached to the results of their actions. That's why nothing causes quite as much suffering, frustration and anger as a mind under the sway of rajas.

If sattva is clear and revealing and rajas is dynamic and agitating, tamas is obscuring and dull. Like someone living with a permanent hangover, tamasic people struggle to see anything clearly. What's worse, because they lack a clear and discriminating intellect, tamas predisposes them to actions that are harmful to themselves and others. Tamasic action tends to be motivated solely by personal gratification and, again, such a person's attachment to results is so strong that grief and misery are never far behind.

Swami Chinmayananda used to speak of three categories of people based on the conditioning influence of the gunas: people of serenity (sattva), people of ambition (rajas) and people of heedlessness (tamas).

This isn't set in stone, of course. While a person may be inclined to the predominance of a particular guna, by taking responsibility for oneself and one's life, it is wholly possible to modify the proportions of these gunas. Krishna spends the best part of the chapter examining this in terms of devotion, diet, self discipline and charity.

You Are What You Eat

Addressing the topic of food, Krishna lays out the basis of the yogic diet. He recommends a sattvic diet that is vegetarian-based and includes fruit and vegetables, legumes, nuts and seeds, fresh juices, honey, oils and non-meat proteins. Traditionally, certain dairy products such as milk and butter are also considered sattvic. With its emphasis on fresh and unprocessed food, a sattvic diet is said to be healthful and nourishing, promoting a strong body and a calm mind.

The rajasic, however, are partial to rich and stimulating foods. These include dishes with onions, garlic, and excessive spice and salt, which may cause inflammation and irritation in the body, as well as contributing to a restless mind. Sugar and caffeinated beverages are also considered rajasic. The effects of a certain food can be observed in the hours and even days after eating it. Anything that disturbs the harmony of the body and mind, causing restlessness and irritation, is sure to be rajasic in nature.

Tamasic food is generally dead, stale, or improperly cooked, and has little nutritional value. Think of a pepperoni pizza that's been left out overnight. Meat is considered tamasic, along with fish, poultry, eggs, bread, pastry, and fermented and sugary foods. Alcohol is exceptionally tamasic, as can clearly be seen by its effect on the body and mind. Tamasic foods are best avoided altogether. They are not beneficial to your health and will almost certainly leave your mind and body feeling dull and lethargic.

When it comes to food, both the quality and quantity are important. The quality is taken care of by sticking to a predominantly sattvic diet, with pure, preferably organic and ethically sourced foods. Food quantity can also be an issue for many people. It's a good rule to only eat when you are hungry, and then to stop the moment you feel full. Food should be enjoyed, but it shouldn't overindulged and treated as a sense pleasure; as a way of feeling good or distracting yourself from emotional problems (as the term 'eating your feelings' implies).

It's not only the type of food that matters, but also the way it is sourced, prepared and consumed. All meals should be prepared and cooked with love. The act of cooking and consuming healthy food mindfully and with full attention and gratitude increases its benefits immensely.

In Vedic culture, the act of eating is treated as a devotional ritual. Every mouthful is offered back to Ishvara with gratitude. A sacred offering should never be given halfheartedly and without due care or attention. Mealtimes should therefore be treated as a ritual; as a way of serving Ishvara by taking care of Ishvara's body—which is, after all, only on temporary loan to you, the indweller. Taking proper care of the body is your way of paying the rent. That said, the body shouldn't be pampered or overindulged, which leads us to our next topic.

The Art of Self Discipline

Krishna next discusses tapas, which might be translated as self discipline or self control. Until you are willing to master your body, mind and senses, you remain a slave to them. Tapas means asserting control over your thoughts, words, impulses, appetites and behaviour. Swami Paramarthananda defines it as "a wilful self-denial to establish mastery over your own body and mind."

The first component of self discipline relates to physical discipline. In any given day, you have only a limited amount of time and energy. Both should be used wisely to in order to maximise their benefits.

As a seeker of liberation, rather than squandering your precious life energy chasing material acquisitions and sense pleasure, Krishna recommends living a devotional lifestyle dedicated to worship of Ishvara, study of the scriptures, and the continual refinement of both body and mind. This process of purification is akin to scraping the mud off a diamond and polishing it to reveal its innate beauty.

Discipline of Speech

Words have power. They can heal, they can enlighten, and they can also lead to confusion, sorrow and destruction. While Vedanta uses words to reveal truth, lesser minds use words to manipulate, deceive and incite conflict. Because words have the potential to inflict such harm, they must always be used with responsibility.

As with our diet, it pays to be mindful of two factors when it comes to our speech: the quantity and the quality of our words.

Swami Paramarthananda suggests that, as a general rule, we should aim to reduce the quantity of our speech. After all, without quantity control, it's impossible to exercise quality control. The problem with talking too much is that you rarely stop long enough to consider the quality of what you're saying. Many years ago, a friend said something I never forgot: "Silence is golden. If you can't improve on it, why even try?"

When it comes to quality of speech, before you say anything, particularly anything that might be emotive or controversial, it's helpful to ask yourself three questions. These are called the three gateways of speech:

1. Is it true?
2. Is it necessary?
3. Is it kind?

If the answer to any of these questions is 'no', it may be best to hold your tongue.

Truthfulness is one of the highest aspects of dharma. Speaking truth creates harmony between your thoughts and words. Any disparity between the two causes an inner conflict, and inner conflict invariably leads to outer conflict.

Impulsive speech—indiscriminately blurting out whatever thoughts arise in your mind—is far from a virtue. Although some people take pride in "telling it like it is", all they're really doing is obnoxiously forcing their opinions on other people, which is always the sign of a childish and immature mind.

That's why it's important to consider the necessity of what you're about to say. Are your words constructive, or are they just pointless noise? Our speech should ideally benefit both the speaker and the listener. Otherwise, why disturb the silence?

Finally, kindness should always be a factor in all communications. Lack of kindness and consideration for the feelings of others only creates hurt and bad karma. Of course, sometimes it's necessary to tell people things they don't want to hear. There may even be situations where you are forced to use harsh words. But that should always be a last resort, and every effort should first be made to communicate in as kind and considerate a way as possible.

Discipline of Mind

As we've seen time and again, the importance of a calm and harmonious mind cannot be understated.

One of the secrets to taming your mind is learning to observe thoughts and feelings as they arise—to be the witness of the mind rather than unquestioningly identifying with it. The mind is, after all, just an object appearing in you; in awareness.

This ability to view the mind objectively will free you from enormous pain. When you identify with the mind, its suffering becomes your suffering. But when you see it as an impersonal mechanism, as an instrument for consciousness, you depersonalise your suffering and become discriminating and dispassionate; two of the primary qualifications for liberation.

Mental discipline is gained by the steady practice of karma yoga, meditation and an attitude of gratitude and devotion to Ishvara. Such a devotee lets go of the past with acceptance and relinquishes any fears and concerns about the future by handing everything to Ishvara. While we can certainly plan for the future, it's important to recognise that the past and future exist as nothing but concepts in the mind. The only sane way of living is to focus our energy and attention upon the only moment available to us—the present moment.

Because the mind is goal-oriented by nature, it must be occupied in a positive and constructive way. That's why you need to provide your mind with some type of noble work; to give it a sense of purpose, meaning, and an ideal by which to live. When this work is aligned with dharma and performed with the proper karma yoga spirit, life becomes an expression of simplicity, worship and joy.

The Cycle of Insecurity

The past two chapters have centred on the refinement of the personality. This refinement involves weeding out unhealthy values and traits and consciously adopting and strengthening positive ones. One of the greatest qualities a person can develop is what the Gita calls *danam*—charity, or generosity of spirit.

The basic problem of samsara is the insecurity born of self-ignorance. Because we don't know that our very nature is wholeness, we fall under the spell of maya and, assuming ourselves to be a limited body-mind entity, experience a deep sense of lack and insecurity.

That's the first delusion of maya. The second delusion is the erroneous belief that the world of objects can somehow bring us lasting happiness and security. This will, of course, never happen, because all objects are themselves ever-changing and perishable. How can we possibly find security in that which is inherently insecure?

The third delusion is an extension of the first two. Because we feel insecure and believe that worldly objects bring happiness, we become obsessed with acquiring, consuming and hoarding—and basically trying to grab as much as we can from the world. It's little wonder that governments now refer to people as 'consumers' rather than 'citizens.' Such misplaced greed brings with it miserliness and anxiety about losing what we have acquired. In fact, Swami Paramarthanada defines samsara as "nothing but the fear of losing things."

The most powerful antidote to this cycle of insecurity, greed and miserliness is to cultivate danam, the spirit of generosity.

The Power of Generosity

Generosity isn't something alien to us. In fact, nature is generosity in action. If you observe the natural world, you'll see that everything gives to everything else in a harmonious cycle of give and take. Trees borrow carbon dioxide from the air and convert it to life-giving oxygen for other beings who, in turn, repay the trees with carbon dioxide. The ocean gives water to form clouds, which then rain down upon the mountains, filling the rivers, which eventually carry this water back to the ocean. Everything takes, but everything also gives.

As an integrated part of this ecosystem, human beings should be no different. We receive all that we need from our environment. Our response shouldn't be one of grasping, hoarding, and always looking for what we can get next. Instead, we should be happy to share what we have in order to repay our debt to life.

The spirit of generosity, expressed through charity and giving, is a way of honouring the flow life. Charity benefits not only the recipient, but also the giver. The ability to give to others breaks down the false sense of ownership at the core of the ego. On the other hand, acting out of greed and selfish desire only strengthens the ego's sense of separation and division.

In truth, we own nothing in this world. It all belongs to Ishvara, who, out of divine benevolence, provides us with everything that we need in order to survive and thrive. Therefore, to give and to share is to align ourselves with Ishvara and the natural laws of the creation.

Krishna states that sattvic charity is giving appropriately to a worthy recipient in a way befitting the situation. However, even charity can be abused. Acts of charity motivated by rajas may be given for ulterior motives, such as the desire to appear virtuous or the expectation of getting something in return. Tamasic people may give to the wrong person or cause, and for improper reasons. Extreme examples include those who fund grossly adharmic organisations such as organised crime rings or terrorist organisations.

Therefore, even charitable giving must be done with a clear, discriminating mind and in an appropriately dharmic way.

Three Sacred Words

The chapter ends with a brief reflection on the words '*Om Tat Sat*'. This is a mantra used in many Vedic rituals, often at the end of the ceremony as a way of sanctifying and dedicating it to Ishvara.

All three words refer to Brahman, the divine Self. The syllable *Om* is the primordial sound of creation. As it represents the prime cause of all things, Om is placed at the start of most mantras.

Tat, or 'That', again refers to the Self; the innermost essence of all things—That which is both transcendent and immanent.

Sat means 'Existence', another synonym for the Self. In this context, sat is the underlying substratum of all existence; the beginning-less cause (satya) from which the world of effect (mithya) arises.

According to Vedic tradition, these three words, when chanted at the end of a ritual, neutralise any mistakes or errors that you may have made, either in the pronunciation of the mantras or the performance of the task.

In 'The Holy Geeta', Swami Chinmayananda writes:

> Acts can be rendered 'good' when pursued and invoked with Om Tat Sat—the Supreme (Om), the Universal (Tat) and the Real (Sat)—the Infinite Brahman. If this chanting is undertaken with faith and sincerity, the seeker's mind expands and overcomes selfishness and arrogance, and karmas are sanctified and purified.

The complete mantra is *Om tat sat Ishvara panam astu,* which means 'let this action be an offering to the Lord, who is Om Tat Sat.'

The point is that any action, however seemingly mundane, can be converted to worship by living a life of karma yoga and offering all your actions to Ishvara with gratitude and reverence.

In this way, engagement with the world doesn't have to be an obstacle to liberation. It can, in fact, be your sadhana (spiritual practice) and your very means of liberation. Swami Chinmayananda called this "maintaining an attitude of attunement with a Higher ideal"—something that can be done even in the midst of worldly activity, by remembering Om Tat Sat.

CHAPTER EIGHTEEN

Liberation

¹ Arjuna had one final question. "Krishna, please tell me the difference between *sannyasa* and *tyaga*, the two types of renunciation."

² Krishna replied, "The first, sannyasa, is to renounce action for the sake of desired objects, and the second, tyaga, is to renounce the results of all actions.

³ "Some believe that all action should be renounced, lest it lead to bondage. Others say that noble actions, such as ritual, charity, and self-discipline, should not be given up.

⁴⁻⁶ "I declare that ritual, charity, and self-discipline should not be relinquished. Such actions purify the mind of those who are discriminating. Yet even these actions should be done without attachment or desire for reward. This is my supreme vision, Arjuna.

⁷⁻⁹ "It is improper to indiscriminately renounce one's duties. Such renunciation, caused by delusion, is tamasic. To avoid action out of fear of physical discomfort is rajasic. Such inaction does not merit reward. But to dutifully fulfil one's responsibilities without seeking personal gain is sattvic.

¹⁰ "Those endowed with a sattvic disposition have clear knowledge. Free from doubt, they understand the true meaning of renunciation. They neither shirk from unpleasant actions, nor do they unduly seek pleasing actions.

¹¹⁻¹² "As long as one has a body, the need for action cannot be avoided. But the one who relinquishes the results of action has mastered renunciation. Those who remain attached to the fruits of their actions will experience the consequences of this karma—whether desirable, undesirable, or a mixture of the two. But the true renunciate remains free from karma.

13-15 "Listen, Arjuna, for Vedanta clearly outlines the five factors necessary for the accomplishment of any action. These factors are the physical body, the sense of doership/ego, the organs of perception and action, the physiological functions, and the environment and elemental forces by which the action takes place. Any action a person undertakes, whether in thought, word, or deed, and whether proper or improper, is the result of these five factors combined.

16-17 "Those who lack clear vision believe themselves to be the agent of action. But the wise understand the self to be free of doership. When taking action, even in fighting these people, such a soul knows that he does not fight, nor is he bound.

18-19 "Knowledge, the object of knowledge, and the knower are the three-fold cause of action. The means of doing, the object of the action, and the agent of the action (the doer), are the three-fold constituents of action. Knowledge, action, and the agent of action can be distinguished according to their conditioning by the gunas.

20-22 "Clear, sattvic knowledge allows one to see the changeless Self in all beings and the indivisible amid the seeming multiplicity of creation. Knowledge conditioned by rajas, on the other hand, sees the manifold forms of creation as separate and distinct. Knowledge filtered by tamas, limited and lacking in perspective, sees one small part and mistakes that for the whole.

23-25 "Action performed in alignment with dharma, without attachment, and free from the influence of binding likes and dislikes, is sattvic. Action driven by lust, self-importance, and performed with intense exertion, is rajasic. Action undertaken without consideration of the consequences or potential loss, its affect on others, or one's own capacity, is tamasic.

26-28 "The one who is free from attachment and egotism, who is endowed with resolve and enthusiasm, and is unperturbed in success and failure alike, is a sattvic doer. The one driven by strong personal desires, who is greedy, aggressive, willing to hurt to others, and whose mind is covetous and subject to elation and depression, is a rajasic doer. The one who is undisciplined, vulgar, immature, deceitful, cruel, lazy, easily depressed, and prone to procrastination, is a tamasic doer.

29-32 "Now I will describe how the gunas affect one's intellect and resolve. A sattvic intellect knows when to act and when to refrain from action; which action is appropriate and which is inappropriate; what is to be feared and what is not to be feared; and what brings freedom and what brings bondage. A rajasic intellect confuses right and wrong action and cannot distinguish between what is to be done and what is not to be done. A tamasic intellect, obscured by ignorance, continually mistakes wrong for right and is utterly unable to discriminate.

33-35 "An unflinching resolve, with which one brings the mind, vital forces and senses into harmony by sustained practice, is sattvic. The opportunistic resolve clouded by selfish craving, which engages in activity only for renown, pleasure, or wealth, is rajasic. The improper resolve, driven by ignorance and distorted by fear, sorrow, depression, sloth and addiction, is tamasic.

36-37 "Listen, Arjuna, as I now explain the three kinds of happiness. By sustained spiritual practice, one will reach the end of sorrow. What first seemed like poison is transformed into the sweet nectar of happiness, born of the clarity of Self-knowledge. That is sattvic happiness.

38-39 "Pleasure arising from the gratification of the senses is always fleeting. Initially it seems like nectar, but soon becomes poison. This is rajasic happiness. The narcotic happiness that is self-deluding and born of sleep, laziness and indifference is tamasic in nature.

40 "There is no being either on earth, or in the heavens, who is free of the influence of these three gunas.

41 "The differing duties found in the social order are determined by a person's nature.

42 "Owing to a predominance of sattva, it is the duty of brahmanas (spiritual aspirants, teachers and protectors of wisdom) to live a life of composure, self-restraint, discipline, purity of heart, patience, and dedication to learning, sharing and embodying Self-knowledge.

43 "Those of rajasic temperament with a degree of sattva have the duty of kshatriyas (those who lead and defend society). The qualities they should seek to embody are courage, self-confident leadership, fortitude, generosity, and the resolve to deal with conflict rather than run from it.

44 "With a predominance of rajas and some tamas, those with a vaishya temperament are suited to preserve the wealth of society through occupations in agriculture and commerce. Owing to a predominance of tamas, the natural duty of the shudra is service.

45-46 "When a person gladly attends to their particular duty, they gain success. Let me explain how. By performing one's own duty, one is worshipping the Creator who dwells in and pervades all forms.

47 "It is better to perform one's own duty imperfectly than to succeed in the duty of another. By performing the action appropriate to one's nature, a person incurs no grief.

48 "The actions that come as result of following your nature should not be abandoned, Arjuna, even if they are not to your liking. One can find fault with any undertaking, just as fire is engulfed by smoke.

49 "He whose mind is free from attachment and longing and who has sublimated the impulses of the lower nature into the quest for Self-knowledge, gains the great freedom of actionlessness by renunciation.

50 "Now, listen as I briefly explain how the pure-minded aspirant becomes firmly established in the ultimate certainty of Self-knowledge.

51-53 "With a clear mind, unerring resolve, firm mastery of mind, body and senses, dispassion with regard to the allure of sense objects, and free from the pull of binding likes and dislikes, one should live a simple and quiet life. Eating lightly, restraining speech and the impulses of the body and mind, and no longer expecting external circumstances to complete oneself, one should remain committed to contemplation of the Self. Relinquishing false notions of doership, ownership and the need for power, one releases all anger and attains a state of harmony. Such a person easily attains and abides in the knowledge that they are Brahman.

54 "By recognition of one's non-separateness from Brahman, one is ever satisfied and beyond the reach of doubt and sorrow. With equal regard for all beings—whom he sees as non-separate from himself—this person attains the highest devotion to Me.

55-56 "This intense devotion leads to the full knowledge and realisation of the eternal non-dual nature of the Self. When one's actions are done as karma yoga, one gains the liberation of Self-knowledge by My grace.

57-58 "Make your every action an offering to Me, renounce all actions to Me, and keep your mind and heart on Me alone. If you fix your mind on Me always, knowing that I am you and you are Me, you will be carried across all difficulties. If, however, out of egotism, you fail to live according to this truth, you will suffer.

59-60 "Even if, through egotism, you assert, "I will not fight", your resolve will not avail you, for your very nature will compel you to act. If, out of delusion, you stubbornly refuse to perform the duty born of your natural disposition, you will still help-lessly end up doing what you did not wish to do.

61 "As the Self, I dwell in the heart of of all beings, Arjuna. By My maya, I cause them to revolve as if mounted on a wheel.

62 "Surrender with your whole heart to Me alone, Arjuna. By My grace you will gain absolute peace and eternal fulfilment.

63 "The knowledge I have shared with you is the great secret of all secrets. Reflect on these words and then do as you wish."

64 After a pause, Krishna continued. "You are dear to Me, therefore, one last time I will share the secret by which you will attain the highest good.

65 "Be aware of Me always. Offer your mind and heart to Me with supreme devotion and you will realise your identity with Me. This I promise you.

66 "Giving up all karmas, take refuge in Me alone. Have no sorrow, for I will release you from all karma.

67-69 "Do not share this wisdom with those who lack disci-pline, devotion, the ability to listen, or those who openly scoff at Me. But those who teach My words to receptive minds realise their oneness with Me without doubt. No one can render Me greater service.

70-71 "Those who meditate upon or recite these words are worshiping Me with great devotion. Those with trust in the teaching, and who do not merely seek to find fault with these words, also benefit greatly.

72 "Tell me, Arjuna, have you listened to these words with unwavering focus? Is your delusion born of ignorance now gone?"

73 Arjuna smiled and lowered his head. "By your grace, my doubts are gone, O Krishna. I will now live with a heart of devotion, guided by the flame of your divine knowledge."

Om Tat Sat.

COMMENTARY

Much like the TV news, the Gita's second chapter provided the headlines and an overview of the main themes, and this final chapter serves as the closing summary.

As you will recall, the Bhagavad Gita can be divided into three sections. These sections correspond with the Vedantic maxim *Tat tvam asi;* the highest truth of the Vedas distilled into three short words: That thou art. If the first six chapters dealt with thou, the jiva, and the middle chapters explored That, the eternal Self, the final section, art, negates any notion of separation between the two. After all, what difference can exist between the waves and the ocean or the pot and the clay?

Arjuna begins the chapter by asking one final question on the topic of renunciation; a familiar theme from earlier chapters of the Gita. In answer, Krishna states that true renunciation is not the abandonment of action, but letting go of one's attachment to the results of action.

Krishna goes on to examine the nature of the Self and discusses six topics in relation to the gunas. The teaching then concludes with a final summary of both karma yoga and jnana yoga, the science of Self-knowledge.

Finally, Krishna asks the million dollar question. Have Arjuna's doubts been resolved? Has the Gita, Krishna's divine song, had its desired effect, or have his words been in vain?

Before we get to Arjuna's moment of truth, we will first explore the key topics of this final chapter.

The Two Life Paths

A theme running through the Gita is the difference between what the Vedas call *pravritti* and *nivritti*—the path of worldly action and the path of renunciation.

Pravritti is a life of karma; of active engagement in worldly life. The vast majority of people are on this path, which encompasses the first three human pursuits: security, pleasure and virtue. The focus of pravritti is worldly endeavours such as work, career, money, family, status and the attainment of various goals and desires.

The other path, nivritti, involves withdrawal from worldly entanglements and renunciation from action (sannyasa). According to the Vedic model of life, the first part of a person's life is governed by pravritti, but nivritti is seen as the culmination of one's life. That's when the renunciant, or sannyasi, leaves behind the outer world and directs his or her focus to the inner world and the final and highest human pursuit—moksha.

While the Vedantic scriptures generally highlight the path of renunciation and enlightenment over worldly action, the Gita states that it doesn't have to be an either-or choice. According to Krishna, a life of worldly action can also be a vehicle for moksha. There's a caveat, however. It must be conducted in the proper way and with the proper attitude—ie., as karma yoga.

True Renunciation

Arjuna's opening question relates to the definition of two words: *sannyasa* and *tyaga*, both of which refer to renunciation. As Krishna explains, sannyasa relates to physical renunciation: the act of withdrawing from the society and living as a wandering ascetic, entirely devoted to the pursuit of enlightenment.

The second term, tyaga, refers not to renunciation of action itself, but renunciation of the results of action. It's this form of renunciation which Krishna recommends. After all, it's impossible to avoid action entirely. Life is a never-ending succession of action. Krishna tells Arjuna that even if he should wilfully decide to abandon action, his very nature will compel him to act, whether he likes it or not.

Because he's desperate to escape the unpleasant duty ahead of him, Arjuna sees a life of sannyasa as a tempting alternative. Krishna, however, strongly dissuades him from this path. He knows that, as someone with a rajasic nature and a warrior's temperament, Arjuna would find himself wholly unsuited to a contemplative lifestyle.

Sannyasa for the unprepared is a recipe for frustration, pain and ultimate failure. Because it requires a highly sattvic temperament, precious few are suited to a life of withdrawal from society. Those whose minds are subject to any excess of rajas and tamas would find the solitude a tortuous experience.

That's why a key part of the Gita's teaching is the importance of purifying and thus preparing the mind for knowledge.

For most people, this means remaining in the world and performing our dharma as determined by our *svabhava* (inherent nature). Doing this as karma yoga and with an attitude of bhakti, or devotion to a higher ideal, gradually neutralises the mind's binding desires and attachments and minimises the influence of rajas and tamas.

Repaying Our Debt to the World

The simple act of living indebts us to the world. We take oxygen from the air, sustenance from the land, and water from the rivers. In addition, many of the things that we may take for granted, such as the food that we eat, the clothes that we wear and the houses we live in have been made for us by the labour of others.

We should therefore seek to repay this debt by performing our dharma, or duty, and in so doing, contribute back to the world. In today's culture, people tend to balk at the word 'duty', but duty is the price that we pay for living in this world.

Some duties are pleasant, and others less appealing. The task ahead of Arjuna is a particularly horrific one. Nevertheless, as a warrior, his duty is to fight and overcome the adharma that would otherwise destroy society.

By performing our duty as karma yoga, we sanctify even the most mundane actions as acts of devotion for Ishvara. When our actions are no longer motivated solely by personal desire, we are freed from attachment to the results, which belong to Ishvara alone.

Life without karma yoga is fraught with stress. Action taken only for self-gratification comes with a deluge of stressful emotions: expectation, anxiety, and—if we don't get the result that we want—anger, resentment and depression.

Whether our actions meet with success or failure, desire-prompted action inevitably disturbs the mind. With each and every result, whether positive or negative, the vasanas are strengthened, cementing our desire to either repeat or avoid that action.

In time, our likes and dislikes become the dominant, driving factor in our psyche. Such a mind, enslaved to psychological forces it may not even be consciously aware of, often pays scant regard to dharma.

That's why the entire psychology of the Gita is based on neutralising the mind's binding likes and dislikes. For the untamed mind, helplessly bound to the wheel of samsara, the higher goal of moksha, liberation, will forever be an unattainable fancy.

Although Arjuna sees a life of renunciation as a preferable alternative to the battle ahead, his nature and temperament are unsuited to sannyasa, as Krishna makes abundantly clear. While the pursuit of liberation is indeed life's highest goal, it cannot be attained by absconding from our worldly duties. We are each bound to our duty, which is our dharma.

We All Have a Contribution to Make

The entire creation is a perfectly ordered and interdependent ecosystem. While the human mind sees only duality and division, in actuality, nothing exists in isolation, nor can it function independently of anything else.

The intelligence behind this creation, Ishvara, is also the very form, shape and substance of the creation; appearing as all the stars, galaxies, planets, mountains, oceans, rivers and trees—and the laws governing them. These natural laws, which are Ishvara in action, form the very order of the creation. Another word for this order is dharma; the basis and foundation of the cosmos.

The natural world, as we've seen, exists in a state of homeostasis in which everything contributes to the whole by following its innate dharma. But what comes naturally to animals and plants is altogether more of a challenge for human beings. We are, courtesy of ignorance, desire, attachment, and the misuse of free will, the only species capable of violating dharma.

The sorry state of the world today is symptomatic of this. At the core of our materialistic, hyper-consumer culture lies the exploitation and weaponisation of our desire, greed and personal attachment. From birth, we're conditioned to be mindless consumers; cogs in the wheel of the capitalist machine rather than warriors of dharma. This has resulted in the degradation of our planet, the systematic annihilation of our natural resources, not to mention the entropic breakdown of society alongside the steady erosion of dharmic values.

We all have a part to play in contributing to society and the world. The Gita makes it clear that this is our duty and our obligation. Instead of raising our children to be mere reflectors of the prevailing culture, we need to teach them to be adherents and defenders of dharma.

Krishna implores Arjuna to follow his path, his dharma, irrespective of his likes and dislikes. These conditioned desires and aversions must be relegated to the background rather than allowed to govern our actions.

Following dharma rids us of our sense of doership. By aligning with dharma, we come into harmony with Ishvara, and we also find that the appropriate action in any situation is already defined for us; not by our personal likes and dislikes, but by dharma. Our choices are already made for us when we simply follow the natural order of life.

Not only that, but by performing our actions in accordance with dharma, which means doing the appropriate thing at the appropriate time in the appropriate way, we are worshipping Ishvara and repaying our debt to life.

Swami Dayananda says:

> Whenever I do exactly what is called for in a given situation, that is worshipping Ishvara. Whenever I do what is appropriate, I connect myself to Ishvara. That is why there is so much joy and satisfaction in my actions. There is a harmony between the law of dharma and my actions and that gives me a sense of peace because of a release from the hold of *raga-dvesas* (likes and dislikes). If I am

doing this day after day, what will happen to my likes and dislikes? What hold can they have over me? They just fall apart. Only non-binding raga-dvesas remain, which are beautiful because they make me a unique individual.

Living solely to satiate our desires is the surest way to scupper any hope of freedom and lasting peace. As we've established, like a ravenous fire, desire only increases when fed and causes misery when obstructed.

Krishna makes it clear that such a wasted life leads only to spiritual disintegration. This might be a hard sell in our deeply materialistic, ego-driven culture, but our lives must be driven not by desire, but by dharma; by performing our duty as determined by our nature and the needs of the situation.

The Four Varnas

The form our duty takes naturally differs from person to person. As the Self, we are all the same—the one, all-pervading consciousness. But as jivas, we fall into different character types according to our *svabhava*, or inherent nature. This nature, in turn, determines our personal dharma.

The Vedic *varna* system outlines four basic character types relating to one's predominant gunas and the roles and jobs they are suited to play in the society.

Sadly, in India, the varna system degenerated over time into a warped and exploitative caste system based upon bloodline rather than a person's temperament. Nevertheless, as a foundational understanding, the varna system remains as applicable today as ever. These guna-based divisions account for the universal differences found in people's character and temperament in all cultures across time.

The four-fold varnas are:

1. *Brahmanas*: the Spiritual/Knowledge-Based Class (Sattvic)
At the top of the Vedic system we find the brahmanas; those with predominantly sattvic minds and dispositions. Owing to the clear, reflective quality of sattva, brahmanas comprise the

spiritual class; the priests, scientists and teachers whose life purpose is to keep the flame of knowledge alive at the heart of society. Brahmanas are expected to teach by example, inspiring and educating the society, and living simple lives of purity, integrity and dedication to their field of knowledge.

2. *Kshatriyas:* the Leadership and Warrior class (Rajasic/ Sattvic)

Those whose natures are primarily rajasic with a touch of sattva fall into the kshatriya class. Such people enjoy the clarity of mind engendered by sattva mixed with dynamism of rajas, which compels them to play an active role in the society. The kshatriyas are intended to be the political leaders, administrators and defenders of the society.

3. *Vaishyas:* the Commerce Class (Rajasic/Tamasic)

Those whose minds are predominantly rajasic with an element of tamas comprise the commerce class. The vaishya mind and temperament is ideally suited to running the society's industry and commerce, and dealing with all matters pertaining to trade and economic or material concerns.

4. *Shudras:* the Service Class (Tamasic)

Finally, those whose disposition is generally tamasic make up the general workforce. Because they lack the clarity of sattva and the dynamism of rajas, shudras find themselves best suited to service work and performing the society's necessary and valuable manual labour.

All Roles Have Equal Value

It should be noted that each varna has equal value and importance. After all, the Vedas view society as a single organism in which all parts are interconnected and must function together in harmony. The knowledge-based brahmanas are likened to the head of society, the administrative and defence-oriented kshatriyas are its arms and hands, the commerce-focused vaishyas are the trunk, and the service-based shudras the legs.

The varna model helps us to identify which profession, which duty, is best suited to our nature. We were each born with a certain role to play in life. Whether it's a grand and celebrated role, such as leading a nation, or a humbler one, sweeping the streets, we each contribute to the creation by playing our assigned part.

Problems arise when a society has no understanding of these varnas. We end up devaluing teachers while glorifying reality TV 'celebrities'. Worse still, instead of voting for competent, qualified and psychologically sound political leaders, we elect tamasic minded businessmen of dubious moral caliber.

Although certain jobs and roles may be more valued and coveted than others, there's little point hankering after a position unsuited to your particular skills and temperament. After all, what could be more stressful than landing a job that you know you're utterly unqualified for?

That's why Krishna stresses the importance of being true to our nature and doing our own dharma rather than anyone else's—and being willing to follow it through, even if it isn't always to our liking.

Living in a desire-based rather than a dharma-based culture, people tend to measure 'success' in terms of the attainment of their personal desires and ambitions. Like avaricious bargain hunters, they seek to squeeze all that they can from the world while spending as little as they can. Those of us with an understanding of dharma, however, see success as contributory in nature: as giving more to the world than we take from it.

Karma Yoga Revisited

While action in the world cannot be avoided, this action can at least be converted to spiritual practice by the application of karma yoga, which is the primary sadhana of any seeker of enlightenment. Only by neutralising the psyche's binding likes and dislikes, and the stresses inherent in worldly karma, will your mind become a fit receptacle for Self-knowledge.

The karma yogi offers all actions, whether sacred or secular, momentous or mundane, as a gift to Ishvara. Your work, whatever it might be, becomes your means of worship; your way of giving back to the Lord and repaying the debt for all you've been given in life.

As a karma yogi, you understand that life isn't about gratifying your personal desires, but about doing what you must, with a steady, single-pointed mind and a heart full of gratitude and devotion.

Karma yoga doesn't just change your attitude towards action; it also changes your attitude toward the results of action. While you obviously still do things with a certain outcome in mind, that outcome is no longer the sole purpose of your endeavour. Your ultimate aim with karma yoga is not the attainment of specific worldly results, but the cultivation of a pure and tranquil mind.

By recognising Ishvara as *karma phala data*—the dispenser of the results of all action—you can gracefully accept every outcome as prasada, a divine gift.

This isn't a license to be fatalistic, however. If you don't get the result you intended, you don't necessarily abandon your efforts. Depending on the dharma of the situation, you may need to redouble your efforts and try again.

Regardless of what happens, as a karma yogi, you learn to adopt an objective and dispassionate view of life. When you get what you want, you no longer inflate with a conceited sense of pride, because you know that whatever happened was by Ishvara's grace. Similarly, when things don't work out as you intended, you never entertain misplaced notions of failure and self-inadequacy—because, again, you know the results were determined by Ishvara.

Whatever happens, good or bad, is an opportunity to learn and grow. Besides, the aim of karma yoga is never the attainment of specific worldly ends. Its ultimate aim is to purify and refine the mind. That's why, whether you experience gains or losses in the outer world, karma yoga can turn even the worst defeats into spiritual victories.

The World Is Not The Source of Your Sorrow

Those whose happiness depends upon the world aligning with their likes and dislikes are slaves to samsara. Object-based happiness not only precludes liberation, but is also the most precarious kind of happiness; given that it is Ishvara, and not the jiva, that controls the world of objects.

Vedanta negates the notion that worldly objects are the cause of our happiness. Were that the case, the same objects would make all people happy, and our joy would be constant and unchanging the entire time the object was there. That clearly isn't the case. What brings us happiness one day is just as likely to bring sorrow the next, as any divorce lawyer will attest.

If the world isn't the cause of our happiness, it cannot be the source of our misery either.

Vedanta reveals that our suffering lies in self-ignorance. By mistaking ourselves to be the conditioning adjuncts of the body, mind and ego, we experience a crushing sense of lack and limitation at the core of our being.

This self-insufficiency drives our desperate attempts to mould the world, ourselves, and others into something favourable—into something we believe will make us whole and complete, not realising that we are already whole and complete.

The Gunas Revisited

Before moving onto Self-knowledge, the middle portion of this chapter returns to a prominent subject of these final chapters: the gunas. As the gunas comprise the field of prakriti, all beings, enlightened or not, are subject to their influence.

Krishna examines seven topics—knowledge, action, doership, intellect, will and happiness—in terms of the conditioning effects of the gunas.

1. Sattva — Your Ticket to Freedom

As the subtlest of the gunas, sattva has a reflective, revealing quality. A sattvic mind, free of the obstructing blinders of rajas and tamas, is capable of clear knowledge, discrimination and creative thinking. This naturally gives rise to dharmic action.

The cultivation of sattva not only aids the seeker of liberation immeasurably, but a sattvic mind is a happy mind; a mind in which the reflected bliss of the Self is experienced as a sense of peace, wholeness, and satisfaction with oneself and life.

Karma yoga comes naturally to the sattvic mind, relieving the stress and strain of continually trying to manipulate situations and people into conformity with our likes and dislikes.

A sattvic person is largely free of egotism and attachment and engages life with an attitude of cheerfulness and resilience. Courtesy of a sharp, refined intellect, such a soul remains clear about their priorities and the ultimate purpose of life. A discerning and unwavering will propels them toward their goal, preventing them from getting lost in what the Tao Te Ching calls life's 'devious side-paths'.

2. Rajas — Your Ticket to Passion and Pain

Rajas, as we've seen, has an agitating effect on the mind and body. It obscures knowledge by extroverting the mind and senses, keeping them hooked on the world of objects.

As a result, rajasic people are generally materialistic and ego-driven, with little interest in spiritual affairs. Because everything gets filtered through the screen of their desires and aversions, the rajasic find objective discrimination almost impossible.

Eternally unsatisfied, and eaten away by their unfulfilled desires and cravings, the rajasic are loathe to sit still for more than a few seconds. After all, there's always more to be done, more to be pursued, and more to be attained.

Under the influence of rajas, desire escalates to greed, and greed often leads to adharma—either knowingly, or because of the mind's impaired discernment.

Smouldering volcanos of avarice and frustration, the rajasic are prone to erupt at the slightest provocation. Such people seek material success, wealth, power and recognition above all else and are utterly dependent on the world of objects for their happiness—the very definition of samsara.

3. Tamas — Your Ticket to Ignorance and Indolence

The quality of tamas, the densest of the three, has a deadening, obscuring effect on the mind and senses.

Like the rajasic, those under the influence of tamas are materialistic to a fault, consumed by their desire for sense gratification, and have no capacity for discrimination. But whereas rajas drives relentless action, tamasic people tend to be undisciplined, lazy and disinclined to act.

The tamasic mind, prone to an unfortunate combination of ignorance and obstinacy, exemplifies what psychologists call the Dunning-Kruger Effect. This is the cognitive bias by which the most ignorant people are often the most confident because they greatly overestimate their knowledge and skill. If someone is ignorant of just how ignorant they are, there's no point even trying to get through to them! Tamasic people are rarely open to new ideas, no matter how self-destructive their current patterns of thought and behaviour.

Fatalistic and prone to addiction, such people have a proclivity for dull, narcotic sense pleasures such as alcohol, drugs, and junk food. As life's great 'takers,' their lives are motivated by sense enjoyment and they have little interest in contributing to others or the world around them.

Guna Management is Essential

All beings are born with a certain physical and mental disposition based on their proportion of gunas. This constitution isn't set in stone, however—otherwise the last few chapters would be pointless. The key is learning to master these gunas by minimising the effects of tamas and rajas and maximising sattva.

As we've seen, an excess of either rajas or tamas leads to suffering. Indeed, our society's pandemic of anxiety and depression could be greatly reduced by teaching people to understand and manage the gunas.

Spiritual practice is basically all about guna management, and creating a sufficiently sattvic mind for Self-Knowledge to take root.

This involves taking a fearless moral inventory of every part of your life. Only then can you make the necessary changes to ensure that your mind, values, actions, diet and lifestyle are as sattvic as possible. Little by little, you cultivate what the Gita calls the 'divine disposition', which is the gateway to a life of happiness and freedom.

The Fire of Self-Knowledge

It's important to note that your sadhana is not an end in itself. While smoothing down the rough edges of the personality is certainly a noble endeavour, the point isn't to make yourself into a 'better' or more 'spiritual' person. Spiritual practise is a means to a specific end: a mind fertile enough for the seeds of Self-knowledge to flourish.

Karma yoga and upasana yoga—unfolded in the first six and middle six chapters of the Gita respectively—purify the mind as one would chisel a diamond free of the mud and polish it to reveal its beauty.

Such a mind, when exposed to jnana yoga, is set alight by the alchemising fire of Self-knowledge. This flame of Truth devours avidya (self-ignorance), burning the ropes of samsara to ashes, and freeing the mind from its self-created torment.

In actuality, everyone already has knowledge of the Self, for it is our innermost sense of 'I'; the ever present and always available awareness in which all objects are experienced. We all know that we are—that we exist and are aware. This is not something that we need to be told, for it is a self-evident fact. Consciousness/awareness is present in every living creature all the time. The existence of the Self is, therefore, never in doubt.

The problem is the erroneous notions we have about the nature of this Self. We take ourselves to be what we are not, superimposing the Self, our sense of 'I', onto the instruments of body, mind and ego, much as the traveller at dusk superimposes a snake onto the rope.

By confusing satya and mithya, we trade the infinite for the finite and seemingly reduce ourselves to an egoic pseudo-self; itself nothing but a mind-created projection.

When we take ourselves to be nothing but the body, mind and ego, we adopt their limitations and their suffering becomes our own. This fundamental self-ignorance creates samsara; a malady that can only be resolved with knowledge.

Vedanta and the Importance of a Teacher

At heart, the Gita is a song of jnanam; knowledge. Jnana yoga, or Vedanta, is derived from the Upanishads, the end portions of the Vedas (the word Vedanta, *Veda* + *anta*, literally means 'end of the Vedas'). Vedanta is a *pramana*, a means of knowledge—specifically, Self-knowledge. It might be thought of as a 'word mirror', for it uses a specific sequence of teaching, logic and discriminative reasoning to remove self-ignorance and reveal to us the essence of our nature.

Vedanta works in three stages, which must be followed sequentially. As you will recall, the first stage is called shravana, which literally means 'hearing'.

Vedanta isn't something that should be self-studied. It requires a skilled teacher. Otherwise ignorance—as tenacious and intelligent a foe as ever there was—will filter and misinterpret the teaching in endless ways.

Perhaps the greatest obstacle a seeker will encounter are the cognitive biases of one's own mind. Confirmation bias is a particularly tricky one, for the student will tend to accept the parts of the teaching that conform to their preexisting beliefs and biases, and reject those that don't. Unfortunately, this leads to nothing but frustration and continued ignorance.

A teacher of Vedanta 2must be Self-realised, well-versed in the teaching and ideally from a recognised lineage in the Shankara sampradaya (teaching tradition).

Most prominent Western teachers tend to cobble together their own teachings by cherry-picking elements of Vedanta, yoga, Buddhism, and so on. Jnana yoga is a science, however, and must be treated as such, and taught with professionalism, clarity and integrity. Just as you would only want to learn physics from a qualified teacher rather than someone who has learned a few things on the internet and come up with their own adapted 'teaching', Vedanta must be taught by somebody capable of delivering the whole picture, and the entire teaching from A to Z.

Modern spiritual gurus and neo-advaita teachers have an embarrassingly poor track record when it comes to getting people enlightened. The simple reason is that they lack a coherent, time-tested teaching. There may be much truth to what they say, but enlightenment requires more than just flowery words. It requires a comprehensive map. Like any other means of knowledge, the teaching must be vetted, its results must be replicable, and it must be guarded from tampering and distortion, which is precisely what the Vedanta sampradaya has done over the millennia.

Once you have both a qualified mind and a qualified teacher, you're all set to go. During the shravana stage you simply expose your mind to the teaching, setting aside your preconceptions and everything you think you already know. You need a certain openness of mind, a willingness to learn and faith in both the teaching and the teacher. This isn't a tamasic type of blind faith. You will go on to investigate what you've been taught through your own process of inquiry.

This inquiry is the crux of the second stage, manana, or reasoning. You may have understood the gist of the teaching, but still have certain questions, doubts or areas of confusion.

Such uncertainty is natural, because Vedanta may at first seem counterintuitive. This stage necessitates a teacher who can answer your questions and help you resolve your doubts. Over time, as you continue exposing your mind to the teaching and working through any doubts or queries that arise, you begin to grasp the fullness, beauty and wonder of this extraordinary vision of Reality.

A New Operating System

Nididhyasana, the third and final stage of Vedanta, means converting your knowledge to conviction. This is done by retraining your mind to shift its point of identification from the limited ego to limitless awareness.

That's when this vision of Truth becomes your mind's new 'operating system'. Krishna's words are no longer just idle concepts, but the basis of your entire understanding and experience of reality.

As Swami Dayananda notes:

> People tell me all the time that they understand this teaching very well, but still they are in pain. Not physical pain, but mental pain. This is only because of [their] incapacity to drop things. What causes mental pain, after all? It is nothing but a particular way of thinking.

Old habits die hard, particularly when it comes to patterns of thinking. A remarkably conservative instrument, the mind will always revert to its set baseline. Without conscious redirection, the mind will keep replicating the same old thoughts and running the same old programs over and over again.

In spite of its stubborn tenacity, the architecture of the mind is certainly not set in stone. Scientists today talk about neuroplasticity; the brain's ability to reorganise itself by forming new neural connections and networks. In short, you don't have to be stuck with the same mental operating system your entire life. Although it takes time and effort, it's wholly possible to update and upgrade your mind's operating system.

That's exactly what Vedanta is for. If the old operating system was based on self-ignorance, the new one is rooted in Self-knowledge.

A new piece of knowledge is unlikely to have much of an effect on the mind unless you invest it with great importance. After all, the mind receives input every second of the day. If you think back to your school days, when you had to sit tests and exams it took a great deal of revision—of time, repetition and practice—in order to get the knowledge to 'stick'.

Because you've spent an entire lifetime thinking of yourself as a limited jiva—a conglomeration of matter and mind, subject to the ravages of time and worldly suffering—it will naturally take time to reorient your identity to pure awareness.

You might intellectually grasp the teaching, yet still feel your identity hinges upon the body-mind sense complex and all its related sorrows. If you have Self-Knowledge, as revealed here by the Gita, yet are still not experiencing its fruits—specifically, freedom from suffering—then you must continue practising nididhyasana.

Swami Paramarthananda offers a cute analogy. When you make a cup of coffee and add a spoonful of sugar, you need to mix it, otherwise you won't taste the sugar. If the first two stages of Vedanta are adding the coffee, milk and sugar, the final stage, nididhyasana, is stirring it all together. Only then can you enjoy the sweetness.

Your nididhyasana might take the form of repeatedly listening to the teaching, meditating upon its meaning, writing it out in your own words, and discussing it with other students.

Another vital part of nididhyasana is observing the content of your mind and practising self-inquiry by questioning any self-limiting thoughts and beliefs in the light of Self-knowledge. Are you identifying with the mind, body, and ego, or are you claiming your nature as ever free awareness?

Meditating on Truth

Nididhyasana is sometimes translated as 'meditation'. This form of meditation, Vedantic mediation, isn't about relaxation and creating a thoughtless state. It's about directing and absorbing your mind in contemplation of your nature as the Self; the eternal witnessing consciousness/awareness that you are.

In 'The Holy Geeta', Swami Chinmayananda writes:

> Diverting the flow of the mind from the world of sense objects and maintaining it in a steady flow towards the Lord in an utter attitude of identification is called meditation. [It means to] bring your entire mind to the contemplation of the Divine, to the total exclusion of all dissimilar thought currents.

Indeed, Krishna tells Arjuna:

> Be aware of Me always. Offer your mind and heart to Me
> with supreme devotion and you will realise your identity
> with Me. This I promise you.

Much of the language of this chapter has a devotional fla-
vour. Krishna qualifies this by again stating that the highest devotion is the pursuit of Self-knowledge; the recognition of the
non-separation between the individual self and Brahman, the
universal Self. Krishna basically sums it up by advising Arjuna
to "Meditate on the imperishable Self always."

Continually bringing your mind back to contemplation of
your nature as awareness is the key that turns knowledge into
liberation, ending the ego's sorrowful dream of separation.

The Highest Truth: You Are Already Free

The Self is limitless and eternally free. You are the Self.
Therefore, your true nature is limitless and eternally free.

The first stage of Vedanta, shravana, reveals this knowledge
to you. Manana, the second stage, offers the opportunity to investigate this claim and resolve any doubts and misunderstand-
ings. The final stage, nididhyasana, is about claiming this identity as your own, thus liberating you from the suffering born of
misidentifying with the world of the maya.

At the relative order of reality, the jiva, the limited entity
struggling in a world of opposing forces, doesn't suddenly vanish. But is seen for what it is: mithya—enjoying only an apparent, borrowed existence—an effect entirely dependent upon an
underlying cause, which is satya, the Self.

The body and mind are instruments through which consciousness expresses. Confused by the murky twilight of maya,
the ego generates an illusory sense of self out of these objects,
and you fall deep under the spell of ignorance.

Everything you then do is an expression of this ignorance;
a vain attempt to overcome the painful sense of emptiness that
comes from believing yourself to be what you are not.

Krishna again addresses the topic of doership in this chapter, saying, "Those who lack clear vision, believe themselves to be the agent of action. But the wise understand the self to be free of doership."

The ego takes itself to be the agent of action, when it is but one factor among many. The performance of any action requires five principle factors: a physical body, the physiological system which grants the body life, the sense organs of perception and action, the ego or agent of action, and the elemental forces, meaning the environment in which the action must take place.

The ego, from which we acquire our sense of doership, is just one component of the subtle body. Under the spell of avidya, we take the ego to be the self, when in fact it is but an object known to the Self. Anything objectifiable cannot, by definition, be the subject; the witnessing awareness/consciousness.

The Self-realised have no sense of doership. They know the Self to be the ever present witness; the light in which all objects appear and function according to their respective natures as determined by the gunas. In other words, all the doing in the field of matter is done by Ishvara.

The Self, the heart of life, is Existence itself; the nature of which is pure consciousness/awareness. Like the sun, the Self is actionless, yet by its presence, it blesses the world of maya with action, with life, sentience and vigour.

By the power of its maya, Krishna says, the Self makes all forms spin around as if mounted on a wheel. Matter itself is inert; the life within it belongs to the Self alone, just as the borrowed light of the moon belongs the sun.

Krishna's concluding words to Arjuna: "Giving up all karmas, take refuge in Me alone and I will release you from all karma, have no fear."

Again, this doesn't mean giving up all action in a literal sense. This is a renunciation born of knowledge—the knowledge that action belongs to the world of matter, as governed by Ishvara.

By knowing yourself to be the actionless awareness in which all form appears, you find release from the false burden of doership and ownership. You are, in Krishna's words, released from karma.

Just as knowledge resolves the snake back into the rope, Self-knowledge resolves the jiva back into the one, all-pervading consciousness from which it was never apart.

Fortunately, ignorance does not die alone. Its byproducts—the crippling sense of limitation and incompleteness at the core of the human psyche—disappear along with it, like shadows subsumed into the morning sun.

The jiva then becomes a jivan muktah; one who is liberated while living. Liberation, you come to realise, isn't something that you gain. It is simply the removal of the notion that you were ever bound in the first place.

Conclusion: Arjuna's Doubt is Resolved

The Bhagavad Gita began with a crisis on the battlefield. About to fight the greatest war the world had ever known, Arjuna's resolve crumbled as he found himself facing his own beloved family and friends across the battlefield. Throwing down his weapon, he turned to his mentor Krishna, begging for his counsel.

Krishna knew that the real problem wasn't the situation at hand. Arjuna was a warrior with a righteous cause and had been well trained for this moment. The real problem was that most universal of human sufferings: the bondage of samsara; the spell of delusion caused by self-ignorance.

And so, the Bhagavad Gita, the shining gem at the heart of the Mahabharata, proceeded to unravel every aspect of the human condition and reality as we know it: the birth and death of the universe, the nature of matter and consciousness, the role of God and the forces of the creation, the necessity of dharma, and the pursuit of enlightenment as life's highest goal.

The breadth and depth of this teaching, distilled into seven hundred poetic verses, is staggering. For the qualified seeker, Krishna's timeless words, which have been recited for millennia, are nothing less than liberating.

Of course, it takes Arjuna time to process this knowledge, for many of his questions retread the same ground. This is why, in the closing verses, Krishna seeks to know whether he has understood the teaching. He asks the Pandava prince if his delusion is now gone.

Arjuna confirms that he has understood Krishna's divine message. By Krishna's grace, his doubts are gone and his sorrow vanquished. Arjuna is now ready to embrace his dharma, his destiny; illumined from within by the eternal flame of Self-knowledge.

Om Tat Sat.

Lightning Source UK Ltd.
Milton Keynes UK
UKHW030912101120
373143UK00013B/989